IMAGES
of America

Bloomington and Indiana University

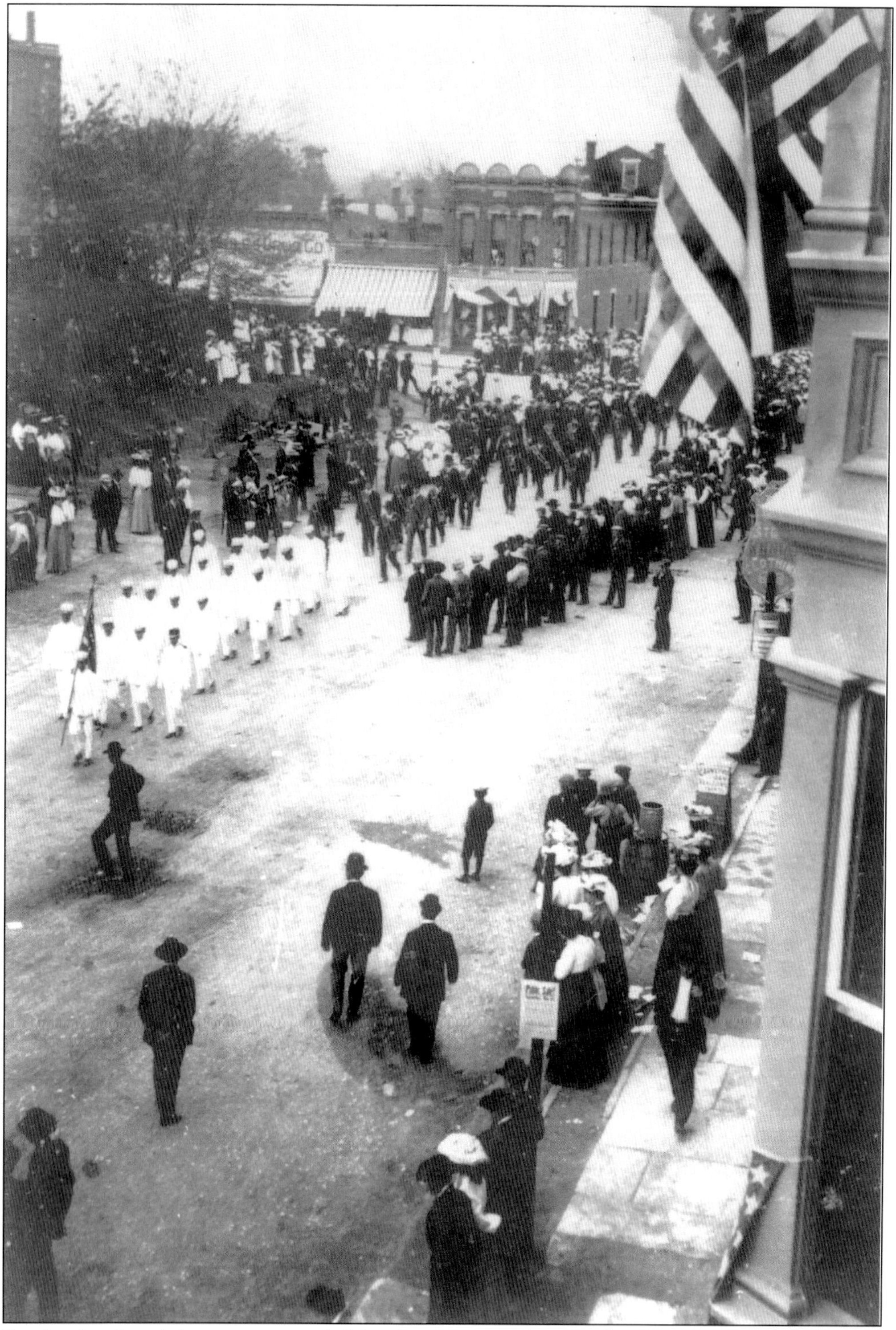

Bands played and dignitaries paraded for the new courthouse, whose cornerstone was laid on May 10, 1907. The building is Monroe County's third courthouse since 1818.

IMAGES
of America

BLOOMINGTON AND INDIANA UNIVERSITY

Bloomington Restorations, Inc.

ARCADIA
PUBLISHING

ISBN 978-0-7385-1940-1

Published by Arcadia Publishing
Charleston, South Carolina

Printed in the United States of America

Library of Congress Catalog Card Number: 2001095421

For all general information contact Arcadia Publishing at:
Telephone 843-853-2070
Fax 843-853-0044
E-mail sales@arcadiapublishing.com
For customer service and orders:
Toll-Free 1-888-313-2665

Visit us on the Internet at www.arcadiapublishing.com

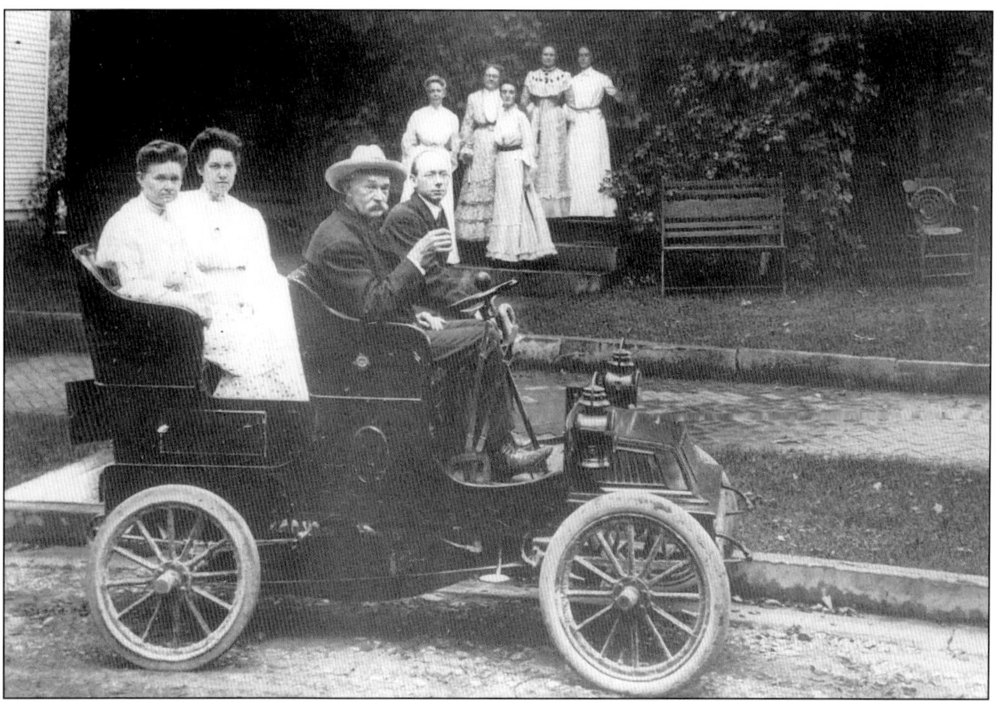

The first factory-built automobile in Bloomington, 1907, succeeded other cars that were hand built by local motoring enthusiasts. In the car (left to right) were Lillie Howe Troutman, Clara Polk, Joshua Howe (owner), George M. Howe. Standing (left to right) were Mrs. Joshua Howe, Mrs. Polk, Grace Philputt Young, Mrs. Frank Hunter, and Juliette Maxwell.

Contents

ACKNOWLEDGMENTS

Bradley D. Cook, Reference Specialist and Photograph Curator at the Indiana University Archives, spent many hours contributing his expertise to this book. Also generous with their time were John M. Hollingsworth, who made six rolls of copy photos, Marian Keith, who posed for her photograph, and Thomas Gallagher, who loaned his collection of glass negatives, glass slides, and ephemera. The Indiana University Geography and Map Library, Paul Ash, Rita Carter, Culver Godfrey, Nancy Hiestand, John Hollingsworth, Eliza Steelwater, and Steve Wyatt also contributed photographs. Chris Sturbaum loaned his original copy of the historical Commercial Club booklet.

Most of the images in the book are reproduced by special arrangement with the Indiana University Archives.

Photo sources are as follows:

INDIANA UNIVERSITY ARCHIVES: pages 2, 4, 8–11, 12 (top) 14, 15, 18, 19 (top), 20–24, 25 (top), 26–35, 37–41, 42 (bottom), 44 (top), 45 (bottom), 46, 47 (top), 48–53, 54 (top), 55 (top), 56–58, 59 (bottom), 60 (top; bottom left), 61, 62, 64 (bottom), 65 (top), 66 (bottom), 67 (top), 69–71, 74 (top), 76, 77, 78 (top), 79, 81–103, 104 (top and center), 105–115, 116 (top), 117–122.
INDIANA UNIVERSITY GEOGRAPHY AND MAP LIBRARY: page 25 (bottom).
PAUL ASH: pages 125, 126, 127 (bottom).
BLOOMINGTON RESTORATIONS, INC.: page 17 (top).
RITA CARTER: page 13 (top).
THOMAS GALLAGHER: cover and pages 43 (bottom), 54 (bottom), 59 (top), 64 (top), 67 (bottom), 68, 72, 73, 74 (bottom), 75, 116 (bottom).
CULVER GODFREY: page 127 (top).
NANCY HIESTAND, Program Manager, Historic Preservation, Bloomington Housing and Neighborhood Development Department: page 16.
JOHN HOLLINGSWORTH: page 36, top left and right.
ELIZA STEELWATER: pages 12 (bottom), 13 (bottom), 17 (bottom), 19 (bottom), 43 (top), 44 (bottom), 47 (bottom), 55 (bottom), 60 (bottom right), 65 (bottom), 66 (top), 78 (bottom), 80, 104 (bottom), 124 (bottom), 128.
CHRIS STURBAUM: pages 36 (bottom), 42 (top), 45 (top), 63.
STEVE WYATT: pages 123, 124 (top).

INTRODUCTION

The pictures and captions in this book tell a series of very brief stories about the shared history of Bloomington and Indiana University. Photographs and a few printed images move forward chapter by chapter through the past, with some excursions into the present to reveal to the reader "how things turned out." Chapters 1, 3, and 7 emphasize Bloomington's history, especially 1880–1930. Chapters 2, 5, and 6 emphasize the history of the Bloomington campus of Indiana University, especially 1916–1960. Chapter 4, 1916–1939, passes back and forth from town to gown. These were the years when historical parts of Bloomington and the university campus took on much of the look they have today. Bloomington is distinctive not only for the presence of a university with a memorable campus but also for an unusually intact courthouse square and a historical limestone industry whose buildings and carvings are found throughout the community. Industries, such as Bloomington's tannery, chair factory, and foundry, brought jobs, wealth, and new neighborhoods. The end of World War II saw trailer housing, the return of veterans to school on the G.I. Bill, and massive physical growth of the university.

The purpose of this book is not to offer a complete timeline of local history. Rather, the book illustrates people and places captured at a few moments through the years. Someone was there who found each of these moments interesting or compelling and happened to record them with a camera. Some favorites will have been omitted, but we sincerely hope that the images presented will provide new favorites for the reader.

This book is written on behalf of Bloomington Restorations, Inc. (BRI), a not-for-profit historic preservation organization whose mission is to rescue historic buildings and revitalize old neighborhoods throughout Monroe County. BRI was founded in 1976. Programs include a revolving fund, an affordable housing program, and tours of historic homes and other sites in Bloomington and county-wide. BRI is a volunteer-based, membership organization open to all. BRI may be contacted at Post Office Box 1522, Bloomington, Indiana 47402. Photographs for this book were selected and captions written by Eliza Steelwater, a past president of BRI, writer, and consultant in historic preservation. BRI's executive director, Steve Wyatt, and current president, Don Granbois, reviewed the material and gave many helpful suggestions. Pat Glushko, secretary of BRI, contributed to publicity.

Excellent historical information including sports histories can be found in several books on Bloomington and Indiana University, but many treasures remain uncollected in local archives. For both current books and vintage materials on a wide variety of topics, the reader is invited to visit the Indiana University Archives, the local-history collection of the Mathers Museum of Indiana University, the library and exhibits of the Monroe County Historical Society, and the Indiana Room of the Monroe County Public Library. The *Indiana Daily Student* and Indiana University's yearbook, the *Arbutus*, have been published since the 19th century. Bloomington newspapers have also been published under various names. Many years of these publications are still available.

Locally published books of particular interest, out of print but available in libraries, include *Bloomington Discovered* (Discovery Press, 1980), an architectural history by Karen S. Craig and Diana M. Hawes, *A Time to Speak* (Pinus Strobus Press, 1985), a history of the African-American community by Frances V. Halsell Gilliam, and the pamphlet titled *The Underground Railroad in Monroe County* (Monroe County Historical Society, 1961), by Henry Lester Smith. Another source of information is the Bloomington and Monroe County *Interim Reports*, publications of the Indiana Historic Sites and Structures Survey sponsored by the Indiana Department of Natural Resources, containing summaries of local and architectural history and lists of historic buildings still standing.

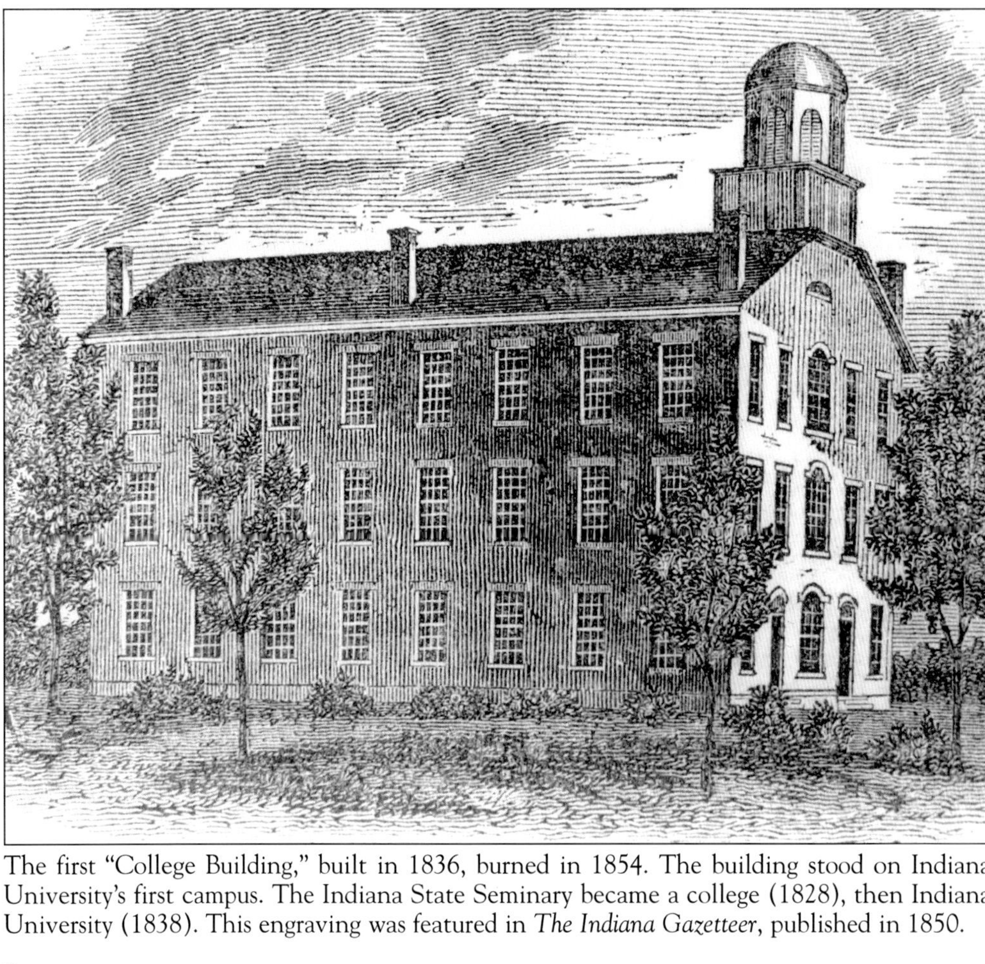

The first "College Building," built in 1836, burned in 1854. The building stood on Indiana University's first campus. The Indiana State Seminary became a college (1828), then Indiana University (1838). This engraving was featured in *The Indiana Gazetteer*, published in 1850.

One

BEGINNINGS

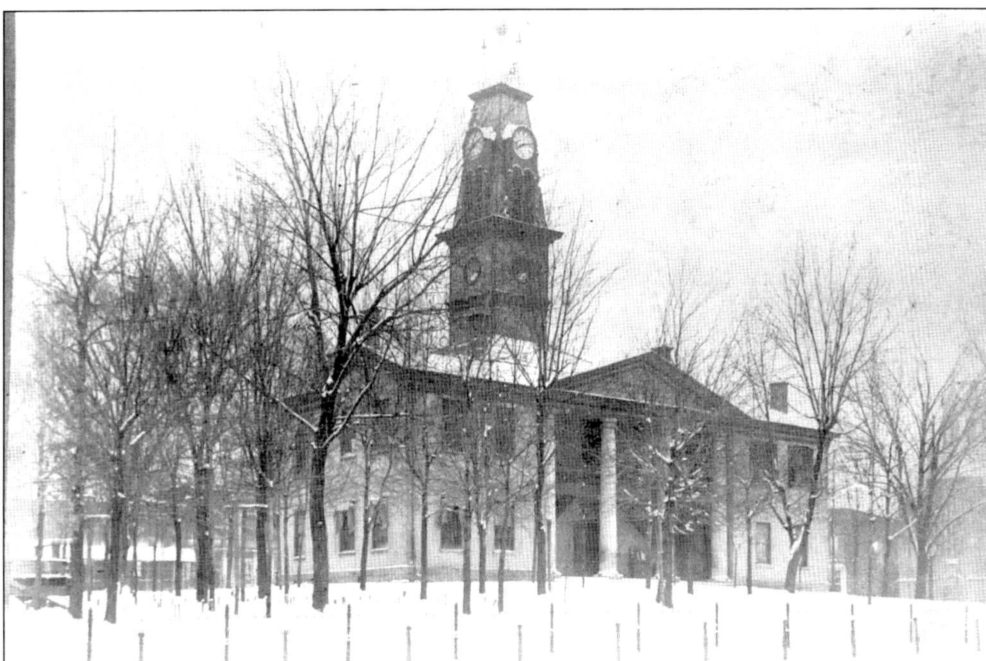

The second Monroe County Courthouse (1826) replaced a log structure from 1818, the year Bloomington was established. Before the railroad reached Bloomington in 1853, a traveler was likely to arrive by stage from New Albany on the Ohio River. Most settlers lived in the southern part of the state. Indians had been in retreat region-wide since battles in 1794 and 1811.

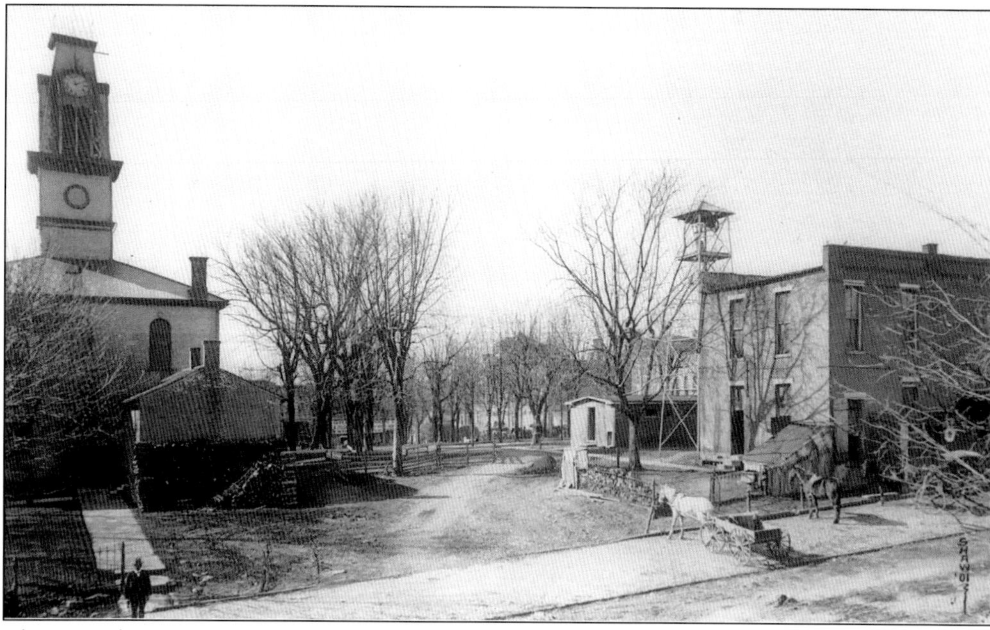

The second county courthouse became the town center, sharing the square on its east side with a two-story brick building (right of this photo, about 1900) that housed the fire engine and city offices. Public restrooms stood west of the firehouse. Between the two buildings was a tower whose bell was rung to summon firefighters.

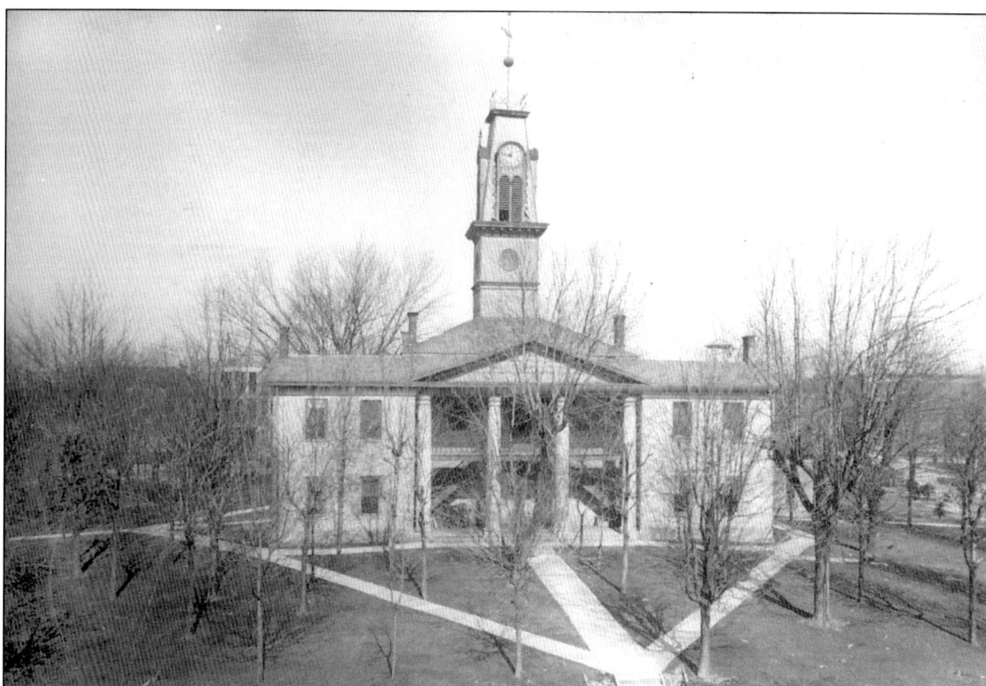

The second courthouse was remodeled in 1856, probably to create the Classical Revival styling shown in this undated photo. In 1906, with a new courthouse in view, the county auctioned the old courthouse. It was purchased for $100.00 and demolished by James A. Pike, the only bidder.

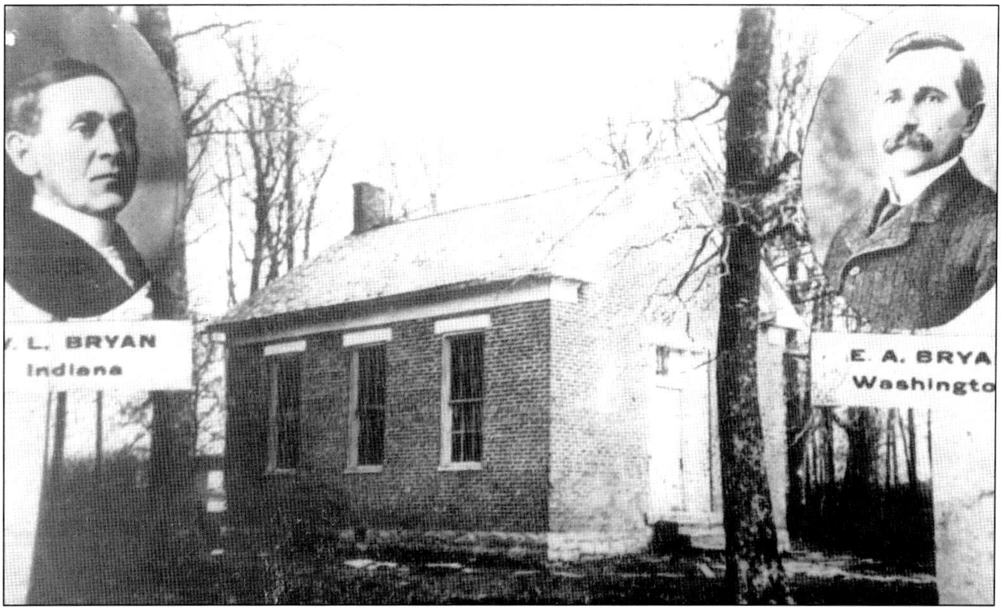

The one-room Philips schoolhouse, location unknown, graduated William Lowe Bryan, 10th president of Indiana University (1902–1937) and William's brother, Enoch Albert Bryan. E. A. Bryan became president of Vincennes University (1885–1893), then president of the State College of Washington (1893–1916).

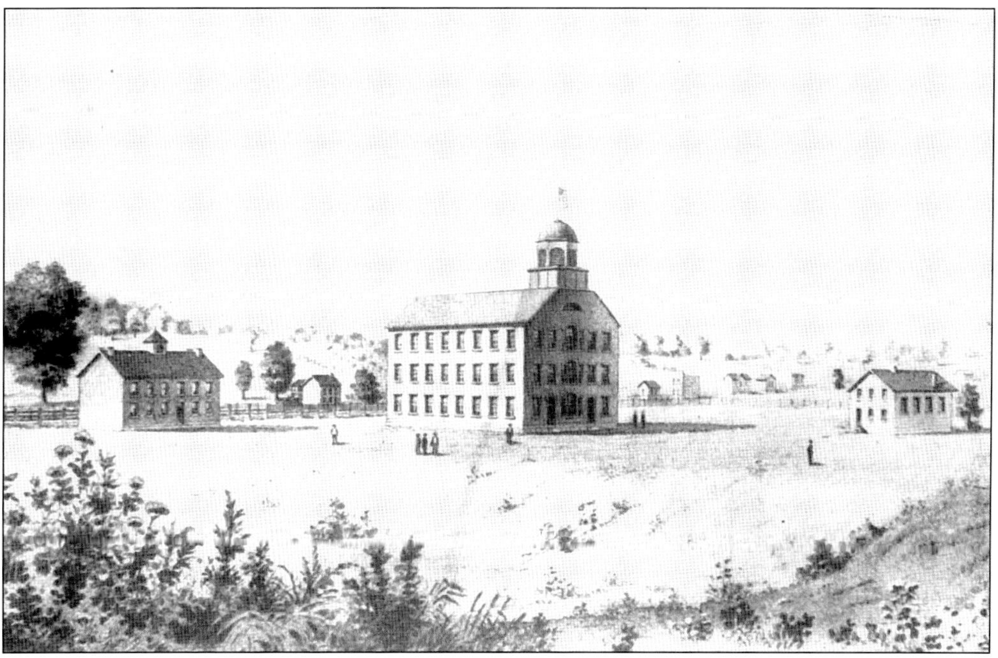

A drawing represents IU's first campus around 1840-1850. Left to right as the viewer looks northeast are the Seminary Building (1824), College Building (1836), and Old Laboratory (1840). The first campus was located near a spring a quarter of a mile due south of Bloomington. Boundaries of the site, today commemorated as Seminary Square, were First, Second, Morton, and Walnut Streets.

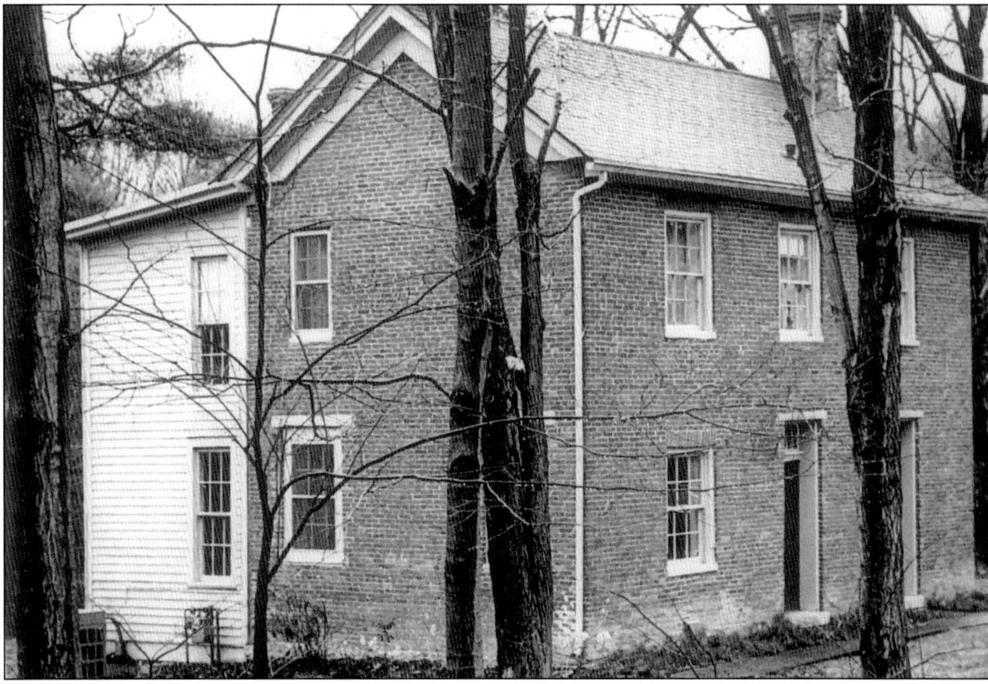

Thomas Smith, farmer, built this brick house (with wood addition) at 1326 Pickwick Place, about 1828. Smith was a member of the Covenanter or Reformed Presbyterian Church, a nationwide movement of anti-slavery Presbyterians. Local Covenanters came from South Carolina to establish their homes, and a stop on the Underground Railroad, 2 miles southeast of Bloomington. These Covenanters secretly conveyed slaves 80 miles from Salem, Indiana, north to Mooresville, then a Quaker community.

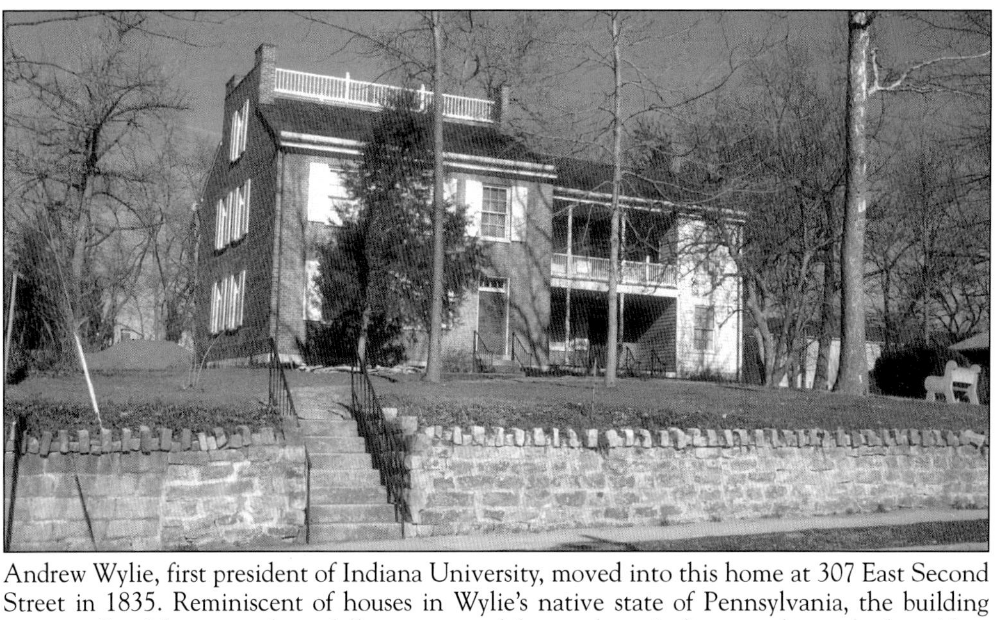

Andrew Wylie, first president of Indiana University, moved into this home at 307 East Second Street in 1835. Reminiscent of houses in Wylie's native state of Pennsylvania, the building is unusually elaborate and carefully constructed for southern Indiana at this early date. Now restored, the home is operated by Indiana University as the Wylie House Museum.

Bob Anderson was a freedman, or former slave, who made his way north from the small town of Westport, near Louisville, Kentucky. He settled in the Covenanter community outside of Bloomington some time after the Civil War. According to Anderson's descendants, he bought a plot of farmland from the church. The land is still owned by the family. Anderson, his son and daughter-in-law are buried in the Covenanter cemetery. Jared Jeffries, IU class of 2003, is a great-great-grandson.

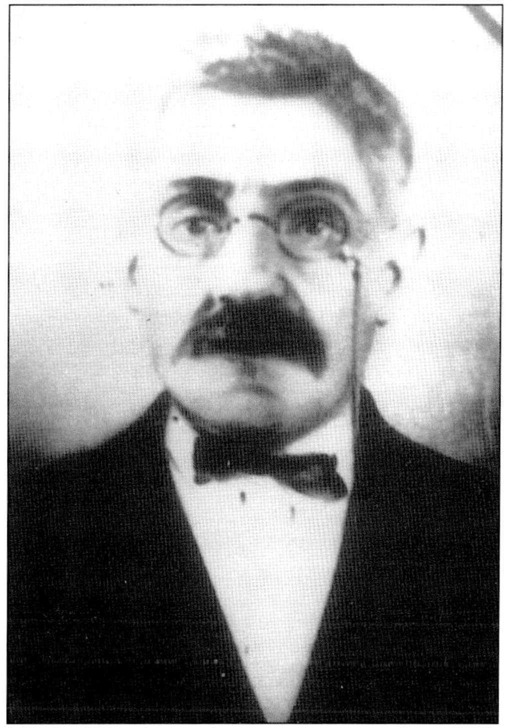

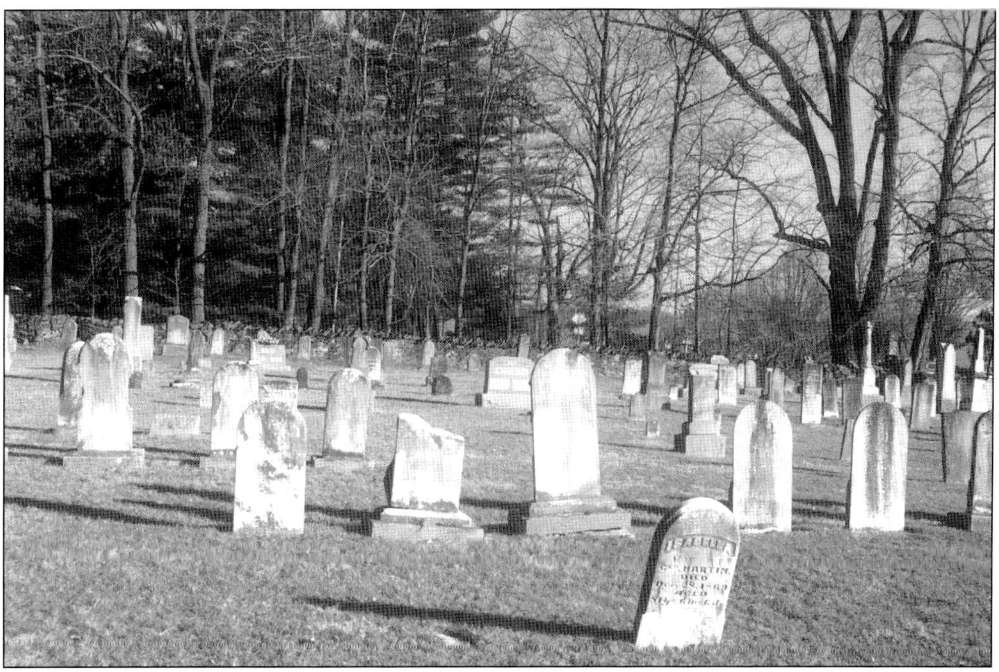

The Covenanter cemetery, with its dry-laid fieldstone wall, stands at the now-busy corner of High Street and Moore's Pike. In 1839, Thomas Smith donated an acre of land near his home for a meeting house or church, charging $10 for an adjoining half-acre where the cemetery was established. The church later burned and was rebuilt elsewhere but the cemetery continues to serve as a burial site.

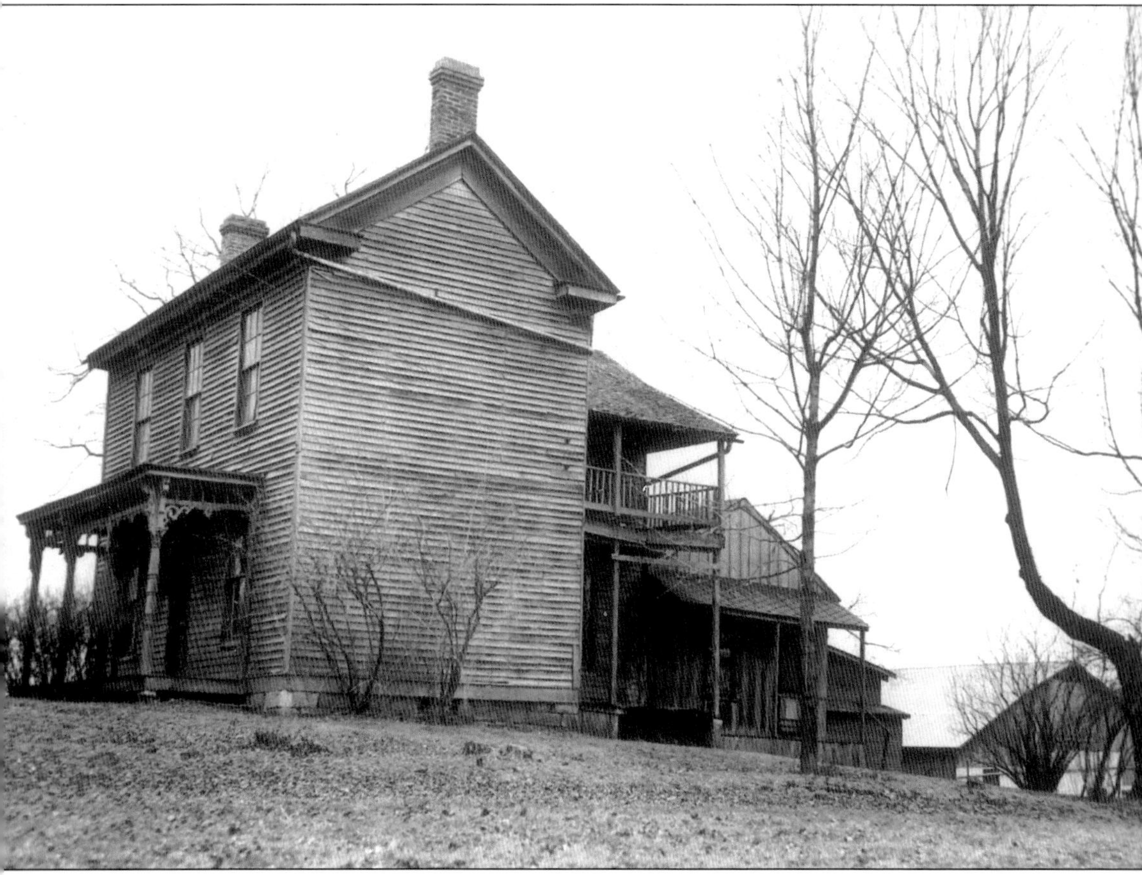

The Faris family, who were Covenanters, acquired this homestead (buildings since demolished) after the Homestead Act of 1862 offered 160-acre quarter-sections of land to settlers. Covenanter pastor James Faris originally owned a house near that of Thomas Smith. Members of the Faris family continue to live in Bloomington. Among other occupations, family members have operated the Faris Brothers Meat Market at several locations since 1923.

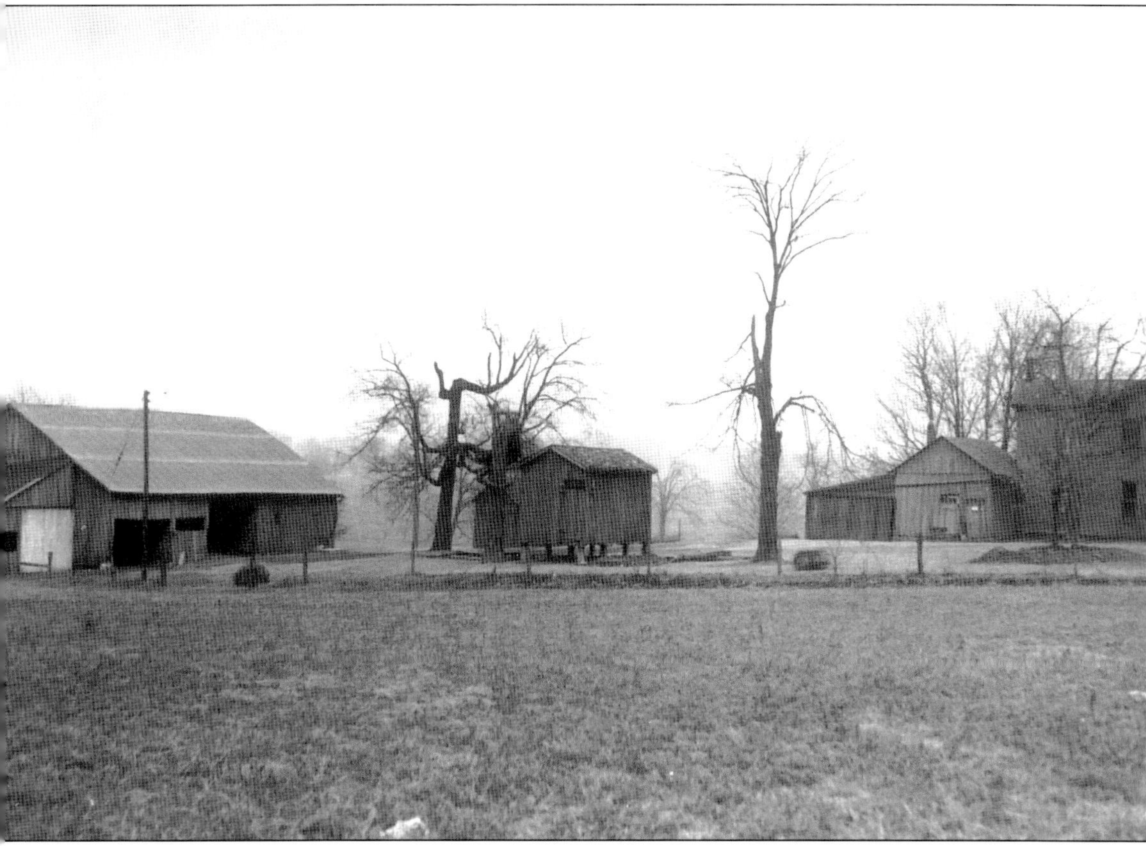

The Faris house and farm occupied the site until 1956, when these photographs were taken and the site was purchased by Indiana University. The site is now bounded by Dunn Street, Fee Lane, Seventeenth Street, and Matlock Road (Ind. 45/46 bypass). The Seventeenth Street Football Stadium was completed here in 1960. In 1971, it was renamed Memorial Stadium. Assembly Hall is located nearby on the east side of the site.

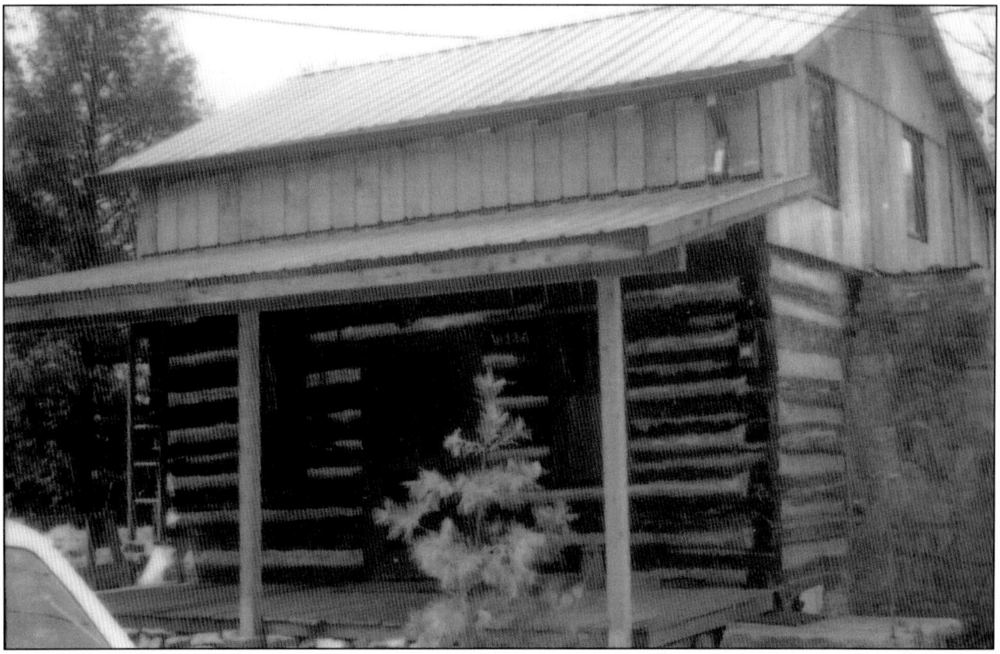

A log cabin on South Park Avenue, much altered, was probably built around 1830. Poplar logs were squared, notched together at the ends, and chinked with stones, wood, mud, or mortar. Whenever possible, logs were covered with hand-split "weatherboarding" (clapboard) to prevent deterioration. Modern preservatives make it possible for log cabin owners to enjoy a rustic look.

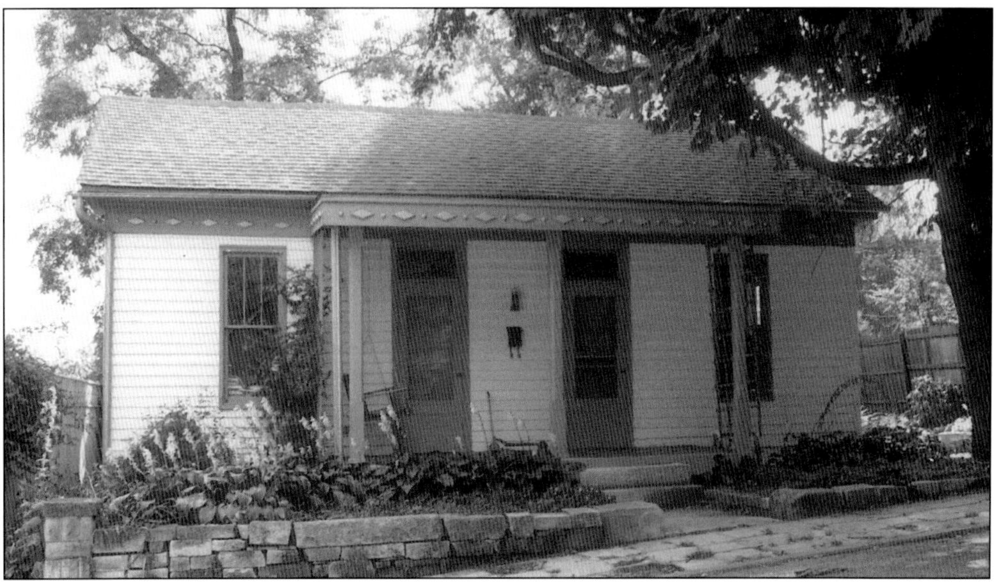

This clapboarded frame house (1890s) is similar to other Bloomington houses built from the 1830s on. Its floor plan—two rooms, each with its own door to the exterior—is sometimes said to be based on log construction, but may also reflect the custom of maintaining separate formal and family entrances. Note the limestone-block sidewalk, a project of the 1930s Works Progress Administration (WPA). The house was moved to its present location on South Jackson Street c. 1927 and recently restored.

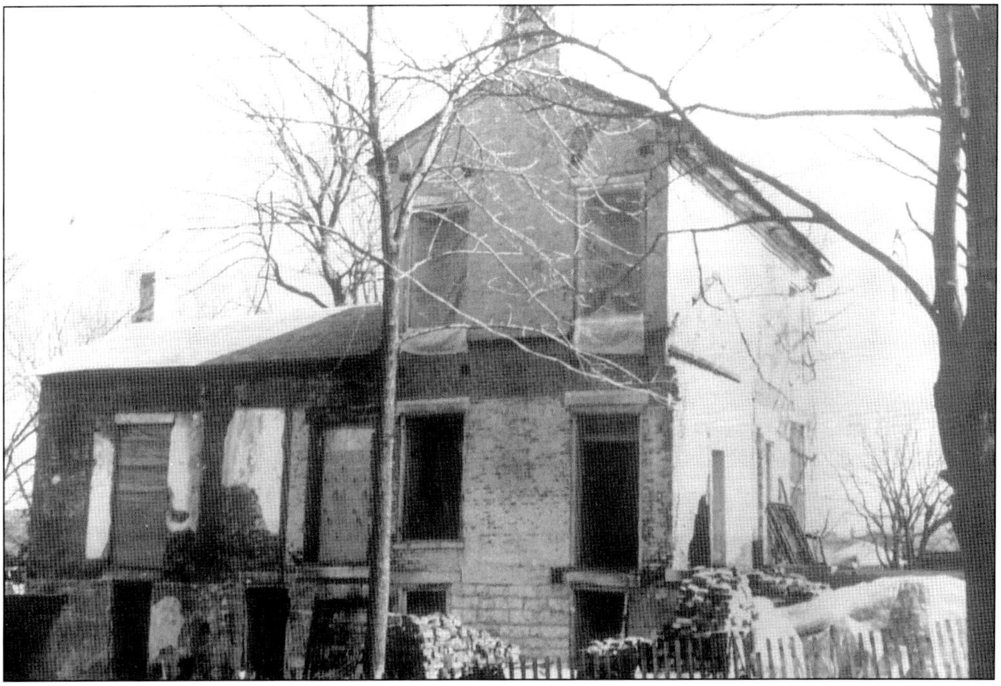

This former home built around 1845 was almost a ruin by the 1970s. Its north wing had collapsed. The house was built of handmade brick on 6 acres on a hill southwest of Bloomington (now 608 West Third Street). Two wings were added during the 1860s. The building's most famous owner, Paris Dunning, served as president of the Indiana University Board of Trustees and Indiana's lieutenant governor (1846–1847), and governor (1848).

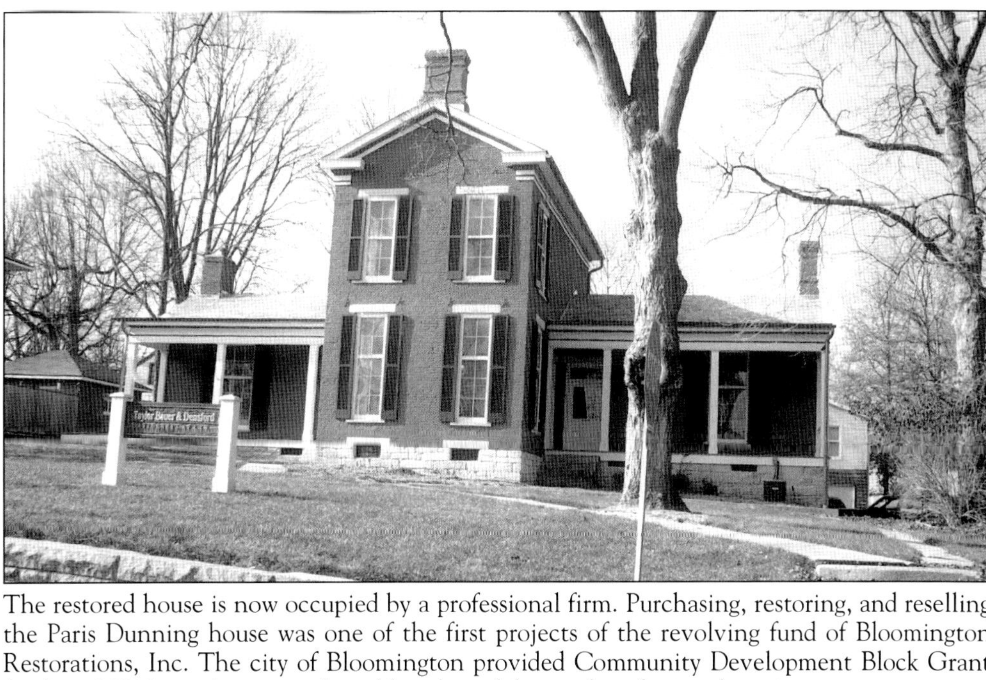

The restored house is now occupied by a professional firm. Purchasing, restoring, and reselling the Paris Dunning house was one of the first projects of the revolving fund of Bloomington Restorations, Inc. The city of Bloomington provided Community Development Block Grant funds and BRI members contributed hands-on labor and professional services.

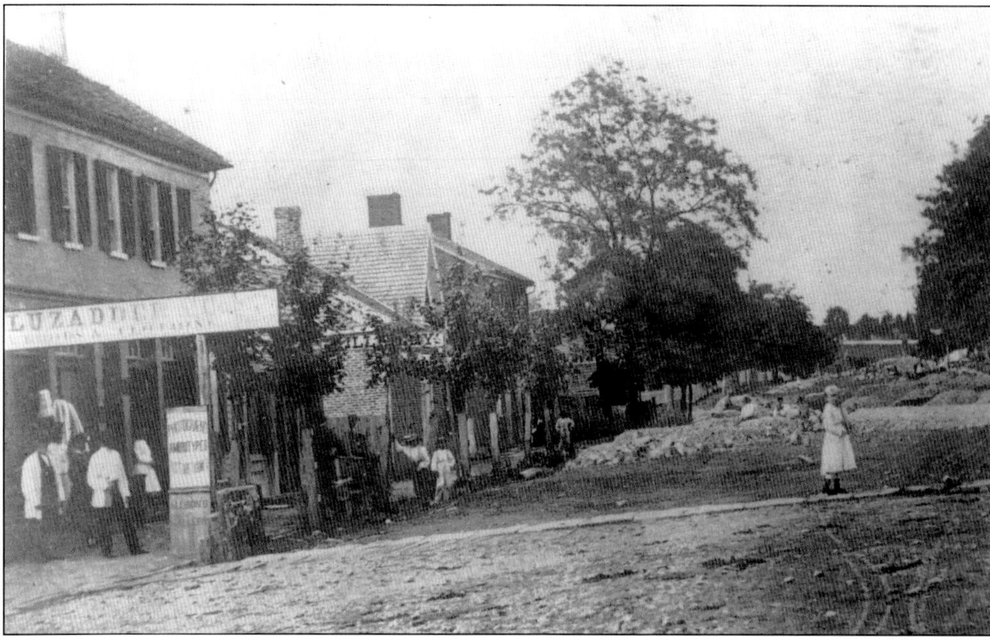

In 1870, the viewer could stand on West Sixth Street, northwest of the old courthouse, and look north along North College Avenue to check the progress of a road-building project. According to local reminiscence, the city dropped rock in front of homes and businesses, leaving each owner to break up the rock and spread it over the street.

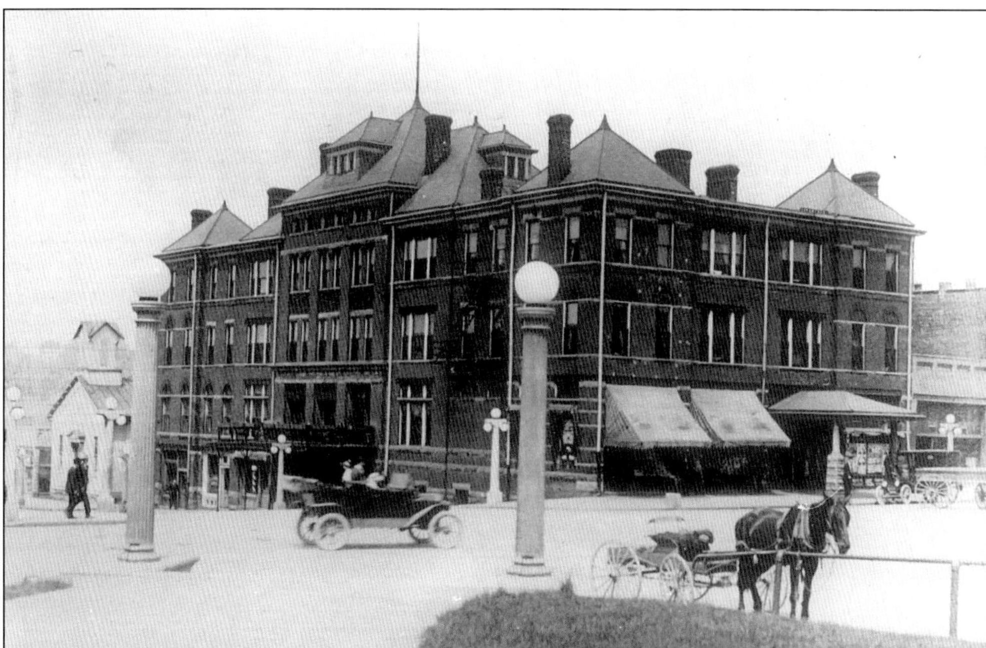

The northwest corner of West Sixth and North College became the site of the Bowles Hotel (later Gentry Hotel) in 1895. On completion, the Bowles took the place of the National Hotel on East Kirkwood as Bloomington's finest hotel.

Walkers going east on Sixth Street in the 1960s passed what was then Alden's Department Store. The corner of the Graham Hotel is just visible at left of the photo. The Graham Hotel replaced the Bowles (1929), which probably replaced the 1870s corner building on the previous page. In the photo below, the Graham Plaza, today an office building, still anchors the corner. It is separated by a parking lot from the mid-1980s Justice Building on North College.

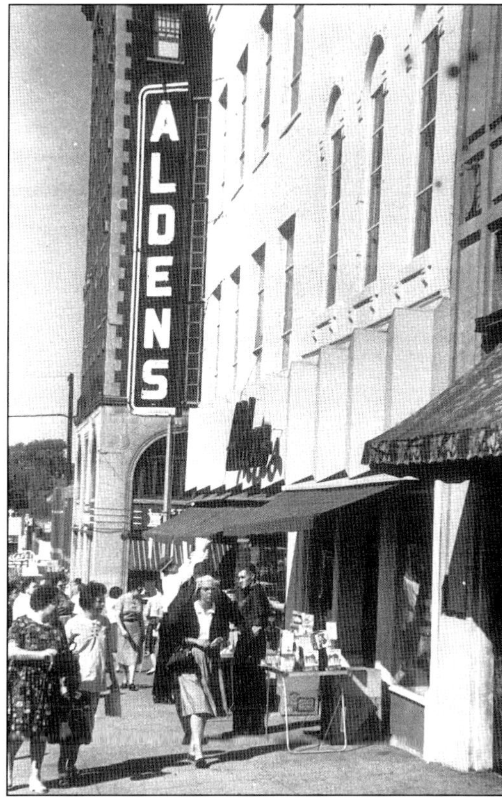

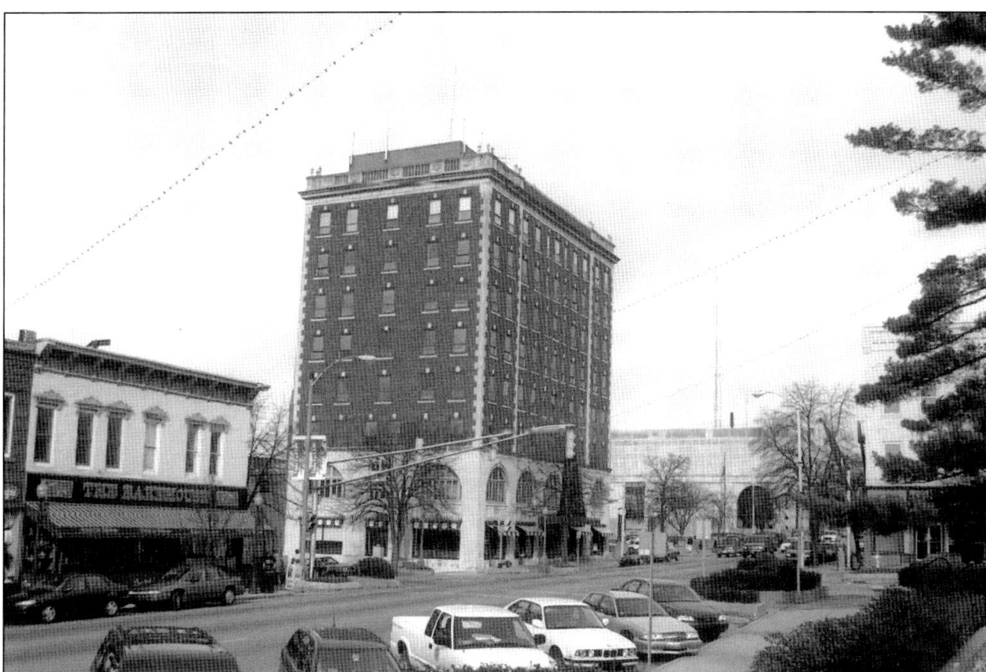

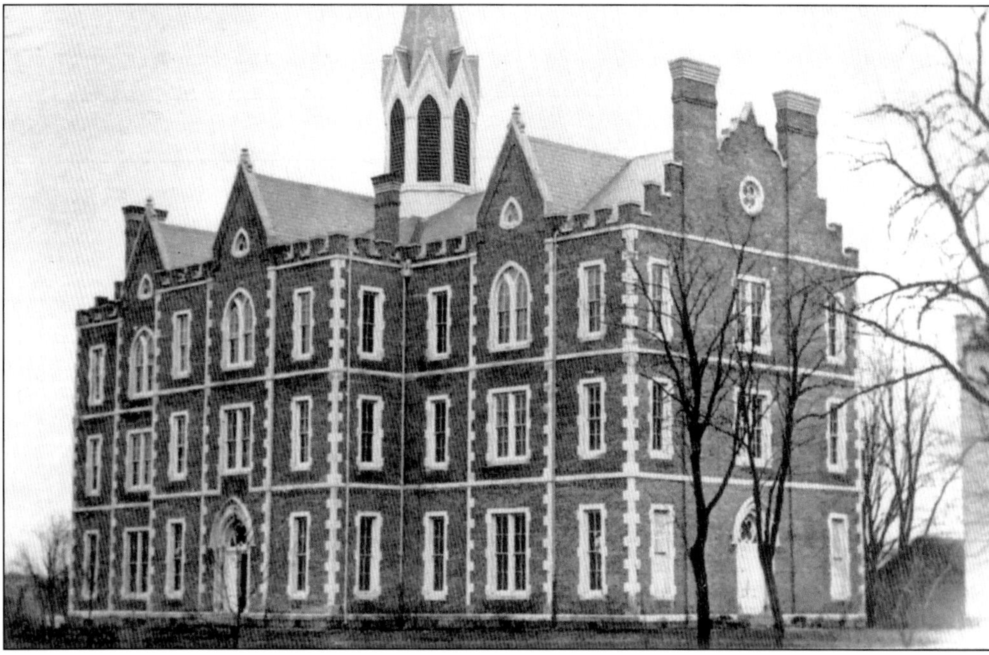

The demands of teaching science and the need for a library led to the construction of Science Hall on Indiana University's Seminary Square campus in 1873. In the third-floor museum, a prized possession was the Owen Cabinet of fossils and other specimens collected by David Dale Owen, professor of geology.

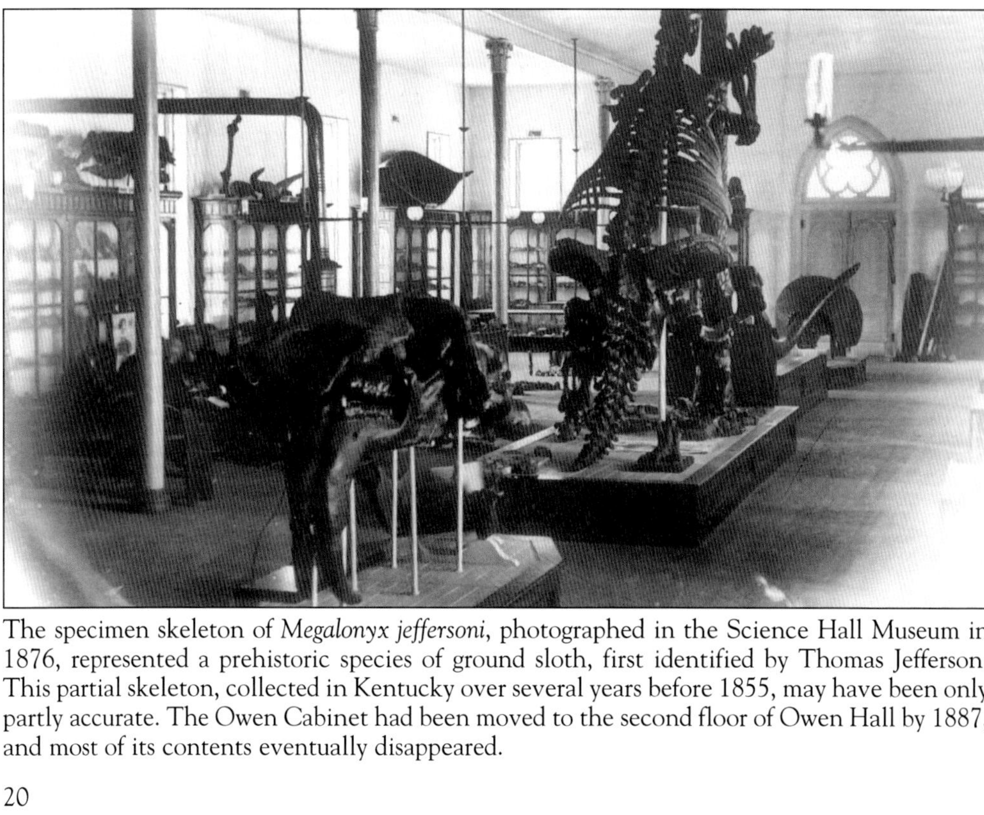

The specimen skeleton of *Megalonyx jeffersoni*, photographed in the Science Hall Museum in 1876, represented a prehistoric species of ground sloth, first identified by Thomas Jefferson. This partial skeleton, collected in Kentucky over several years before 1855, may have been only partly accurate. The Owen Cabinet had been moved to the second floor of Owen Hall by 1887, and most of its contents eventually disappeared.

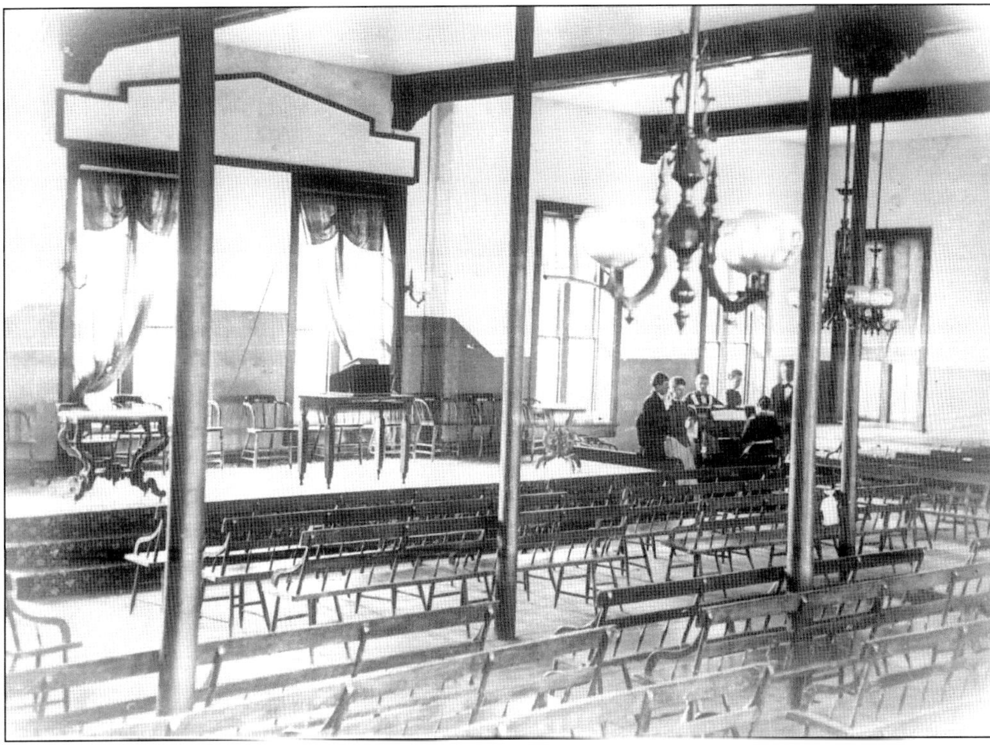

A small group, probably university students, stood around the keyboard in the chapel of the Old College Building (1855; also known as the first University Building) in this photograph c. 1880. High school graduation was also held in this second-floor chapel.

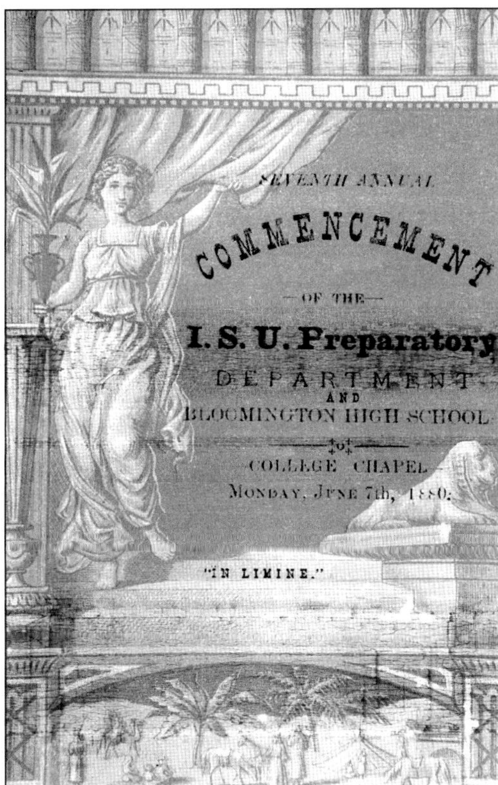

Graduation ceremonies began at 8:00 a.m. for the Preparatory Department and Bloomington High School class of 1880. Until 1890, university professors continued to staff the department where secondary students prepared for higher education.

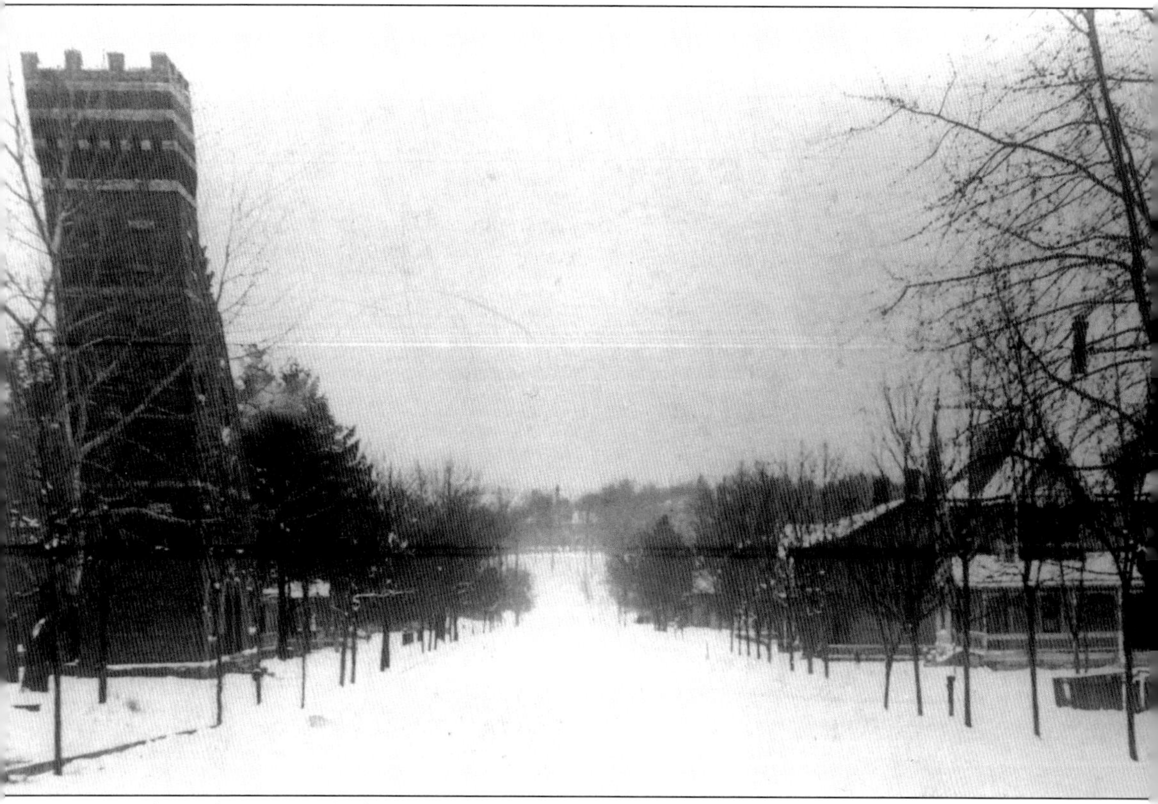

Kirkwood Avenue, looking east on a snowy day in the 1880s, was mostly residential. The Christian Church stood at the southwest corner of Kirkwood and Washington, and its 60-foot tower was the street's major landmark. The church later burned.

Two

FIRE REDRAWS THE IU MAP

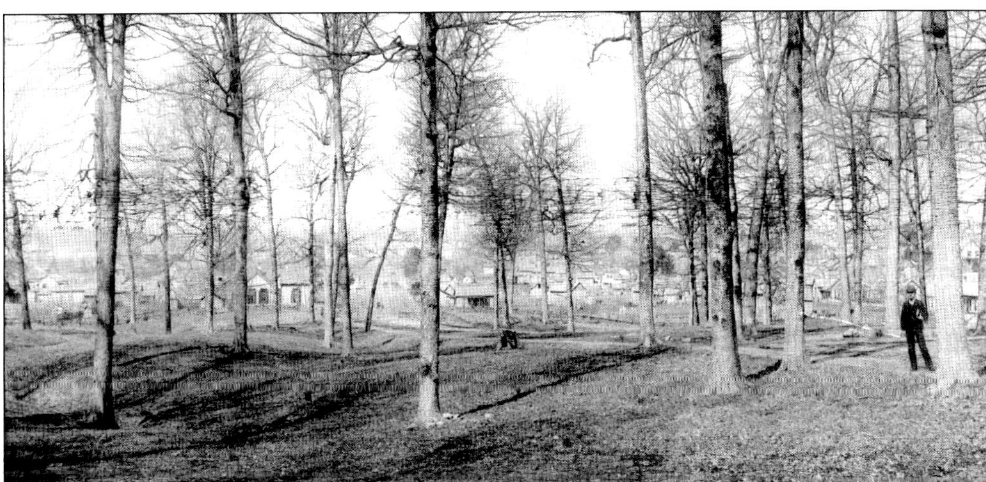

Indiana University moved to 80 wooded acres east of downtown after fire raged through Science Hall on the Seminary Square campus on July 12, 1883. The citizens of Monroe County pledged $50,000 to help rebuild. The new campus, called Dunn's Woods, was photographed looking west in 1891. Kirkwood stretched away toward the courthouse. The houses in the distance would have been located along the future Indiana Avenue.

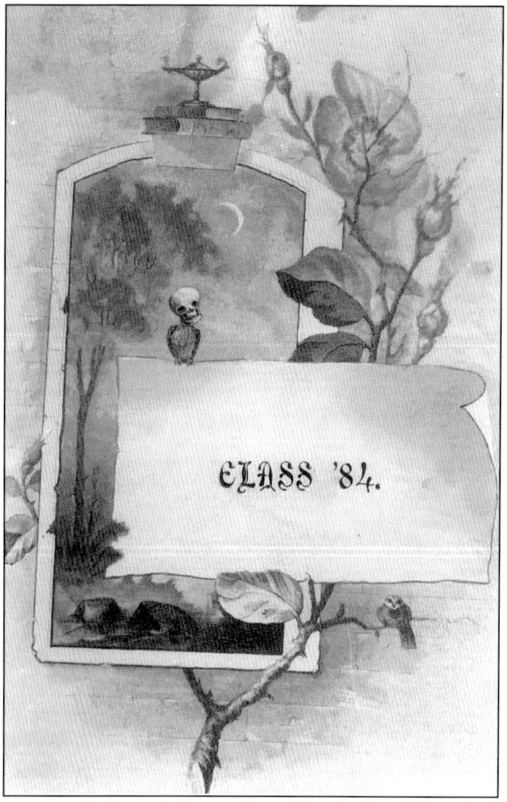

The class of 1884 was the first to graduate after fire destroyed part of the campus that Bloomington High School shared with Indiana University at Seminary Square, between First and Second Streets on the south side of town.

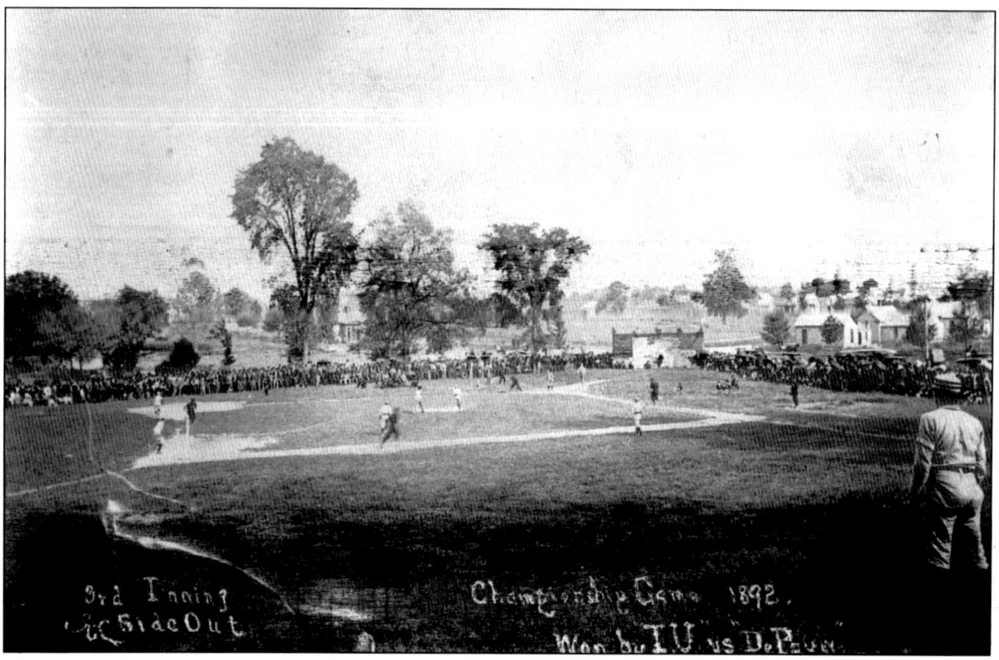

University baseball games, the first varsity sport at Indiana University, were still played on the Seminary Square campus when IU beat DePauw for the championship in 1892.

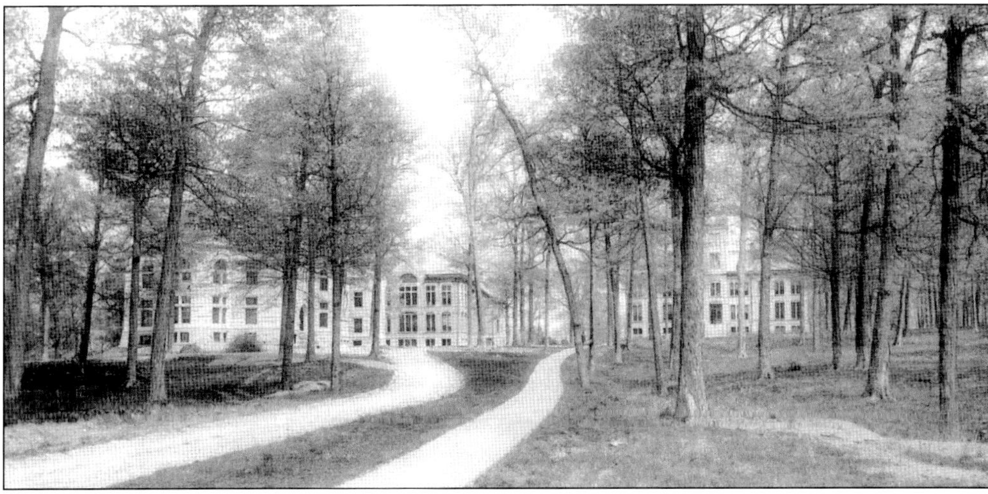

Indiana University's new campus had four main buildings in 1891. Left to right, as photographed through the trees of Dunn's Woods, are Maxwell Hall (then Library Hall), Owen Hall, and Wylie Hall. The original, small Maxwell Hall (1884; later named Mitchell Hall) is off-camera at right. A small gymnasium was completed in 1892. The map bellow is a page from the Sanborn Fire Insurance Map of Bloomington in 1892. These maps, created so that insurance adjustors could set rates, record the details of many historic buildings around the United States.

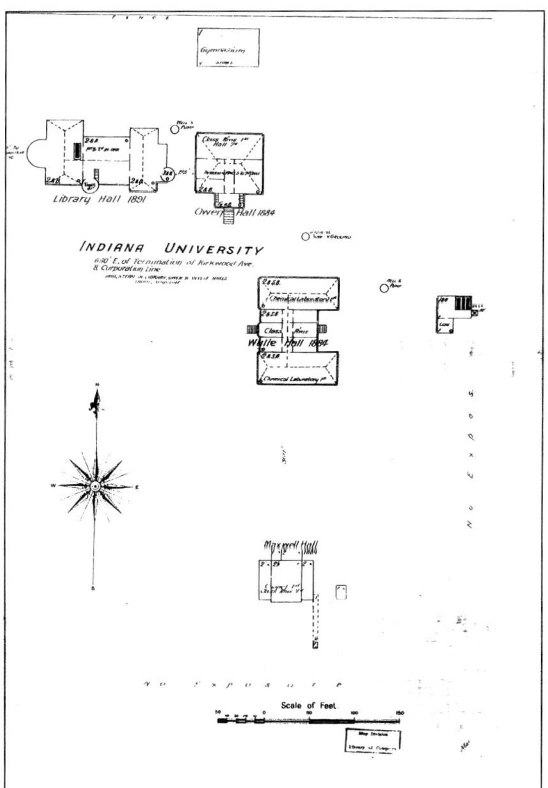

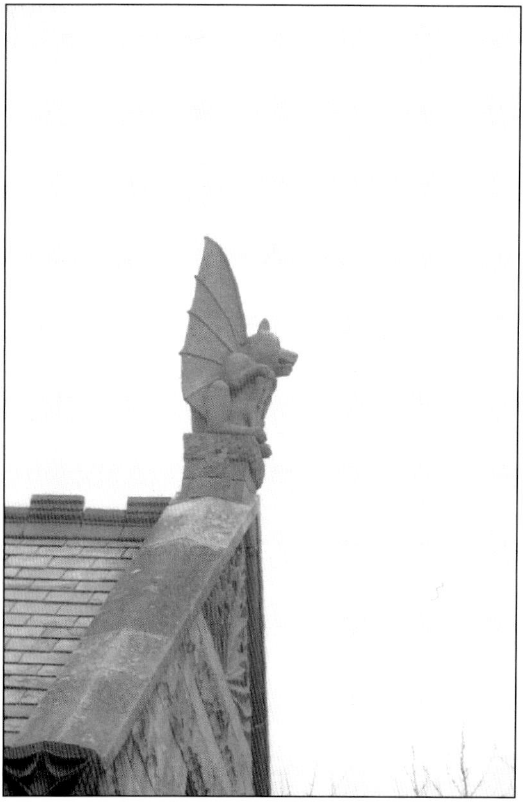

Maxwell Hall, with gargoyle atop the roof, was built west of Owen Hall in 1891 as the Library. It was the first campus building entirely constructed of limestone. Designed by architect George W. Bunting, Maxwell Hall has the towers, rough stonework, rounded arches, and decorative roof flashing of the Romanesque Revival (or Richardsonian Romanesque) style.

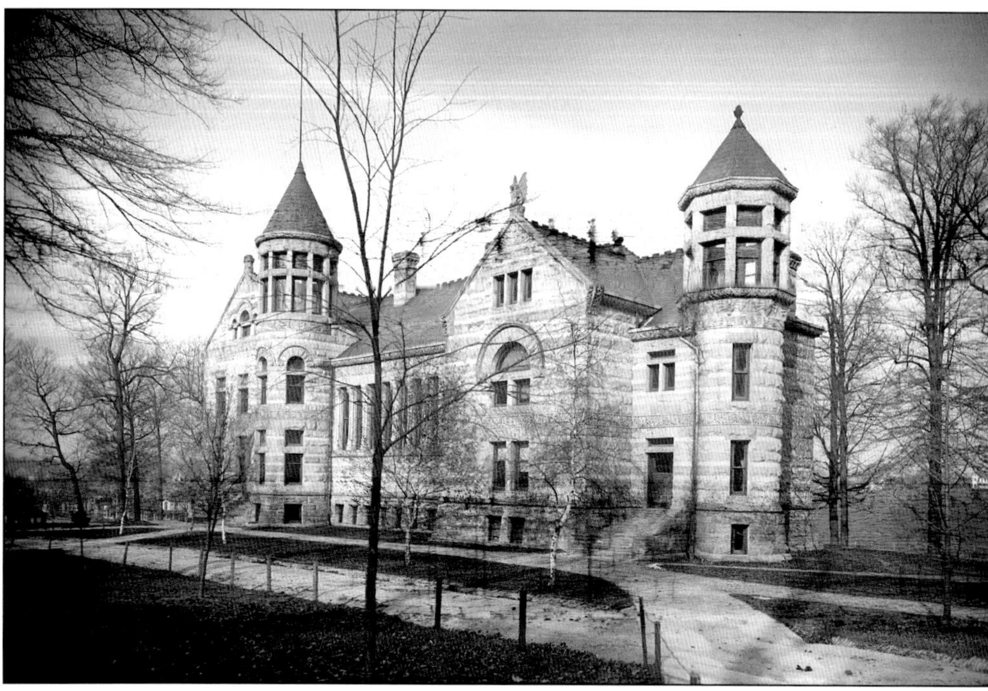

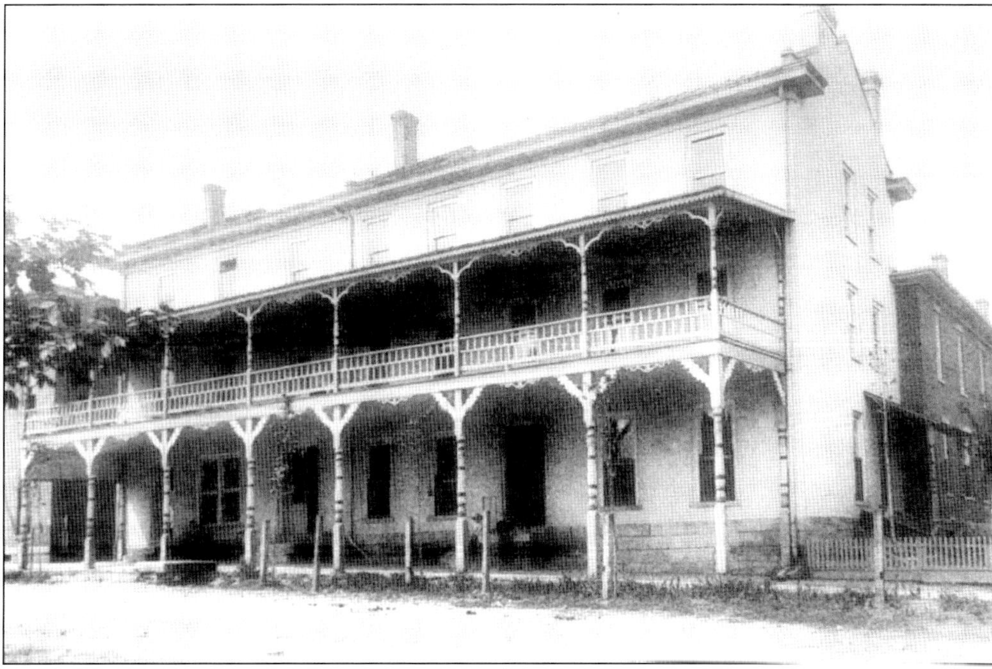

The National Hotel on East Kirkwood Avenue (then Fifth Street) was the closest business to the university when it was shown on the Sanborn Map of 1883. The National was then considered Bloomington's best hotel.

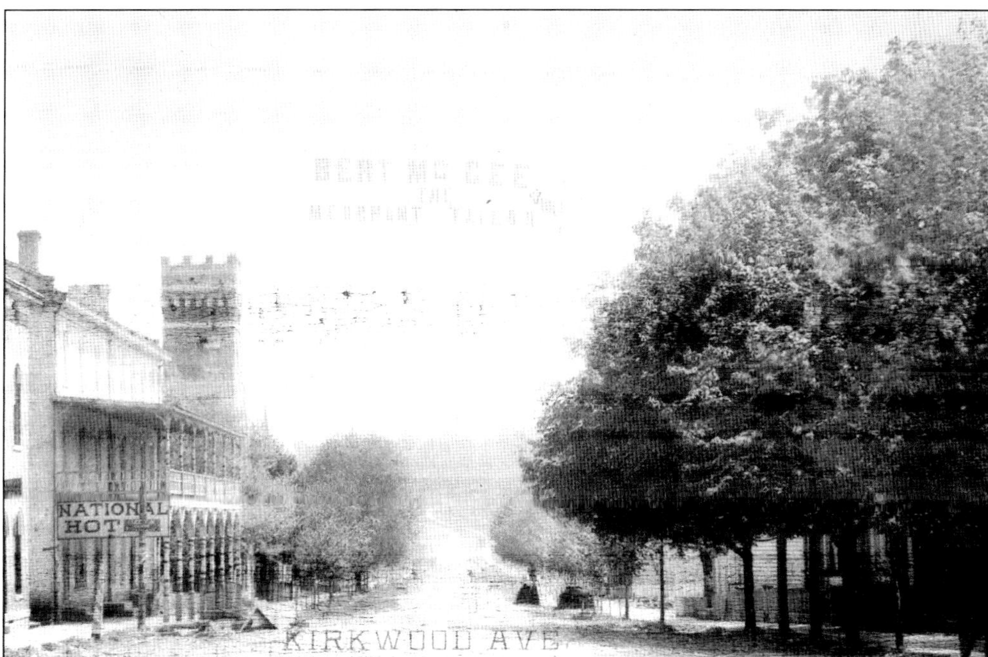

An aerial sign for "Bert McGee, the Merchant Tailor," was strung on a wire above Kirkwood Avenue. This photograph looking east appeared in the 1891 Burford booklet, a promotional brochure for the city of Bloomington.

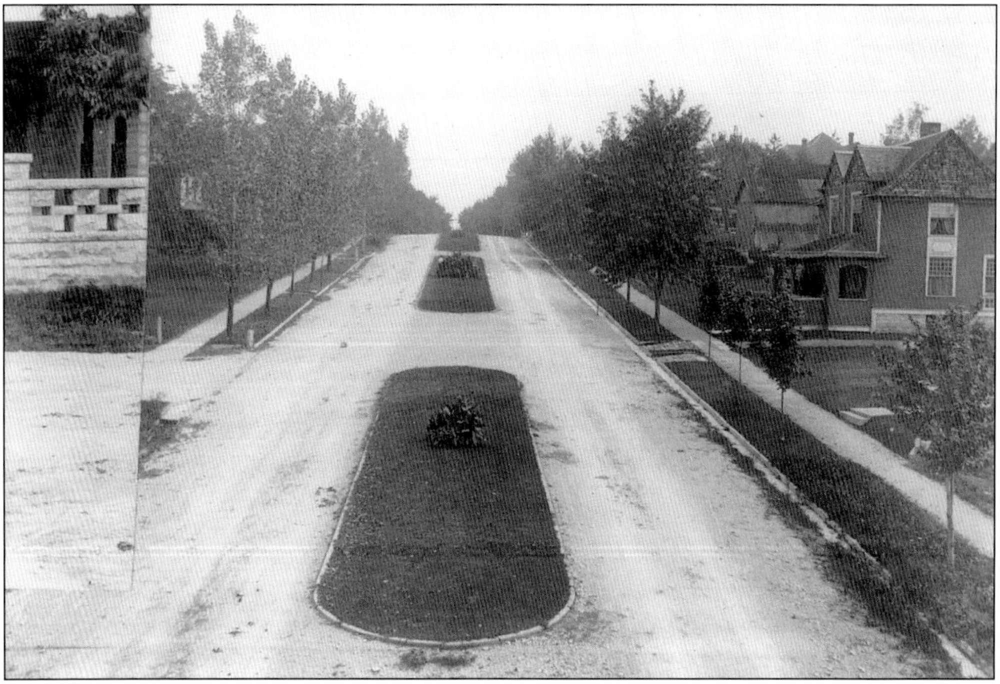

Bloomington business leaders promoted their city through the Burford booklet and the 1912 "Souvenir of Bloomington" published by the Commercial Club, a forerunner of the Chamber of Commerce. This handsome divided street is probably either South College Avenue or South Walnut Street.

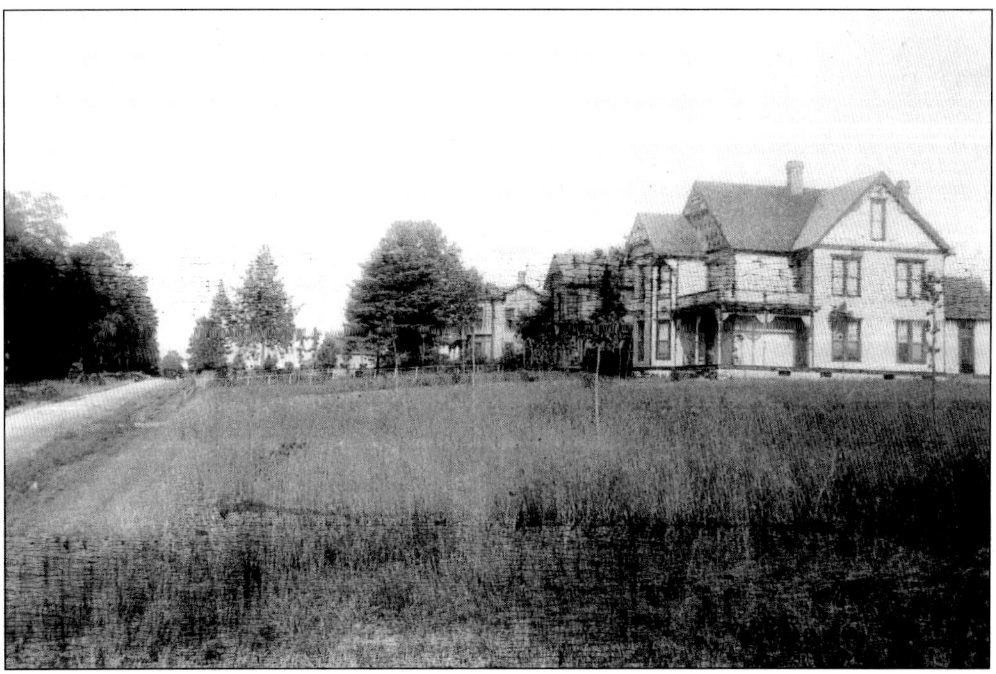

Homes sprang up in the new subdivision of University Heights south of the university during the 1890s.

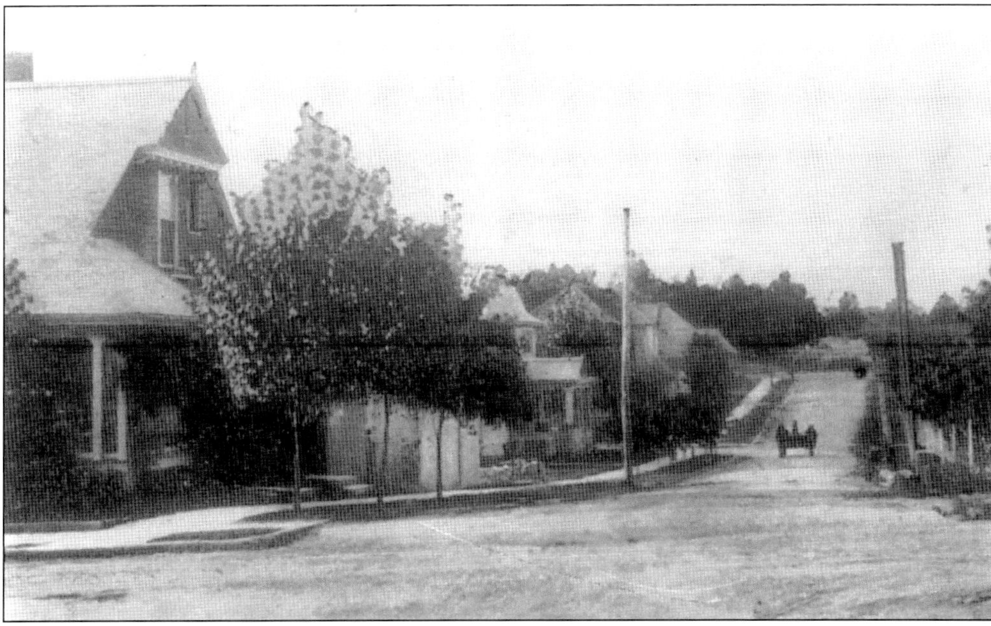

A postcard mailed in 1916 showed Indiana Avenue, at a somewhat earlier date, as the viewer looked south from an unknown cross street. Indiana Avenue was a desirable residential street near the university.

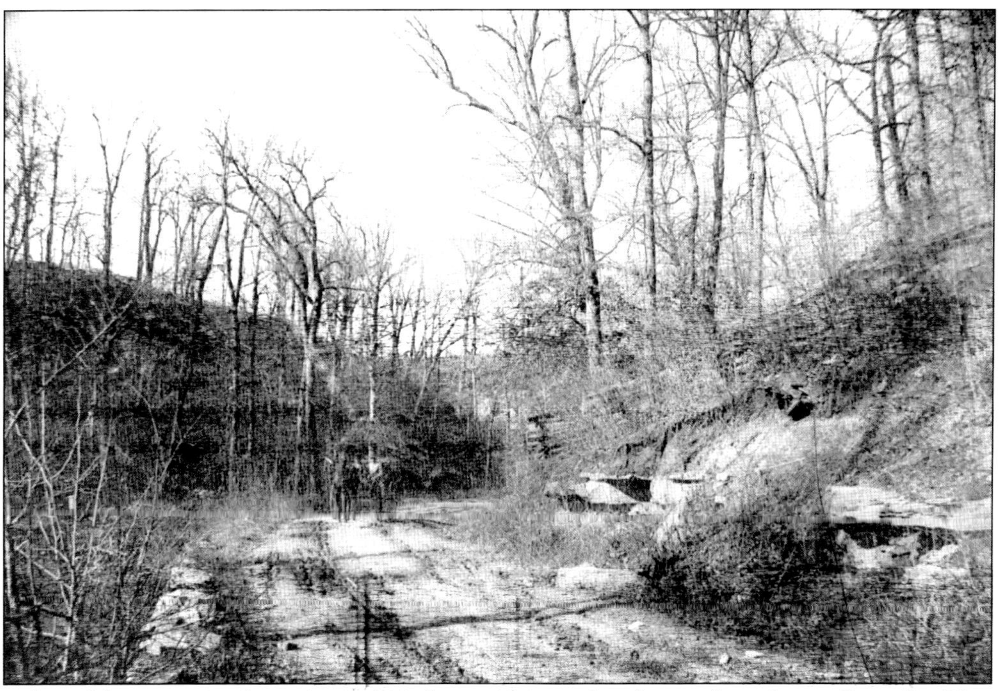

Indiana University students were advised to appreciate the charm of nearby rural scenery. This "scene on the North Pike" was miles away from campus when it was photographed for the 1891 Burford booklet, but is probably part of Bloomington today.

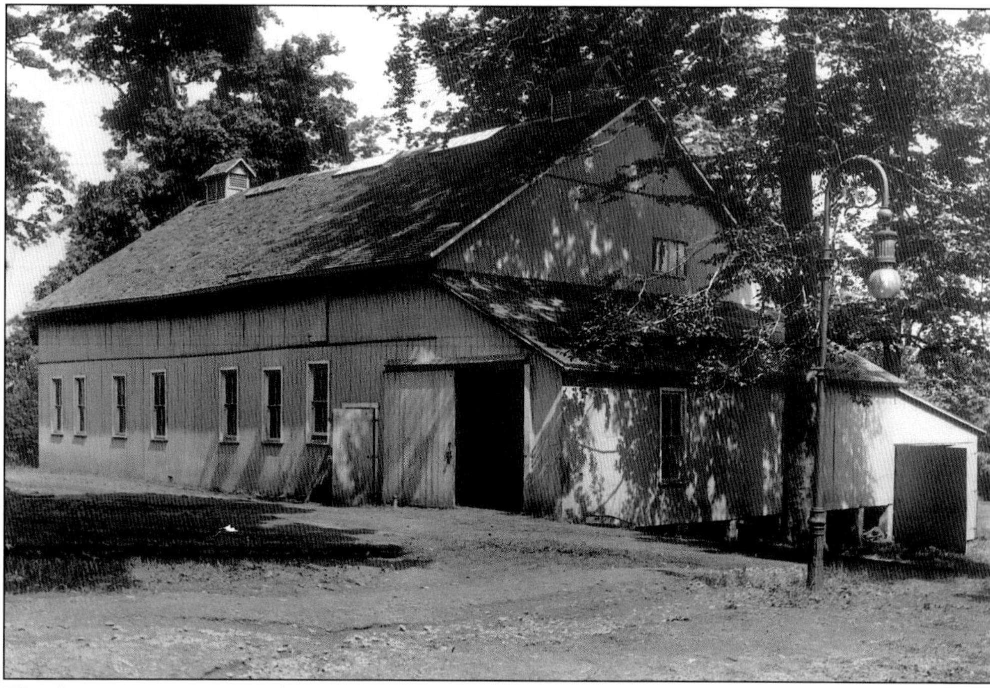

The first gymnasium at Indiana University, built in 1892, was a barn-like wooden building that stood north of Owen Hall. Only four years later, the building was pronounced too small. The first gym became a carpentry shop and was demolished in 1932.

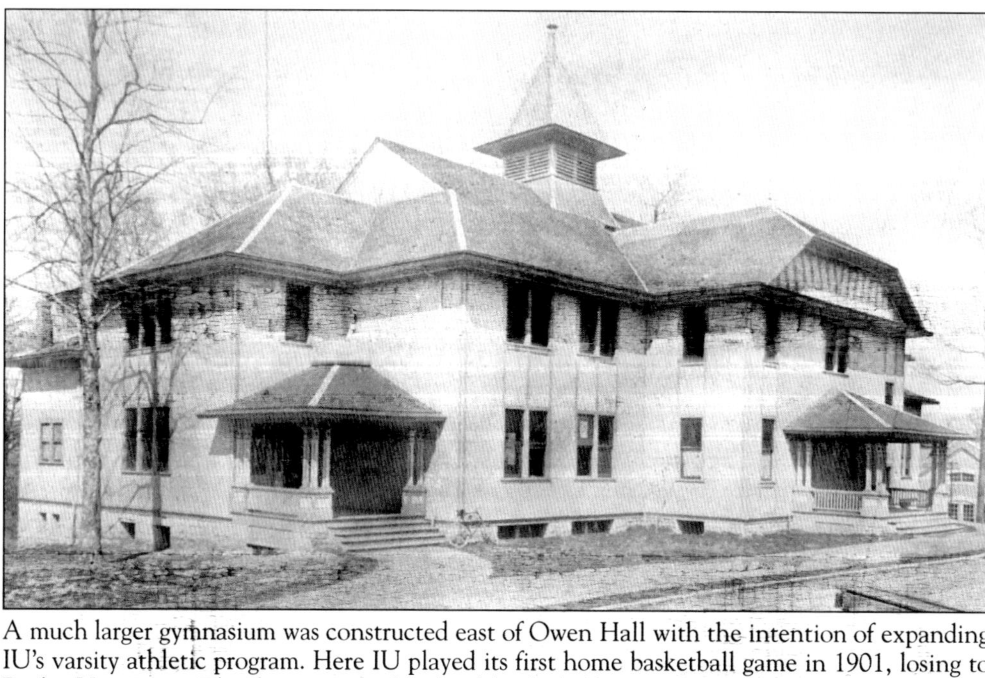

A much larger gymnasium was constructed east of Owen Hall with the intention of expanding IU's varsity athletic program. Here IU played its first home basketball game in 1901, losing to Butler University. The first state high-school basketball tournament was held here in 1911; Crawfordsville beat Lebanon 24-17. The second gym, later known as the first Assembly Hall, was demolished in 1938.

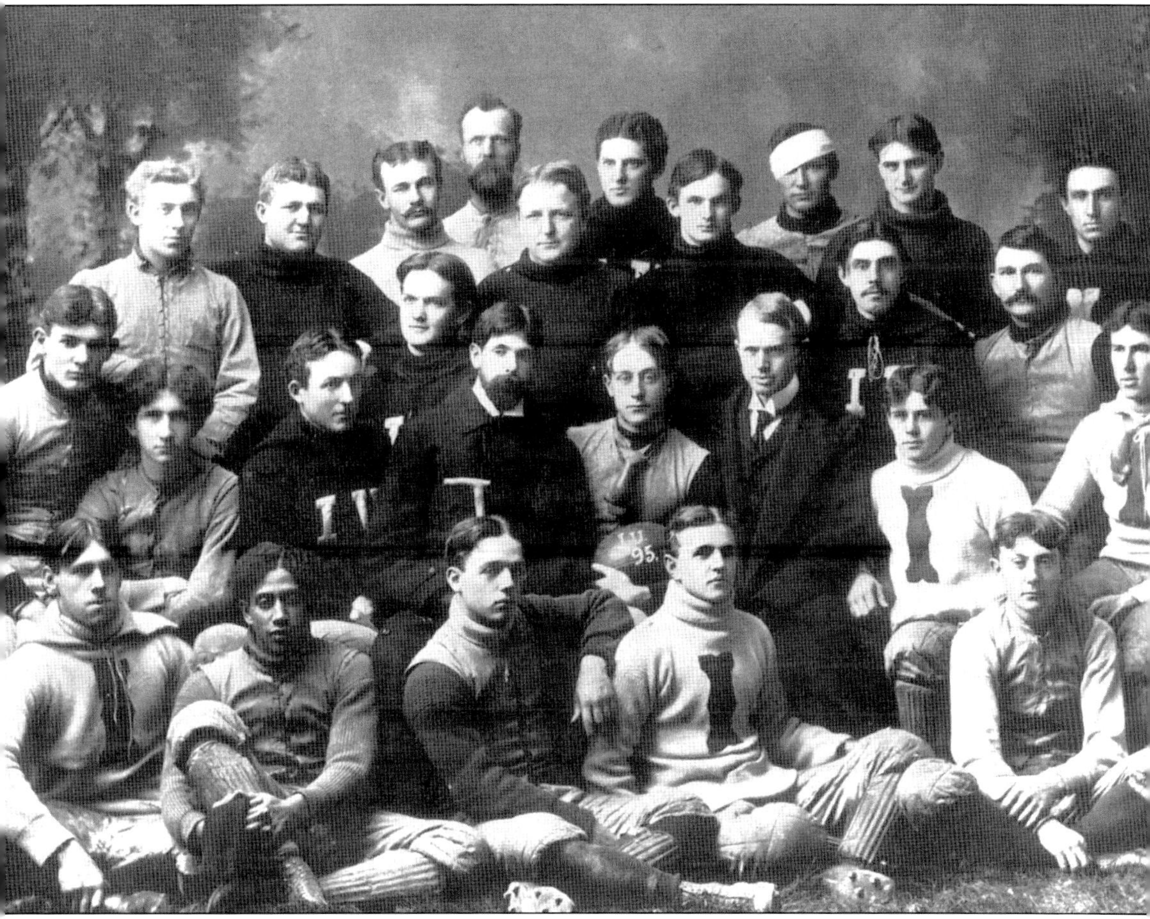

Indiana University's varsity football team posed in letter sweaters and jerseys in 1895. At this date, games were still played on the field at IU's Seminary Square campus south of town. Second from left in the front row of teammates is Preston E. Eagleson of Bloomington, the first African American to play in intercollegiate athletics at IU. Eagleson was also the first African American to receive a master's degree from Indiana University and one of five children sent to IU by his father.

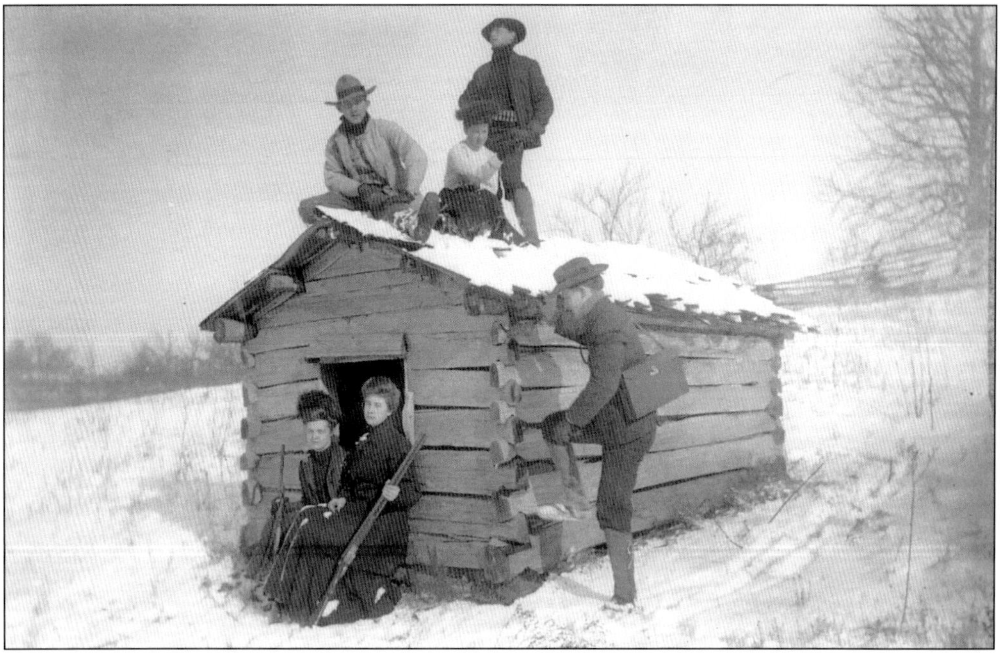

The scrapbook of Indiana University student Harry A. Hoffman, who attended IU from 1904 to 1906, included a photograph of students engaged in winter activities, including hunting rabbits in a meadow.

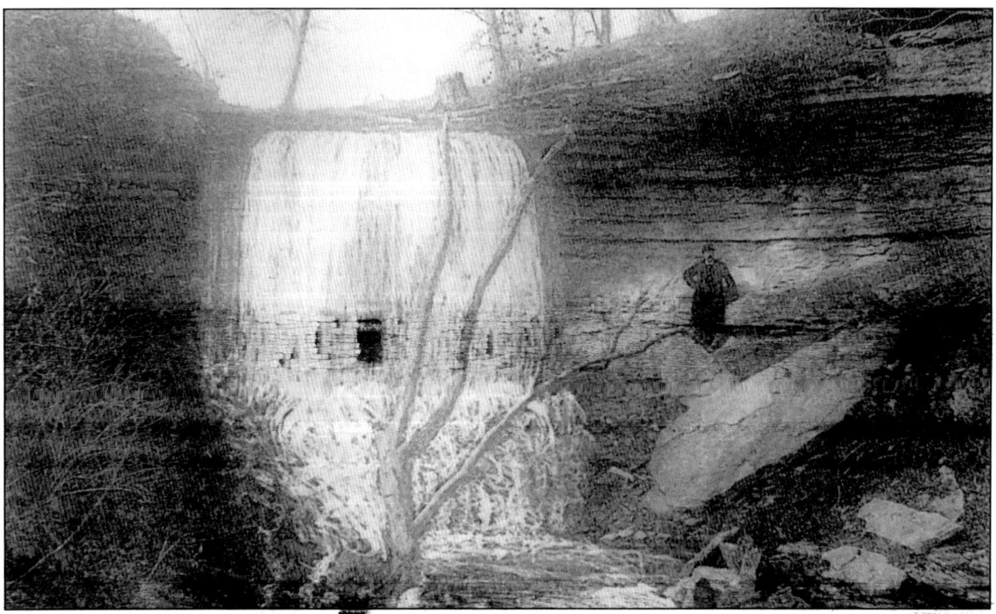

Cascades Park, not yet designated, was still a remote part of Monroe County north of town when its frozen waterfall was photographed around 1890. The popular spot for scenic excursions was opened as Bloomington's first park in 1924. It was upgraded as a Works Progress Administration (WPA) project during the Depression of the 1930s, but suffered from overuse and neglect in later years. Some restoration has been carried out since the 1970s, including rebuilding the walls of the stream bed.

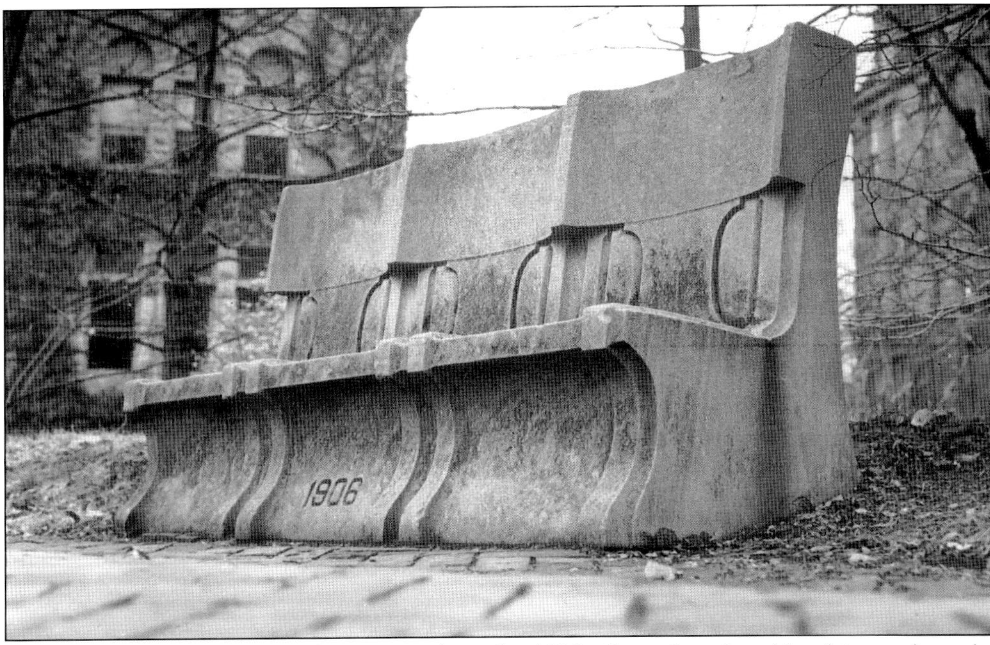

The "class gift" was an IU tradition as early as the 1890s. Stone benches, like this one from the class of 1906, were popular gifts. Choices in 1897 were a cast of the *Venus de Milo* and a portrait for the Trustees' Room. Several classes gave money toward buildings.

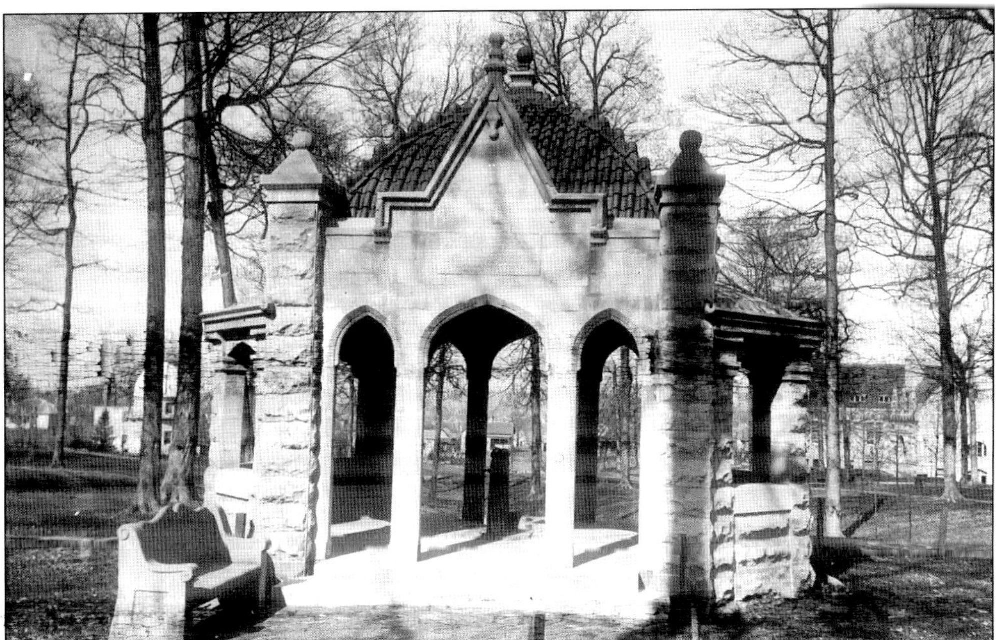

The Rose Well House (1908) in Dunn's Woods was a gift of alumnus and trustee Theodore Rose in honor of the class of 1875. When the Old College building (page 48) on the Seminary Square campus was rebuilt after a fire in 1900, its triple-arched entryways, tucked into the front façade at left and right, were removed. The stonework was incorporated into this small shelter, on the site of a functioning well since IU came to its new campus.

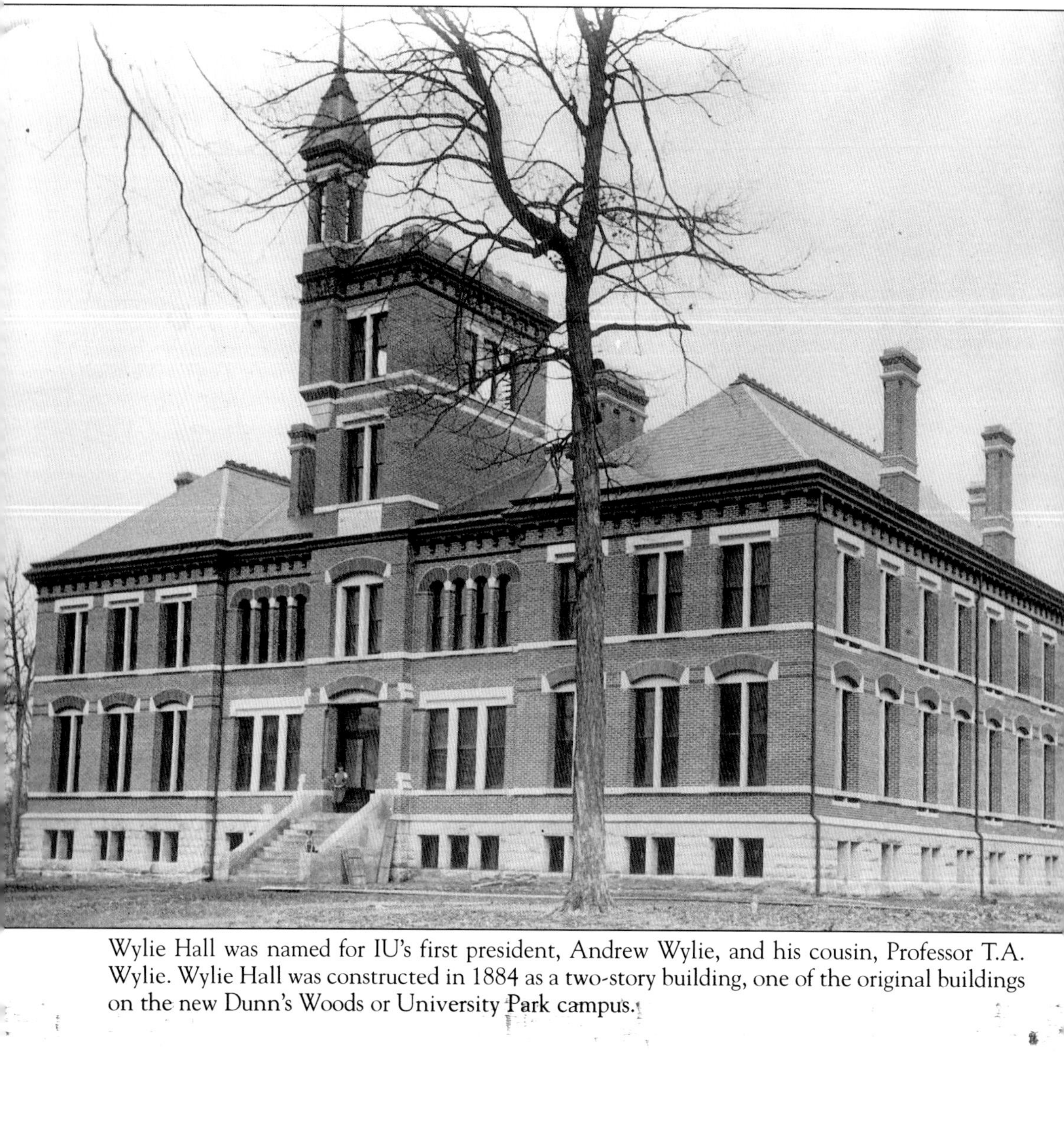

Wylie Hall was named for IU's first president, Andrew Wylie, and his cousin, Professor T.A. Wylie. Wylie Hall was constructed in 1884 as a two-story building, one of the original buildings on the new Dunn's Woods or University Park campus.

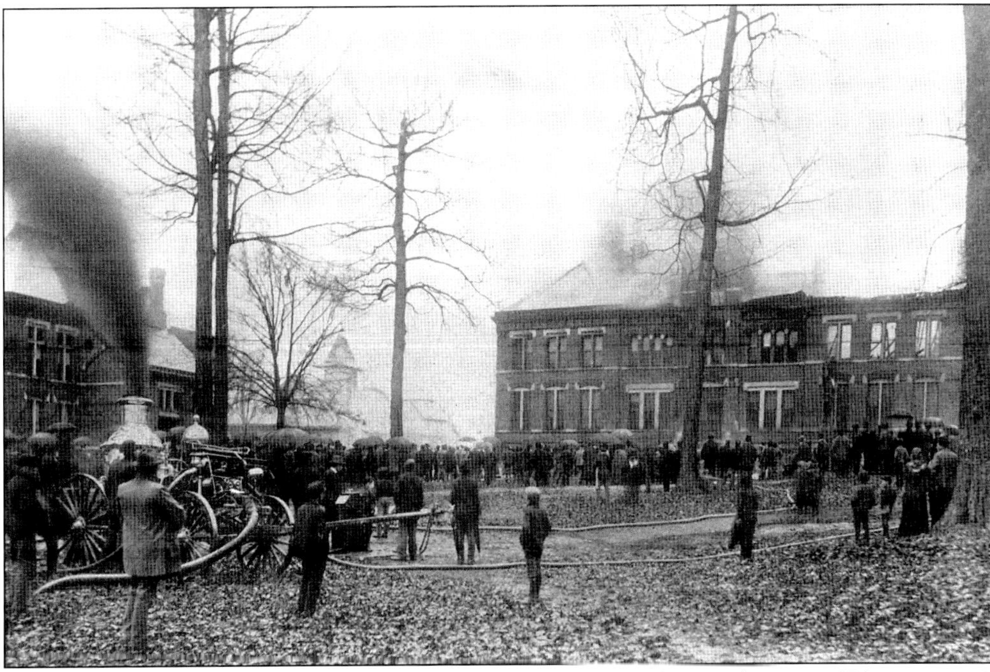

When Wylie Hall caught fire in 1900, the fire was extinguished using the city of Bloomington's horse-drawn, steam-powered pumper (left of photo). Wylie Hall is at right, Owen Hall at left, and the 1896 gymnasium (later the first Assembly Hall) in the center distance.

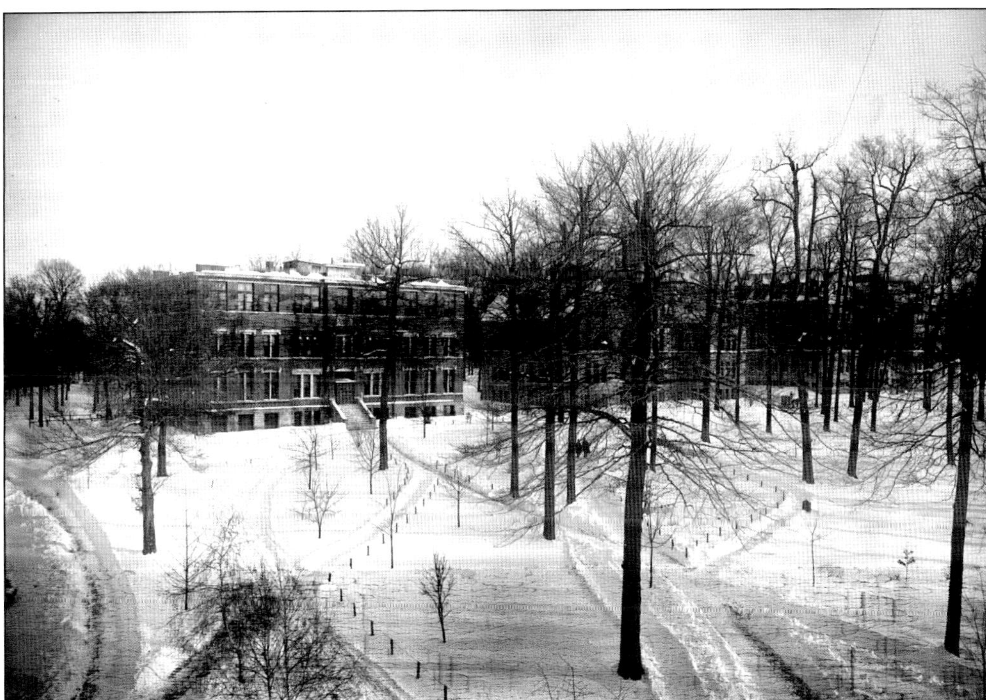

Wylie Hall was rebuilt in 1900 with a third story, a flat roof, and only the suggestion of its old tower. Left to right are Wylie Hall, Kirkwood Hall, and Science Hall c. 1900–1905.

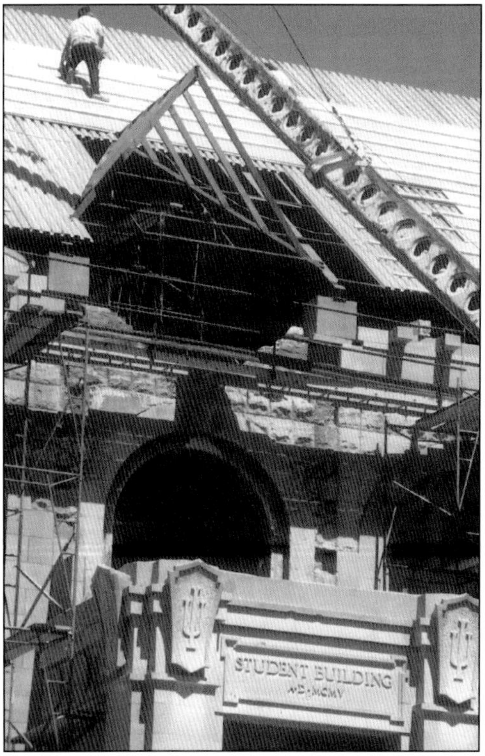

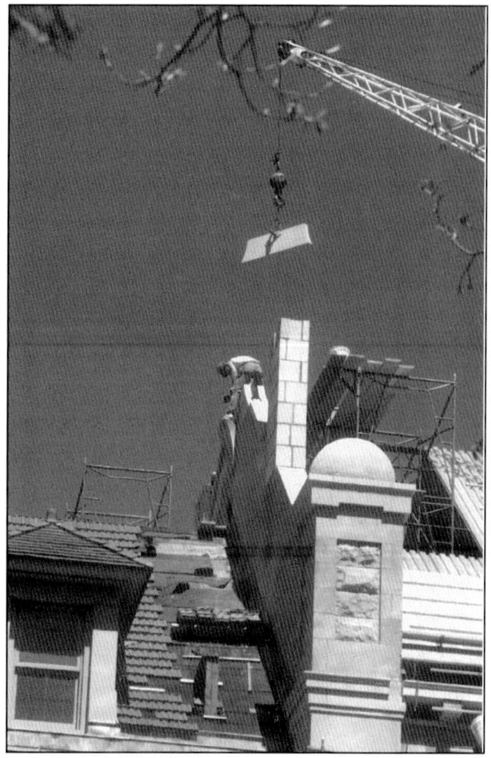

The Student Building (1905; shown below as originally constructed) was built by private contribution, including several class gifts. The Student Building was being restored and its interior modernized in 1990 (upper photos) when a fire occurred. Although work had to be redone, restoration was completed.

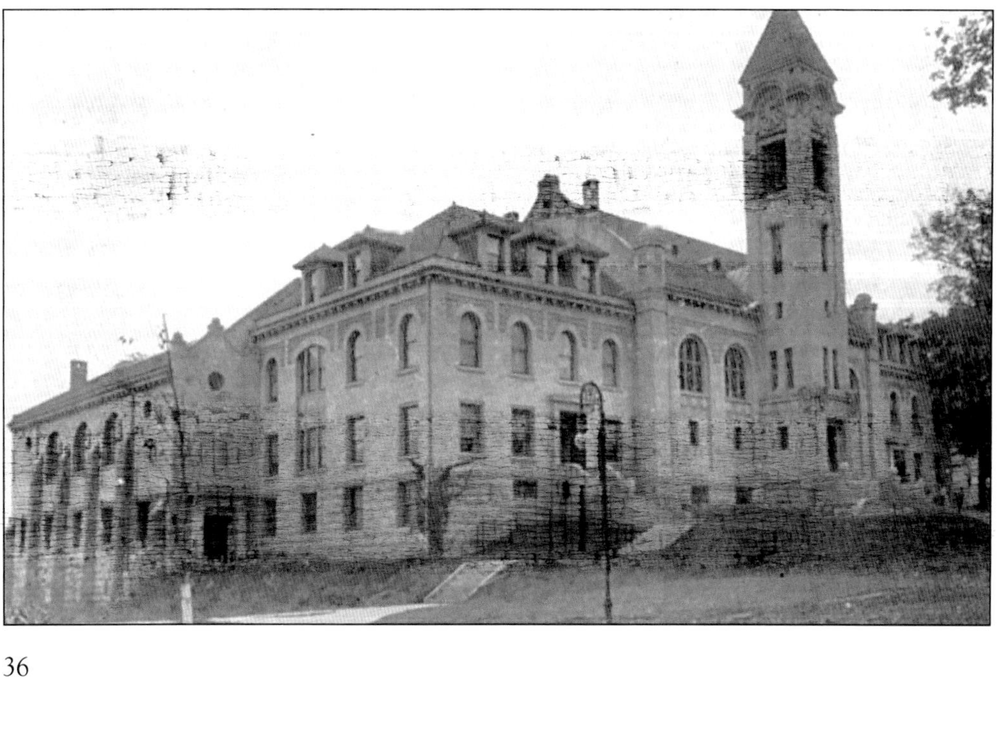

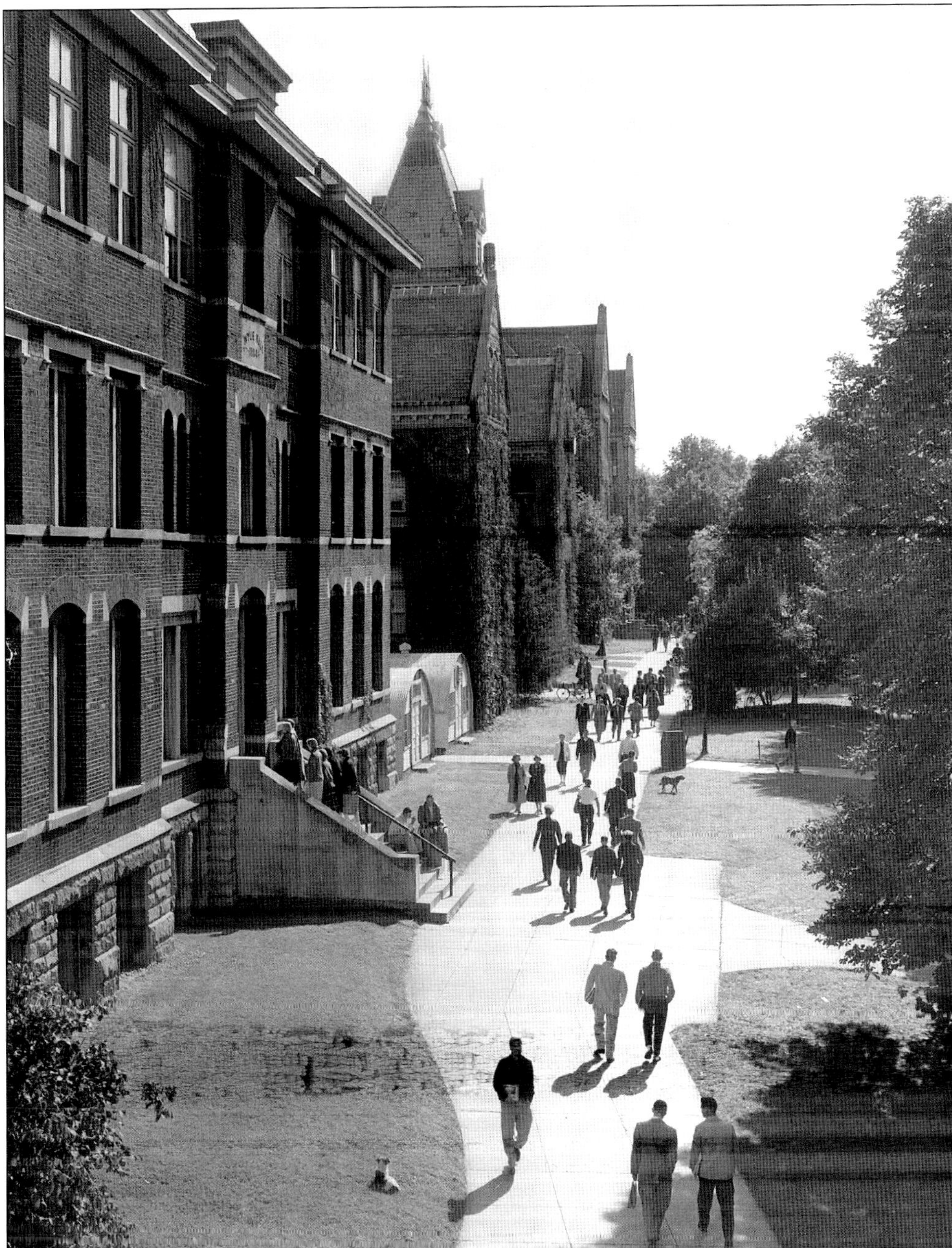

The east side of IU's Old Crescent in 1955 looked much as it does today, including Wylie, Kirkwood, and Science Halls, except that two Quonset huts between Wylie and Kirkwood attest to the university's rapid expansion after World War II.

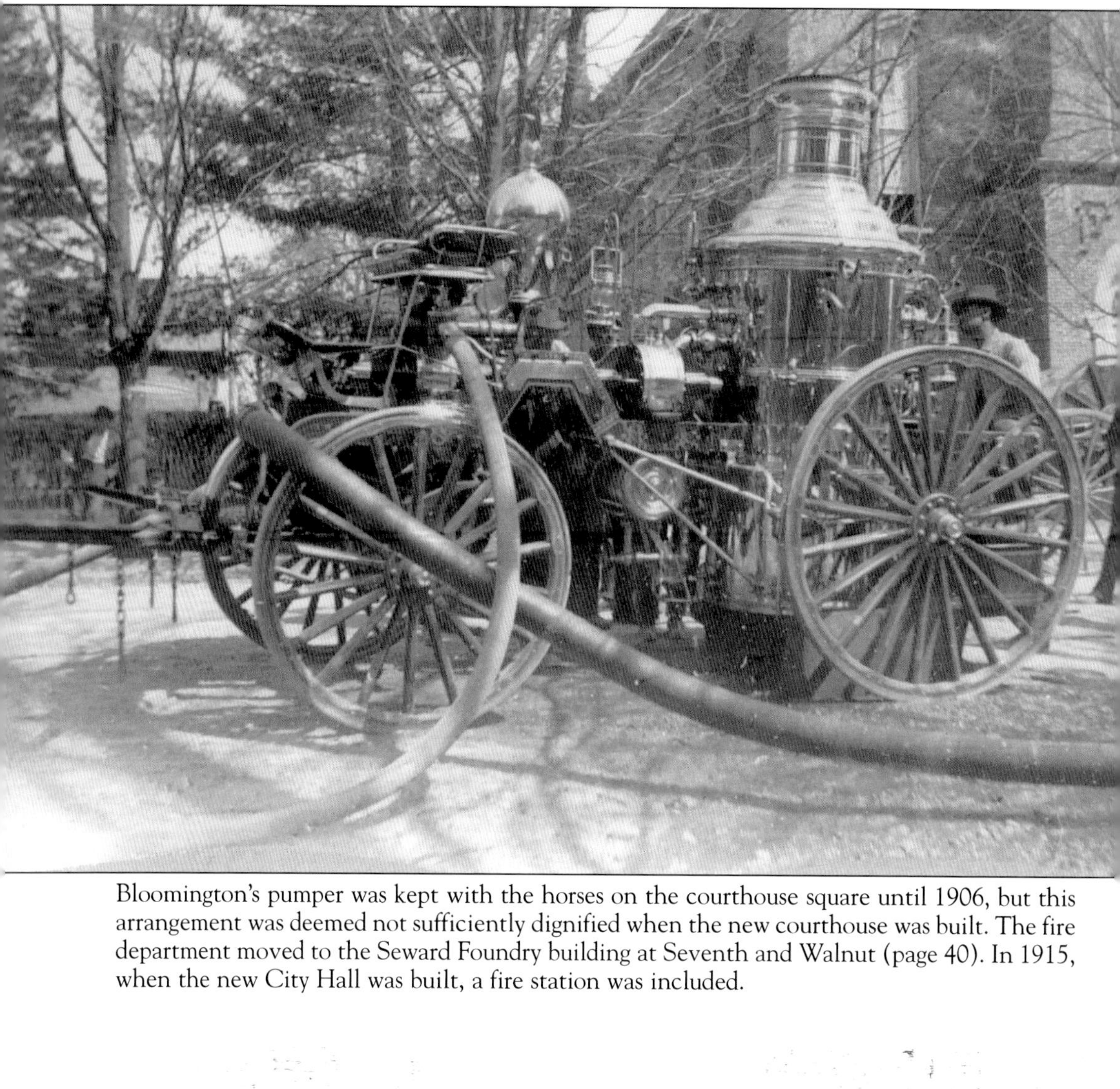

Bloomington's pumper was kept with the horses on the courthouse square until 1906, but this arrangement was deemed not sufficiently dignified when the new courthouse was built. The fire department moved to the Seward Foundry building at Seventh and Walnut (page 40). In 1915, when the new City Hall was built, a fire station was included.

Three

BECOMING A CITY

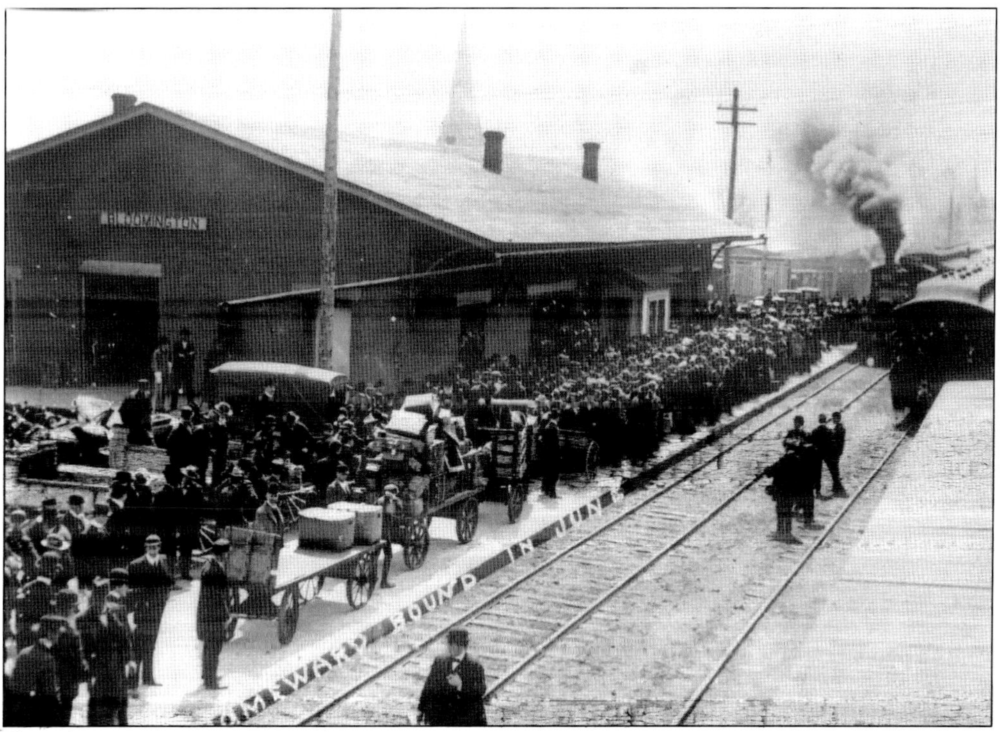

Summer quiet was about to descend on Bloomington as IU students and other passengers waited for a northbound train c. 1906. Above the slogan "Homeward Bound in June," written along the curb of the platform after the photograph was taken, carts held tagged valises and wicker baskets ready for loading. The railroad gradually brought a town-centered economy to Monroe County. By 1910, there were some 40 factories in Bloomington, and more people lived in town than in rural areas.

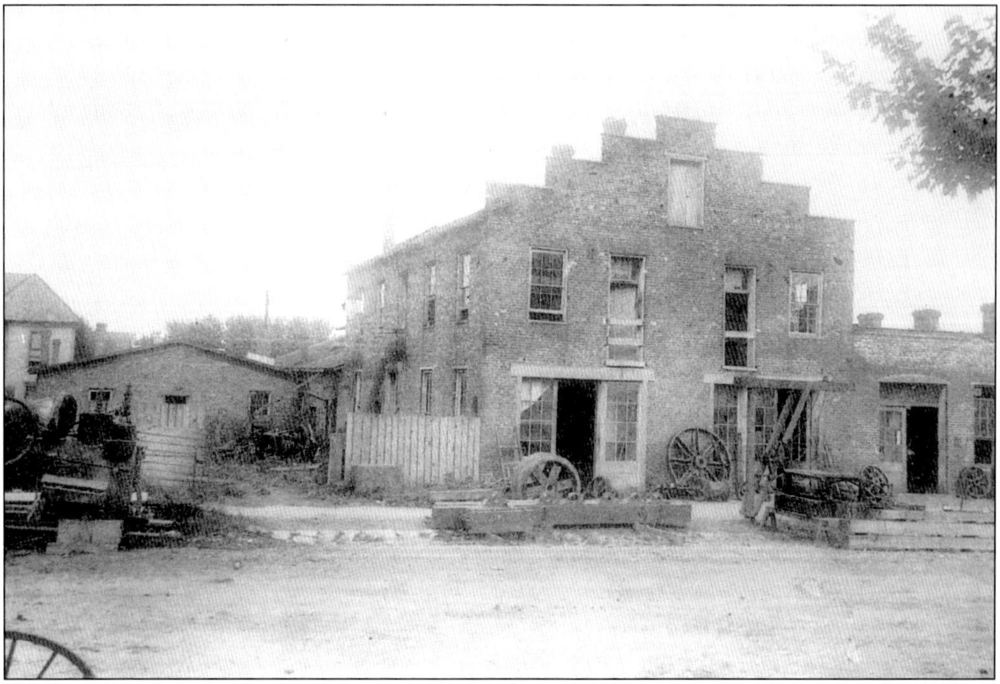

This modest, early factory building with stepped parapet wall, chimneys, and smokestacks was Seward's Foundry and Machine Works at Seventh and Walnut Streets, a firm that began with blacksmith Austin Seward in the 1820s.

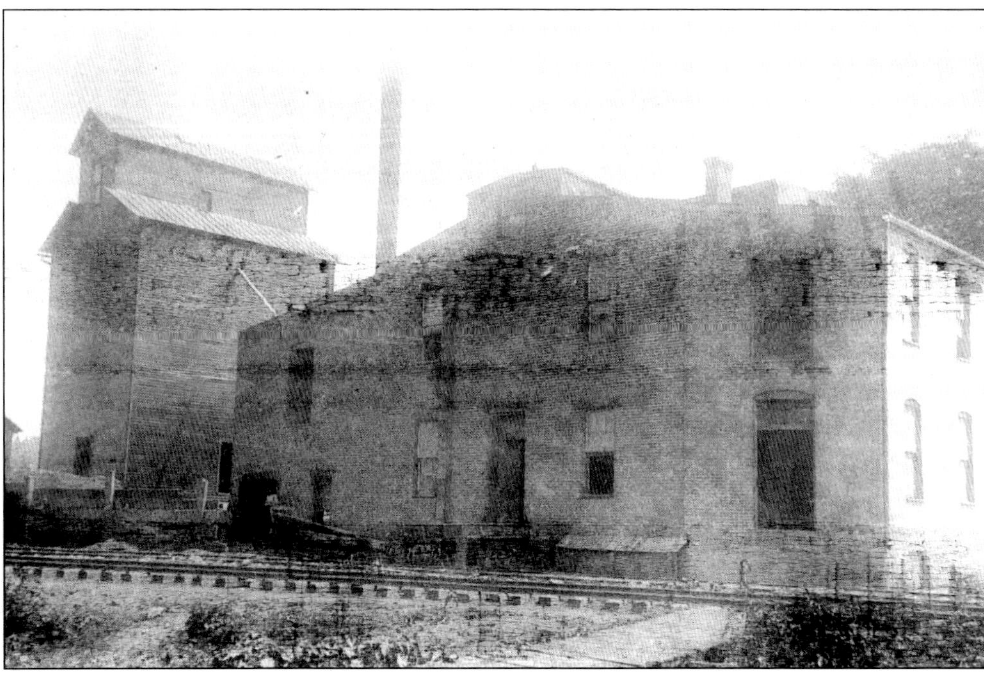

The flour mill and grain elevator, photographed *c.* 1891, was one of the industries that congregated on Bloomington's west side near the railroad tracks.

Workers in aprons, executives in business suits and hats, and a small child pose in front of the Waldron Tannery, a four-story brick building at the southeast corner of Madison and Fifth Streets during the 1880s or 1890s. The clapboarded family home stood beside the tannery building.

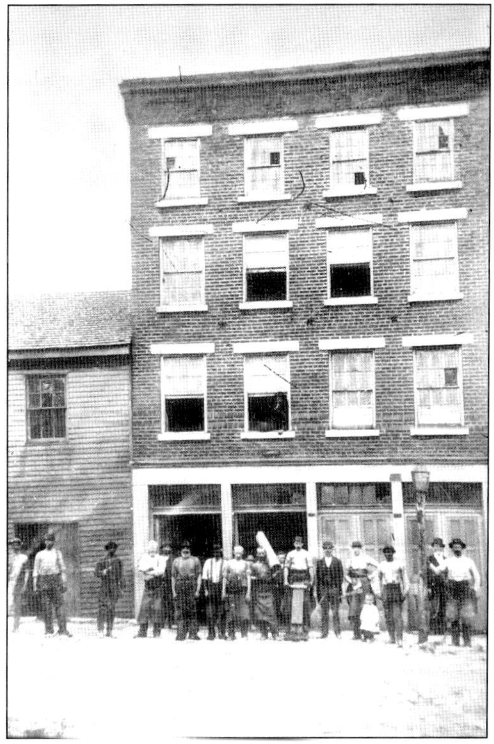

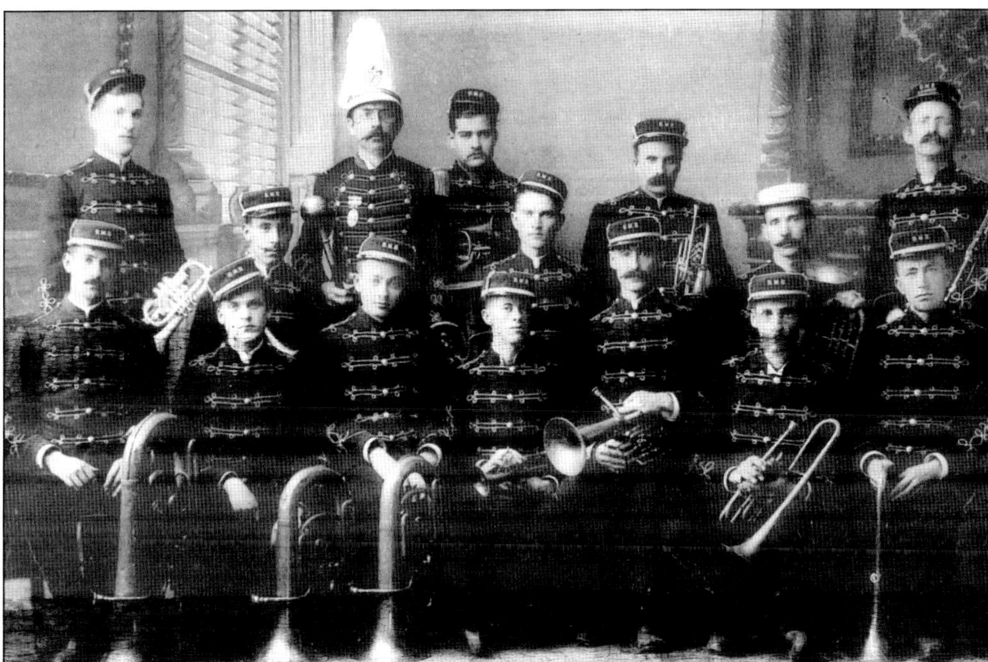

The "Bloomington Mechanics' Band," complete with drum major at left end of third row, showed off their splendid uniforms and their instruments for this formal portrait, included in the 1891 Burford booklet. The band was obviously a marching group made up of local "mechanics" (artisans or workingmen) but is otherwise unidentified.

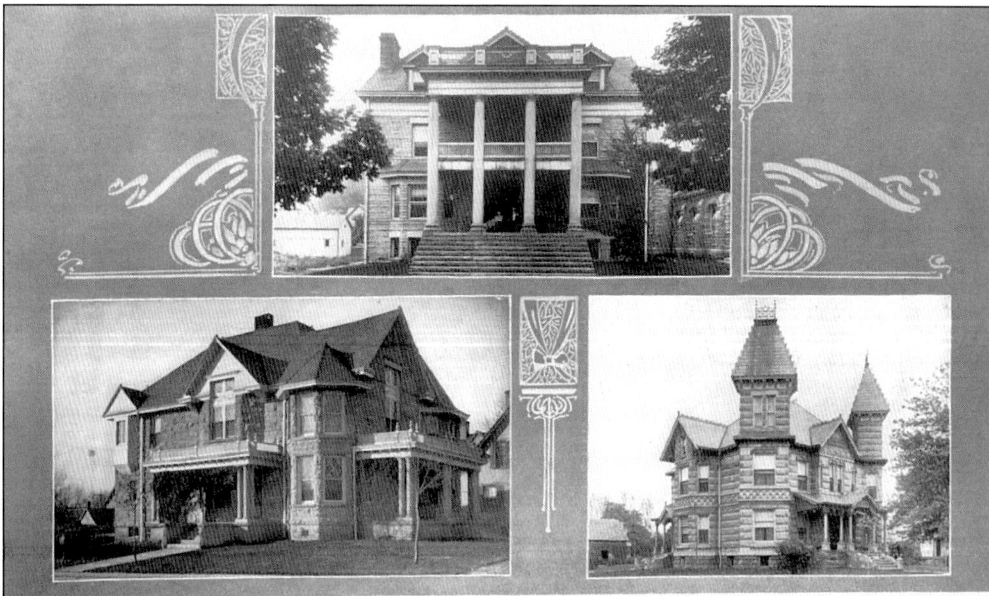

Representative Bloomington Residences.

Limestone fantasias, towered or turreted in early years, were popular among Bloomington's well-to-do from the 1890s through 1920s. "Representative homes," whose architects are unknown, were included in the Commercial Club booklet of 1912.

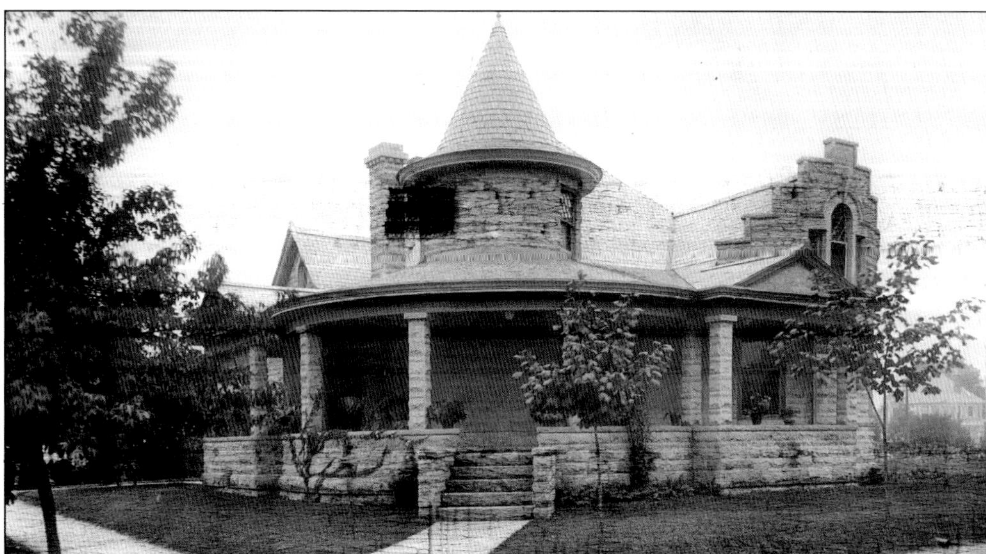

Another local mansion was the now-vanished Bradfute house. Walter S. Bradfute, who graduated from Indiana University, remained in Bloomington to start a newspaper, *The Telephone*, in 1877.

The Knights of Pythias fraternal building (1903) on the east side of the courthouse square, now remodeled as living space, was designed by John L. Nichols (1859–1929), Bloomington's first native architect. Nichols designed buildings in many styles for many purposes, completing 632 architectural commissions in 1908. Prosperity and a larger population brought work for architects and builders.

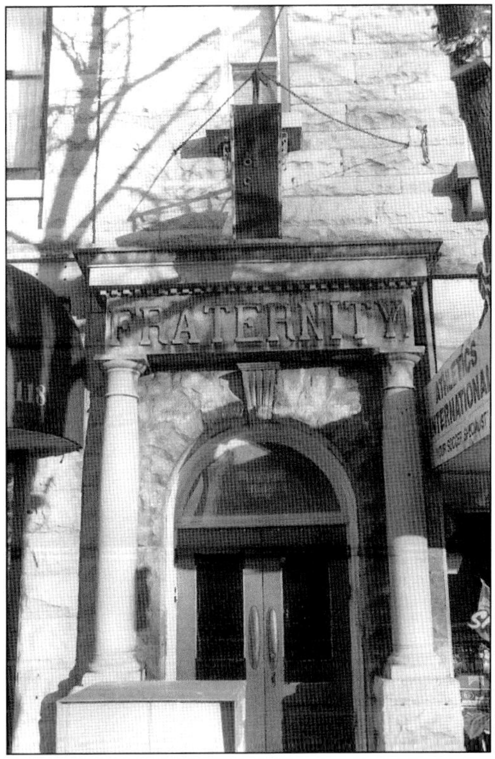

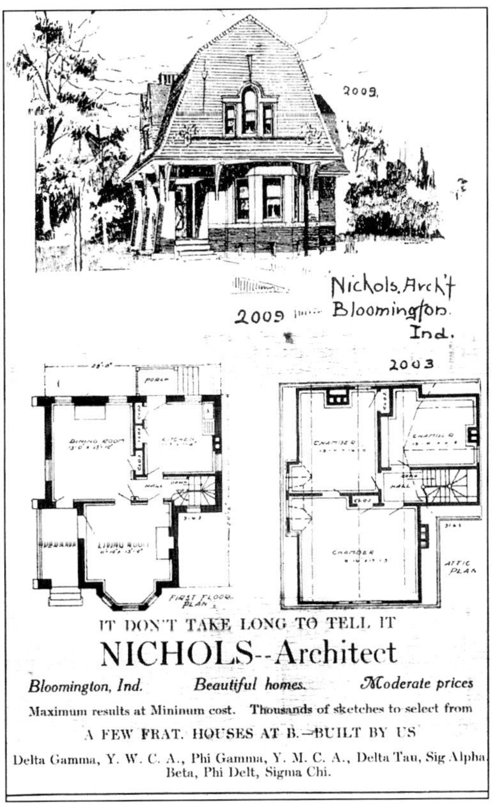

Houses in Colonial Revival style with a gambrel or Dutch roof like that pictured in Nichols's catalog were popular in Bloomington. They were built both from architects' plans for individual clients and from pattern books whose designs could be purchased by a builder. Nichols trained by working with his father, a contractor, and apprenticing to other architects.

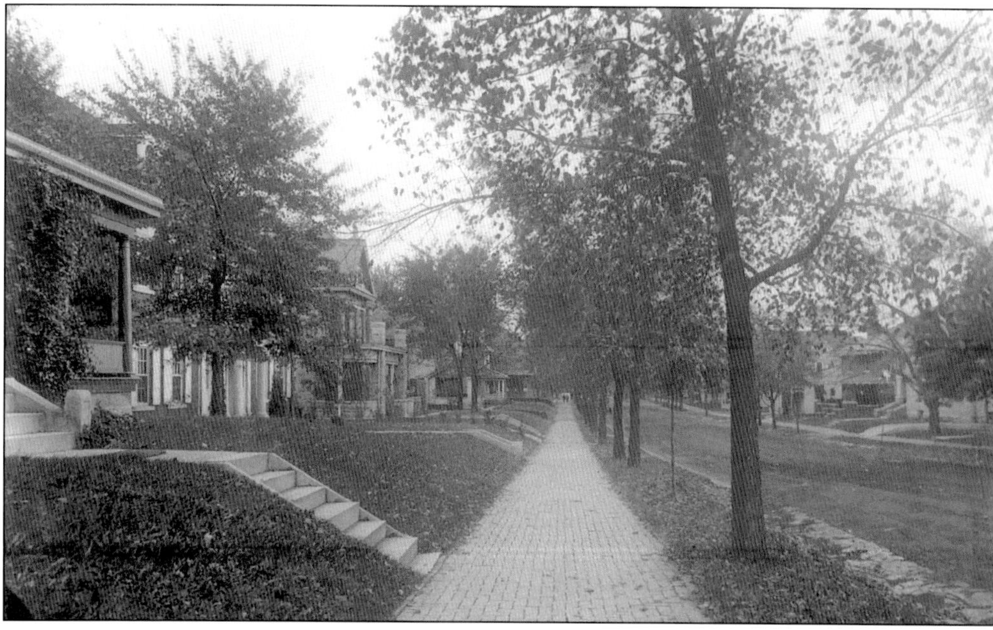

The viewer looks south along North Walnut from East Tenth Street, in the early 20th century and some 100 years later (below). The Showers family, who came to have the largest factory in Bloomington and branches in two other cities, pioneered a residential district on North Washington Street and North Walnut Avenue. The three houses nearest the camera at left above are the Morgan House (1892), the Teter House (1913; not visible in lower photo), and the Buskirk-Showers house (1897). The Morgan house was the first restoration project undertaken by the revolving fund of Bloomington Restorations, Inc.

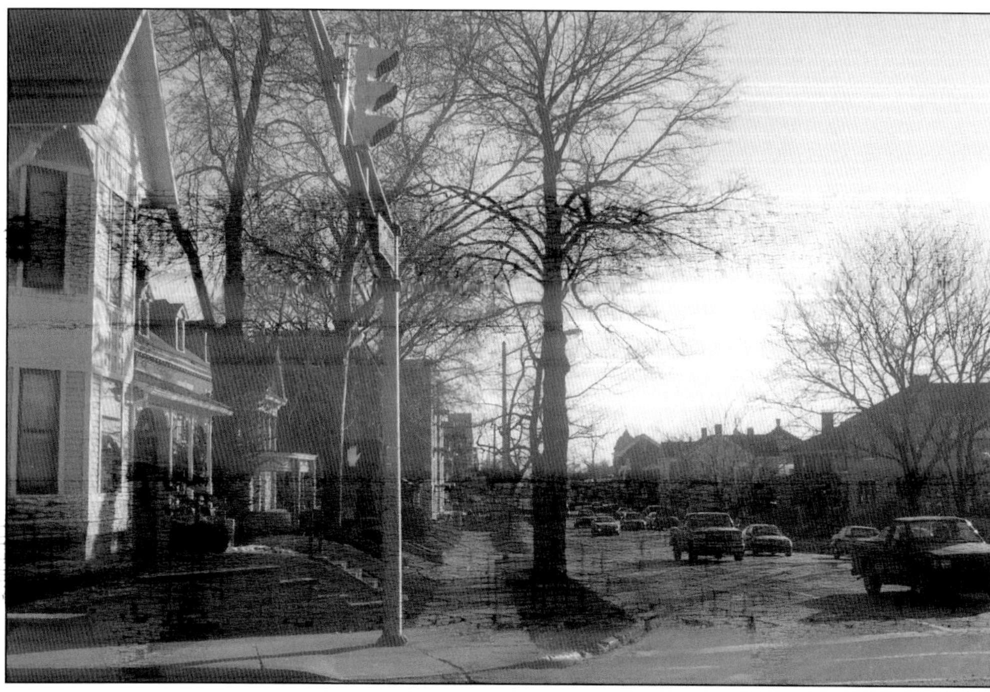

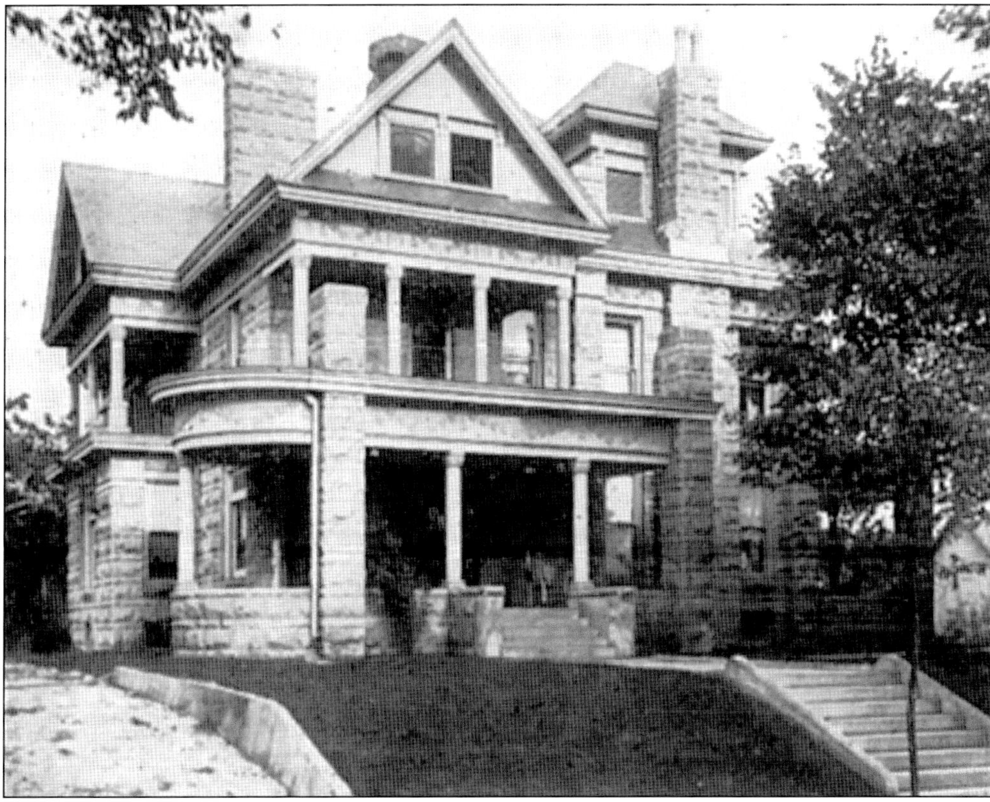

The Buskirk-Showers House, once described as the most beautiful house in town, is located at 520 North Walnut Street. Philip Kearny Buskirk was president of the First National Bank and owned stock in both Indiana limestone quarries and California gold mines. The house was later lived in by members of the Showers family.

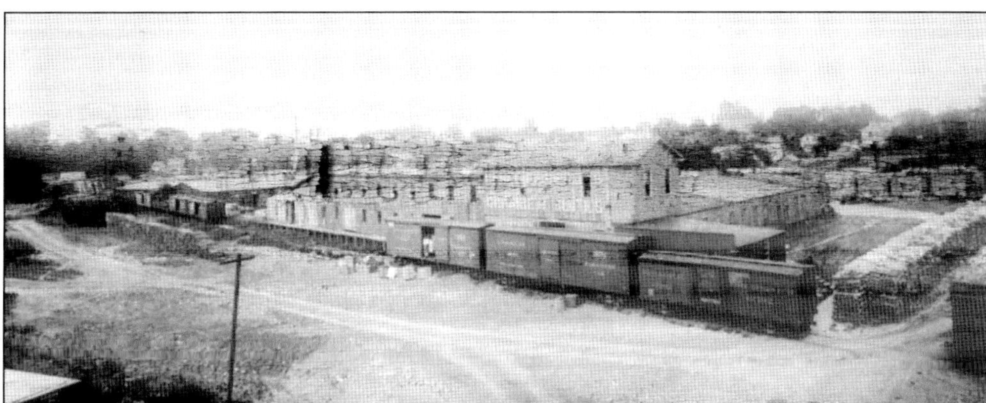

The Showers factory relocated near the railroad on Morton Street after an 1884 fire, and the city paid half the cost. Charles C. Showers located his first cabinet shop on the east side of the courthouse square in 1856, then moved to Ninth and Grant Streets about 10 years later. Because Showers was willing to hire African Americans, a 19th-century black neighborhood developed between Fifth, Lincoln, Tenth, and Dunn Streets. Some African Americans as well as other factory workers later moved near the new plant.

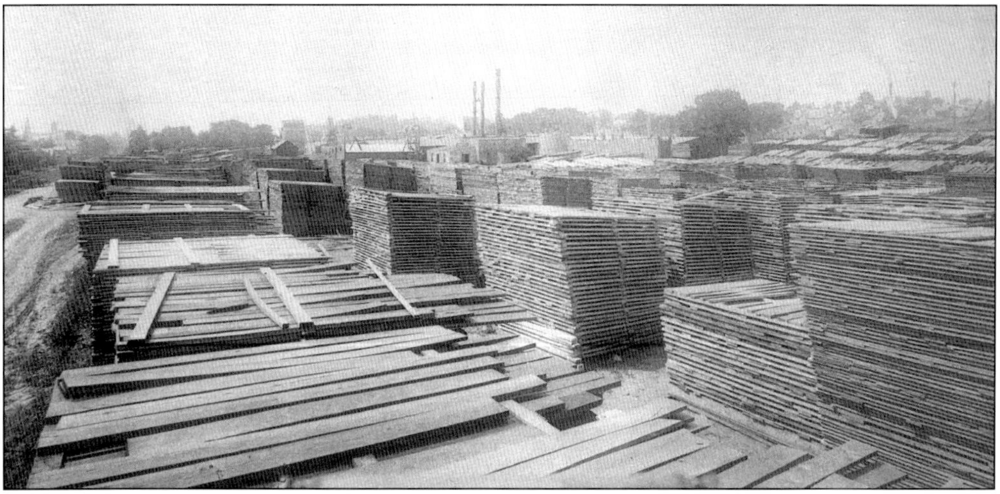

The Showers Brothers lumber storage area was included in the 1891 Burford booklet. New factory buildings (1910; below) replaced the old ones on the same site. The viewer looks west across Morton Street and the railroad tracks toward Rogers Street. The factory's seemingly endless row of saw-toothed roofs was a feature of the 1912 Commercial Club booklet. Coincidentally, the Morton Street site was the 1910 center of population, as determined by the U.S. Census Bureau.

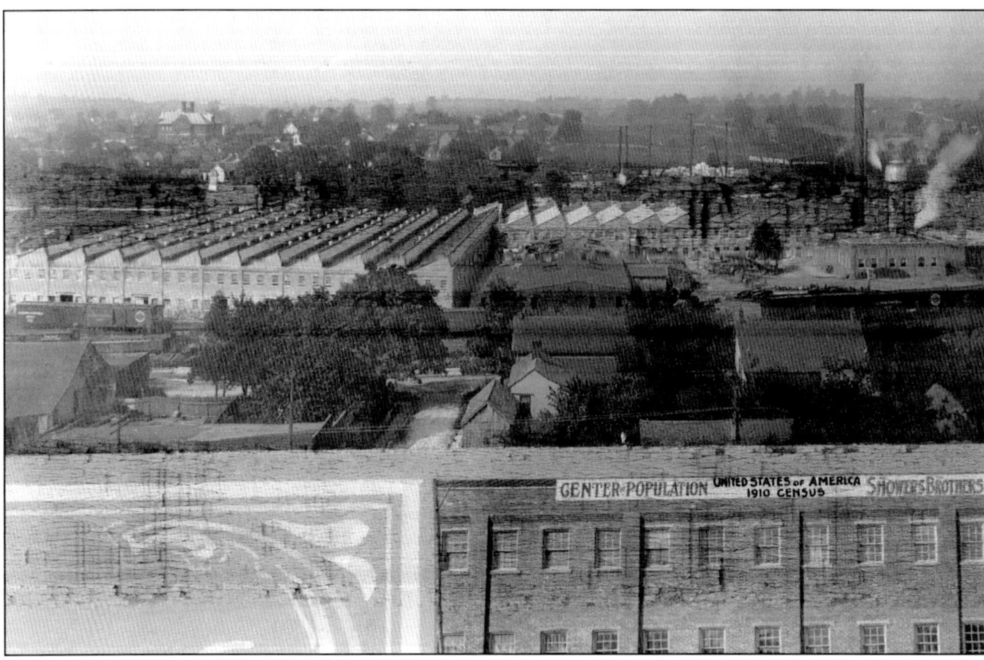

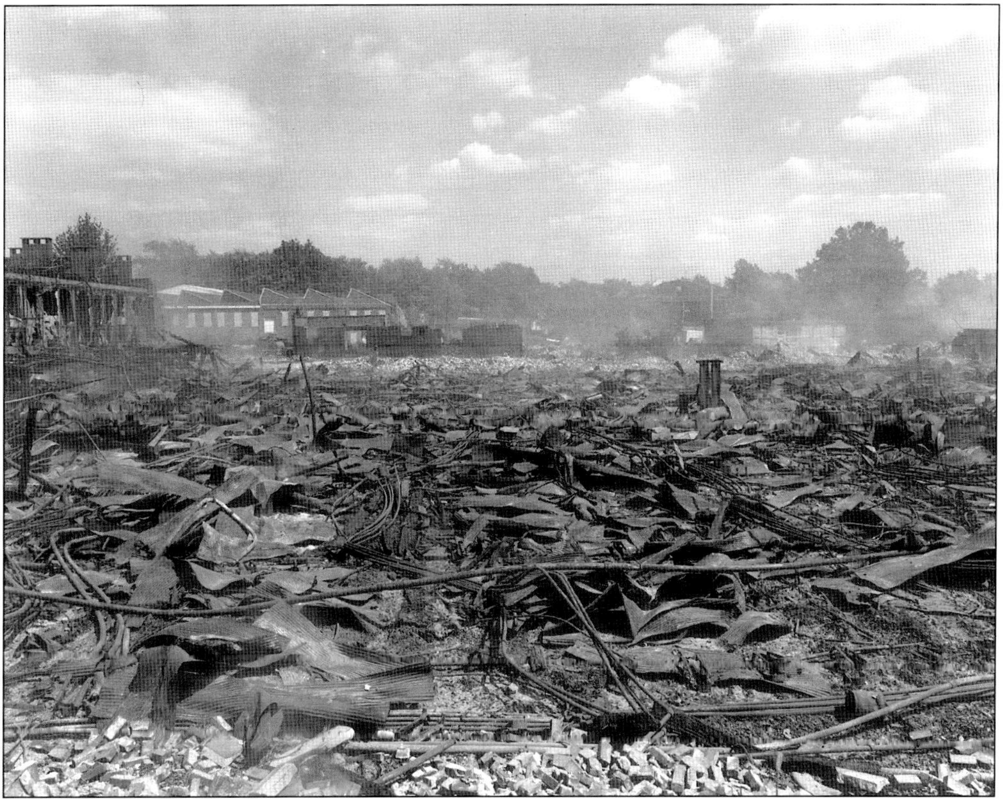

Fire trucks from surrounding communities helped answer the call in August 1966, when fire destroyed part of the former Showers factory. Indiana University had purchased the factory in 1959 to use as storage space. At its greatest extent in the 1920s, the Showers factory site was bounded by Rogers, West Eleventh, Morton, and West Eighth Streets.

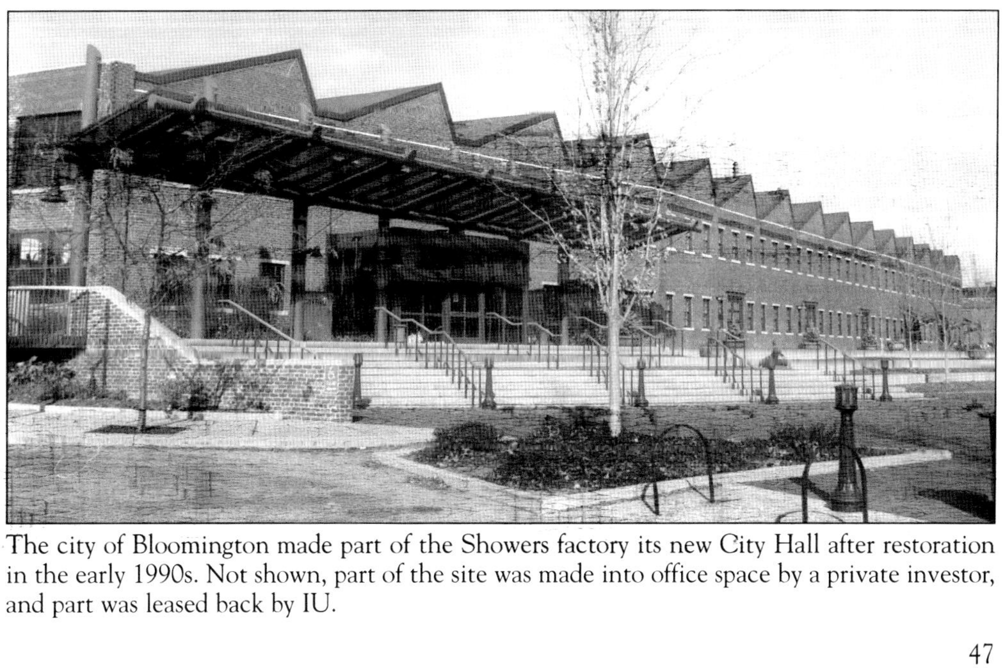

The city of Bloomington made part of the Showers factory its new City Hall after restoration in the early 1990s. Not shown, part of the site was made into office space by a private investor, and part was leased back by IU.

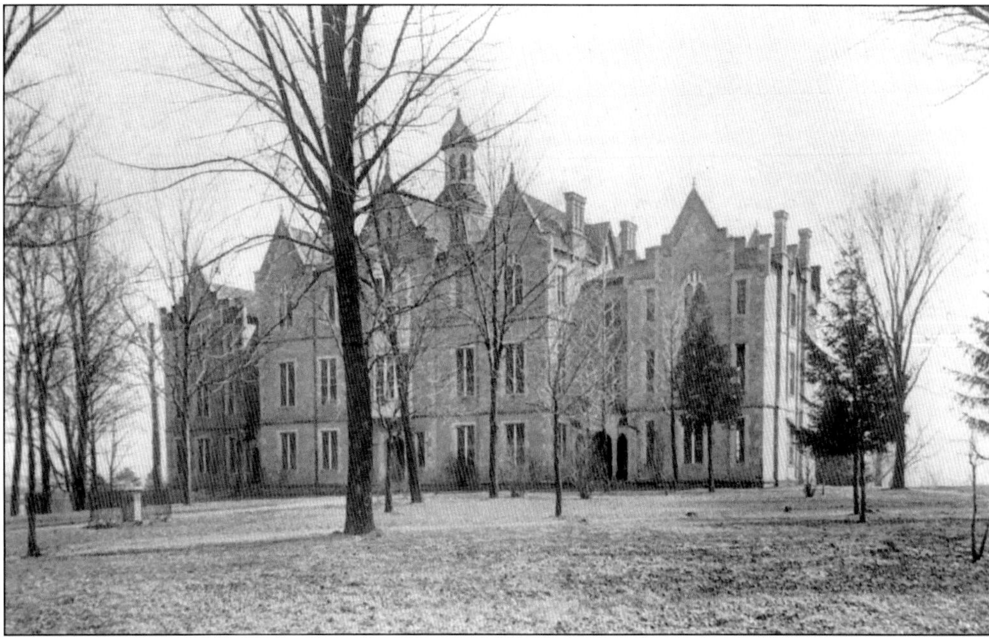

The High School Building, built in 1855, was formerly known as the Old College Building or first University Building. The building was sold to the city of Bloomington as part of the high school in 1897. It was rebuilt after a fire in 1900, the top floor was removed in 1935, and the building was razed in 1965.

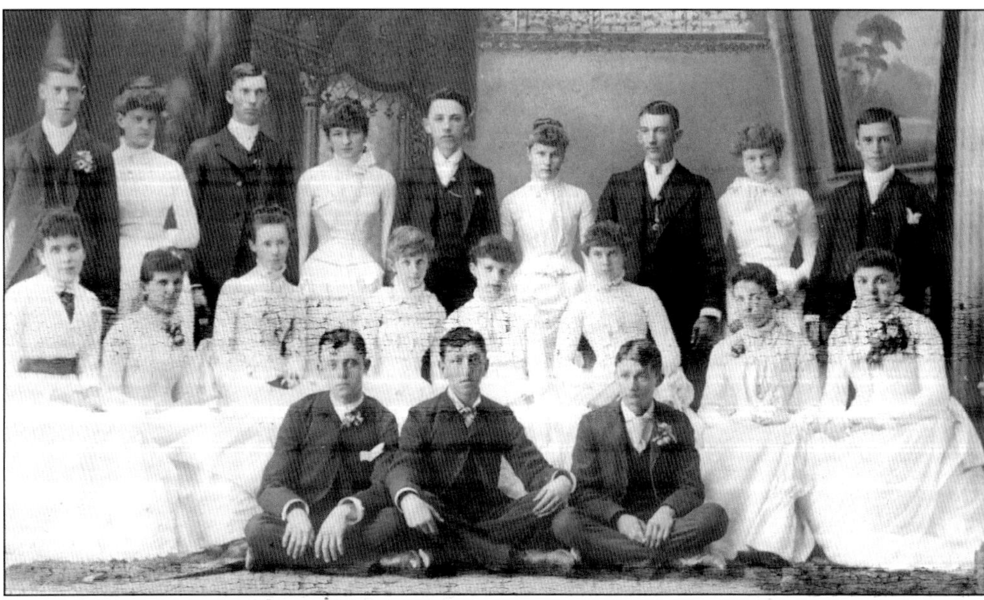

Thirty-five members of Bloomington High School's class of 1888 are shown here and opposite. Standing are Wade Dinsmore, Mayme Lindley, Oscar Cravens, Olive Hughes Miller, Tom Braxton, Nora Robinson Helton, Charles Bolden, Flora Kreuger Moore, James Weaver. Middle row: Lula Grimes Anderson, Amanda Hanna Rogers, Louise Mathers, Bertha Miers Cravens, Louise Rogers, Birdie Roseberry Cravens, Carrie Dodds Holsapple, Julia Dinsmore Bauer. Seated on floor: Eugene Clayman, Otto Rott, Ezra Borland.

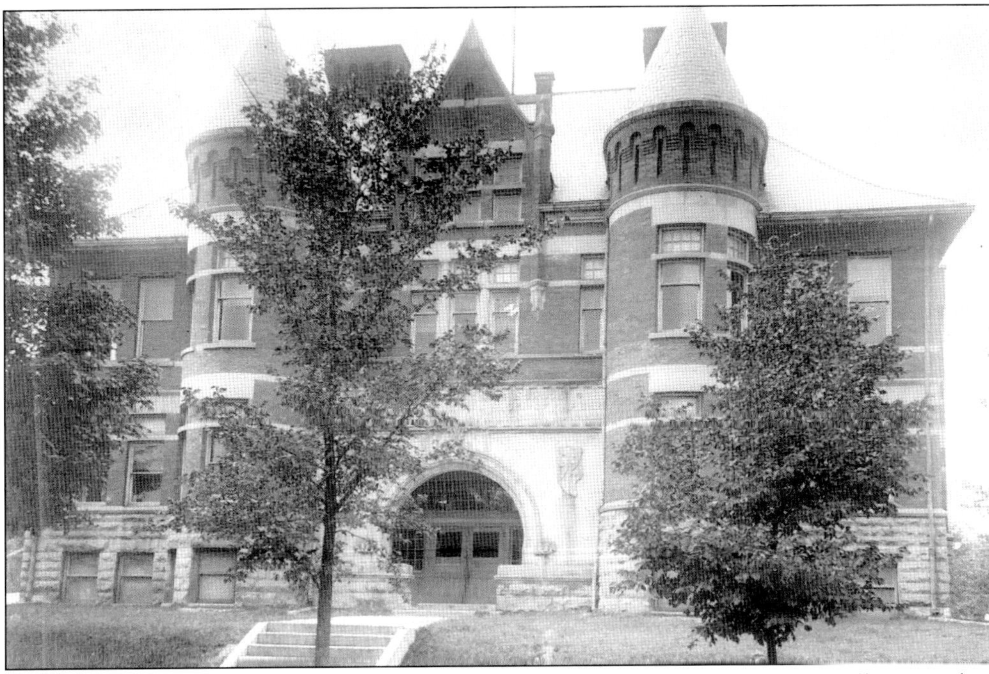

The original Fairview School on West Seventh Street served Bloomington's rapidly expanding west side. The school was built in 1893 at a cost of $17,000. Financed by a bond issue, the school relieved congestion at "Old Central" school on South College Avenue and also took white students when the school on Sixth and Washington was made African American only. Over the arched entryway was inscribed, "What sculpture is to a block of marble, education is to the human soul."

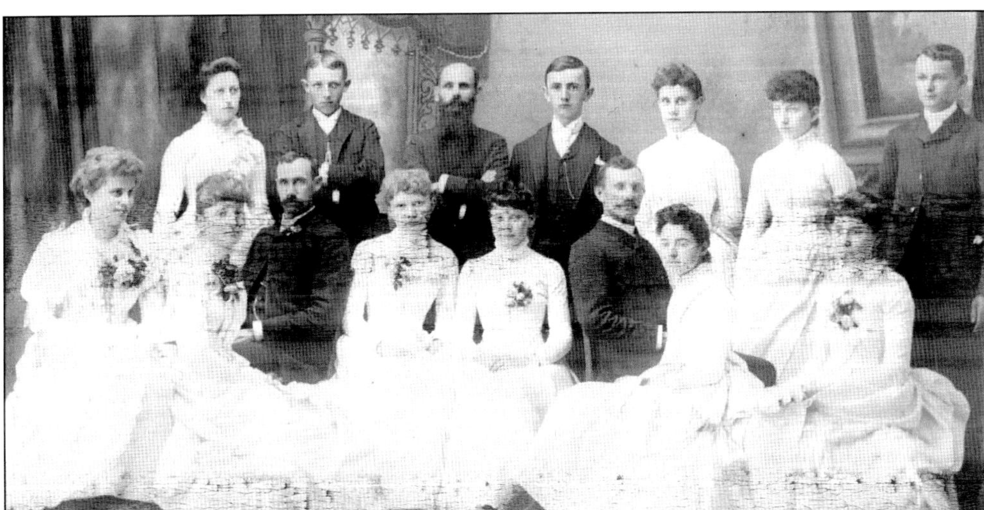

More members of Bloomington High School's class of 1888 were (standing) Mary Nicholson, John Campbell, Professor J.K. Beck, Tom Stephenson, Helen Shields, Etta Stephenson, John Kelley. Seated were Edith Hall Owens, Lela Rogers Curry, Prof. Wylie, Adele Bond, Anna Denaree, Prof. Mitchell, Fannie Woodward, Matt Burgoon.

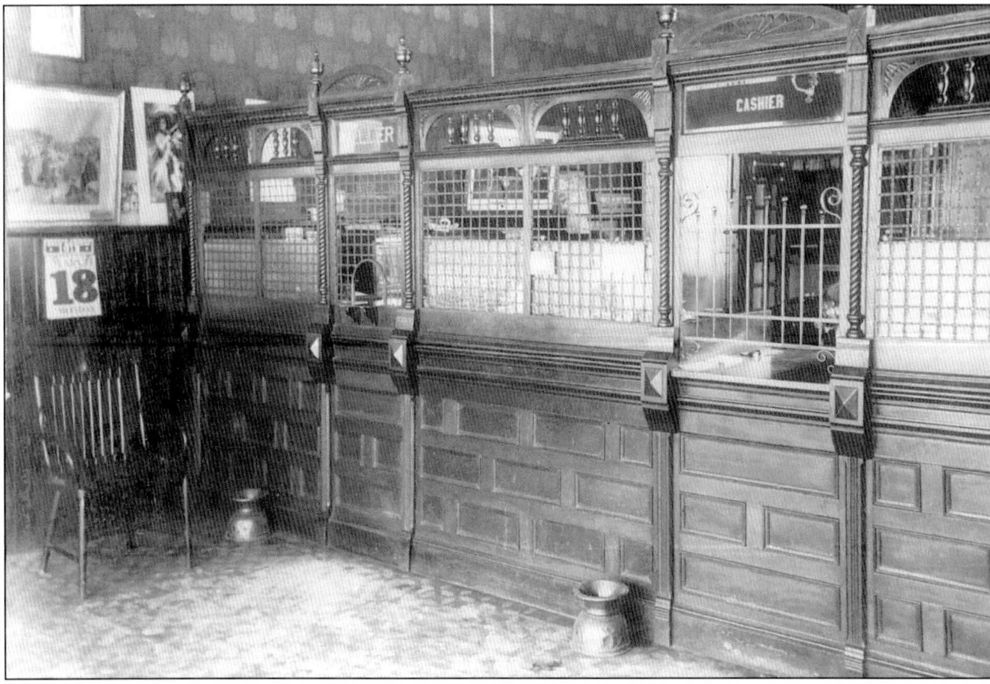

The interior of the Monroe County State Bank was shown off in the Commercial Club booklet of 1912. The bank then occupied the building on the northeast corner of North Walnut and East Kirkwood. More banks came to Bloomington following industrial growth in the late 1800s.

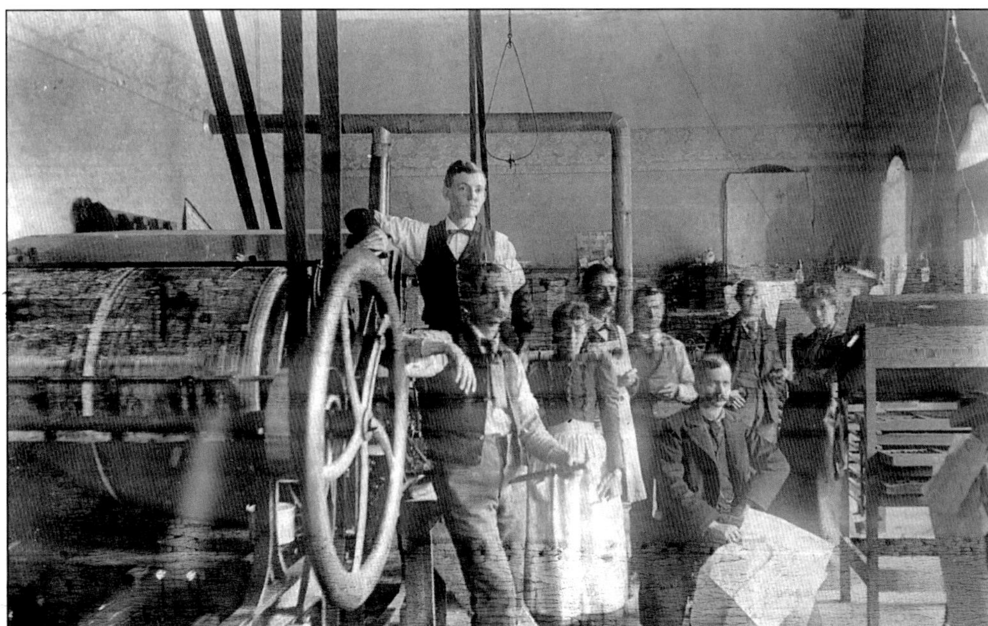

Publisher John W. Cravens, seated holding a newspaper, posed with staff members in the pressroom of the *Bloomington Daily World and Weekly Courier* during the early 1890s. Tentatively identified are (left to right) "Spider" Hentworth, Bert Harris, Miss Southerland, W.H. Harris, Charles Krueger, Cravens, William Shock, and Miss Smith.

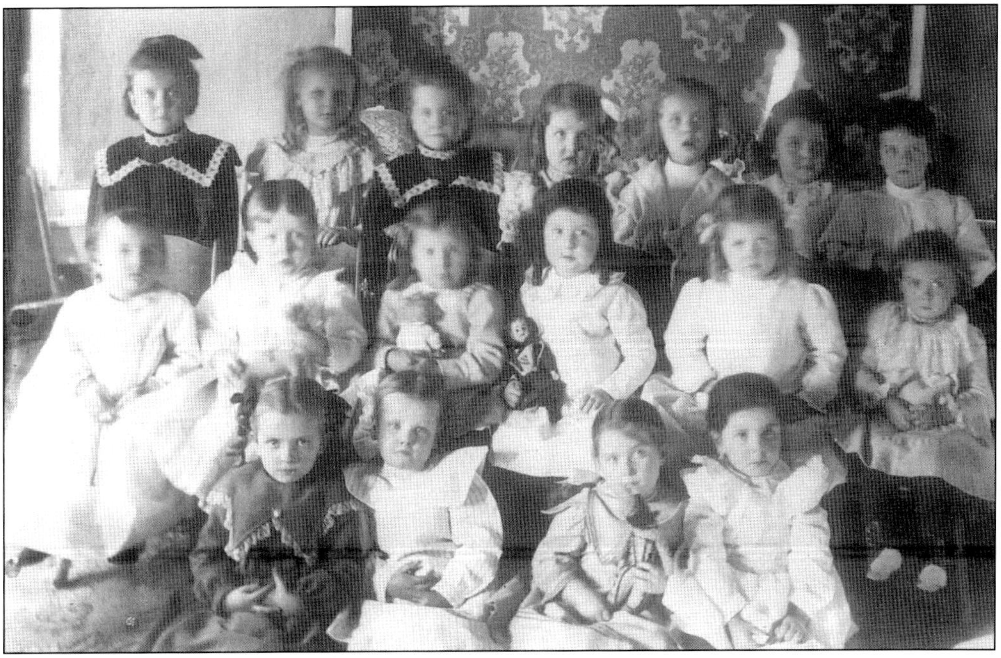

The invitation read, in part: "I do not want you to bring or send me any presents. I just want you to come and play with me." The young guests at Ruth Ralston Cravens's fourth birthday party, 1902, were each presented with a souvenir copy of this photo. Standing were Mary Woodburn, Doris Hoffman, Martha Woodburn, Marjorie Davis, Dorothy Cunningham, Mary Louden, Agnes Joiner. Seated in chairs: Elizabeth Miller, Martha Buskirk, Ruth Dill, Carol Hoffman, Frieda Hershey, Ruth Cravens. On the floor: Margaret Faris, Pauline Reed, Dorothy Clough, Catherine Fletcher.

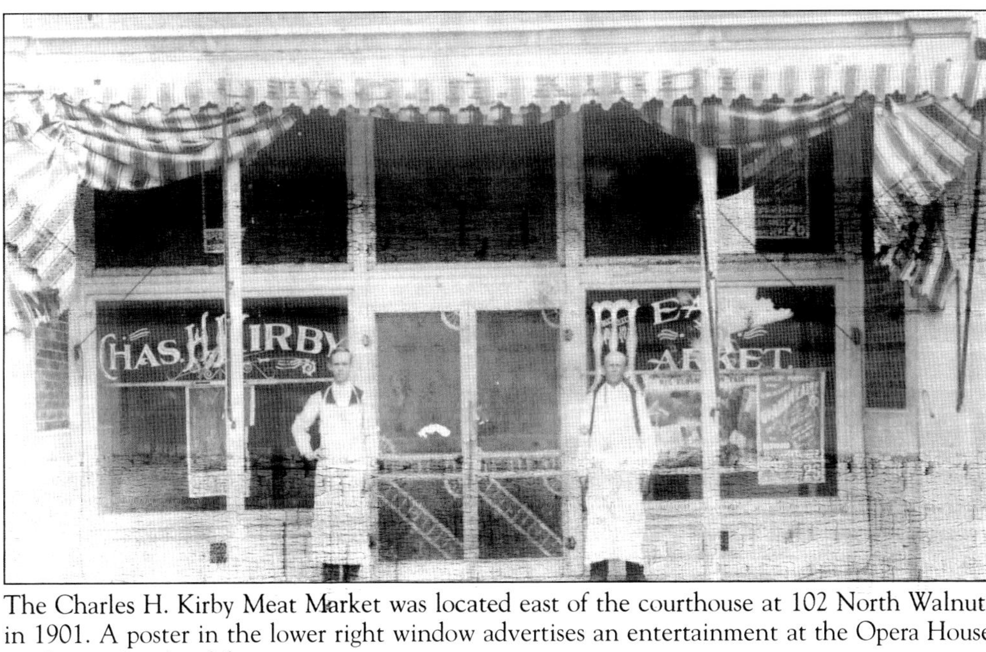

The Charles H. Kirby Meat Market was located east of the courthouse at 102 North Walnut, in 1901. A poster in the lower right window advertises an entertainment at the Opera House on the south side of the square.

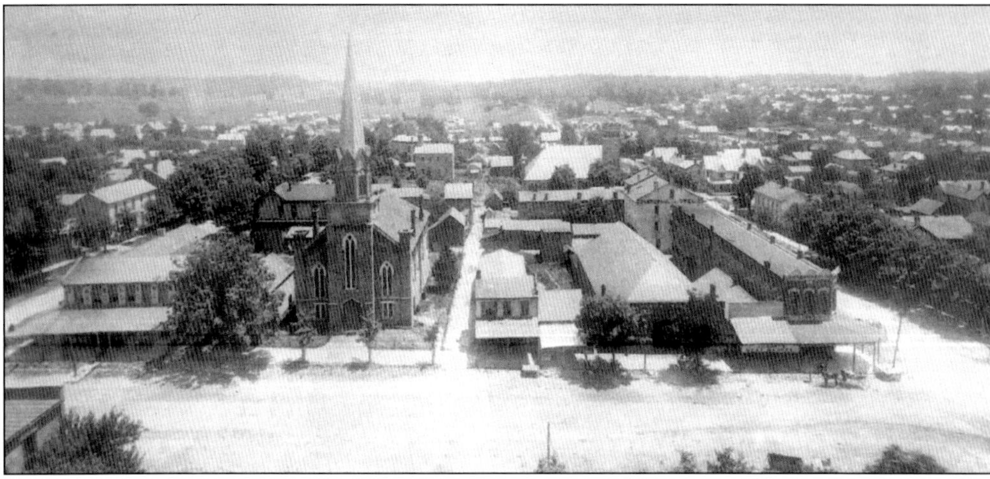

Four bird's-eye views of the courthouse square were made around 1891 for the Burford booklet. On the east side (North Walnut Street), the most conspicuous building was the First Presbyterian Church. It was one of eight churches shown on the Sanborn map of 1892. Others, besides the Christian Church on East Kirkwood, were the College Avenue Methodist Episcopal Church, the Colored Methodist Episcopal Church, St Charles's Roman Catholic Church, another Christian Church, and two more Presbyterian Churches.

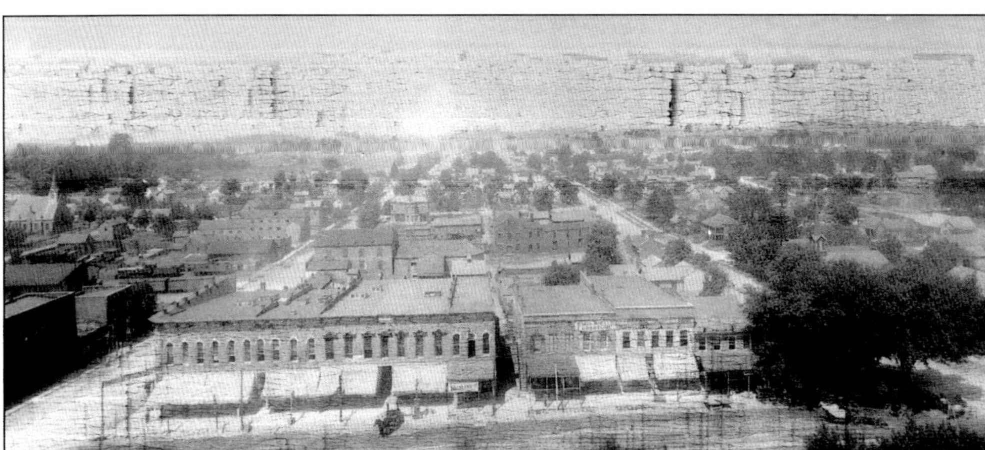

The west side of the square (North College Avenue) retains some of its Victorian-era appearance from 1891. Factory buildings and workers' housing lay beyond.

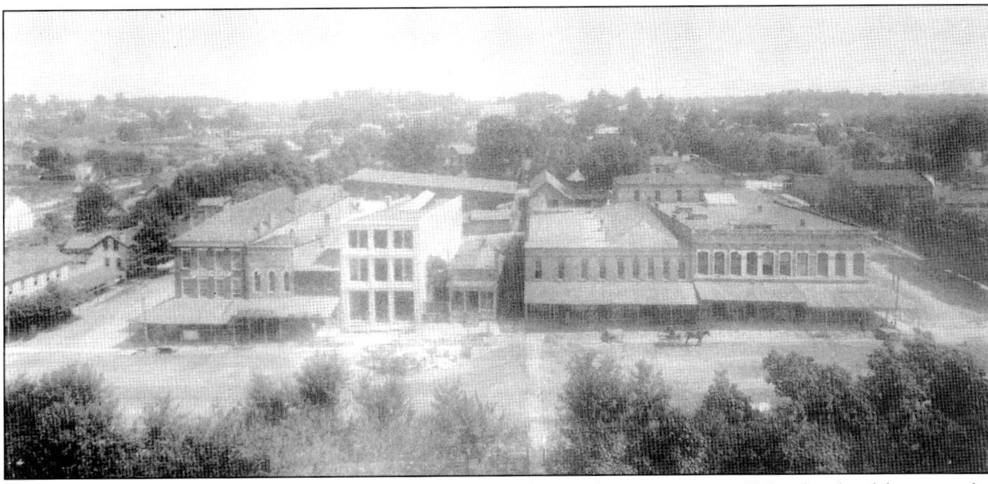

The north side of the square (West Sixth Street), in about 1891, still had a building at the center of the block that was originally a house. Livery stables were located on the north side of the block away from the square (West Seventh Street).

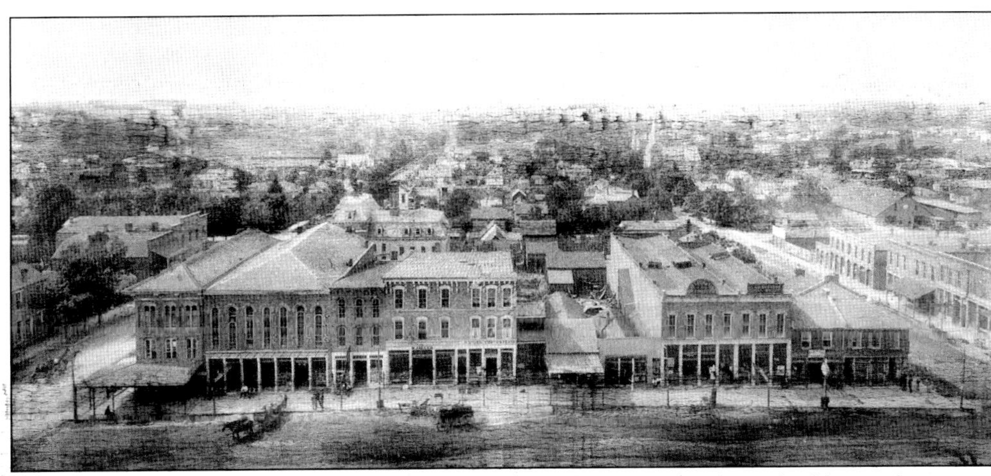

The south side of the square (West Kirkwood Avenue) also retained two buildings of one story in 1891. Non-residential uses extended one block south along College and Walnut to West Fourth Street. Almost 100 years later, in 1988, buildings on the block facing the square were extensively rebuilt and joined together to become Fountain Square Mall.

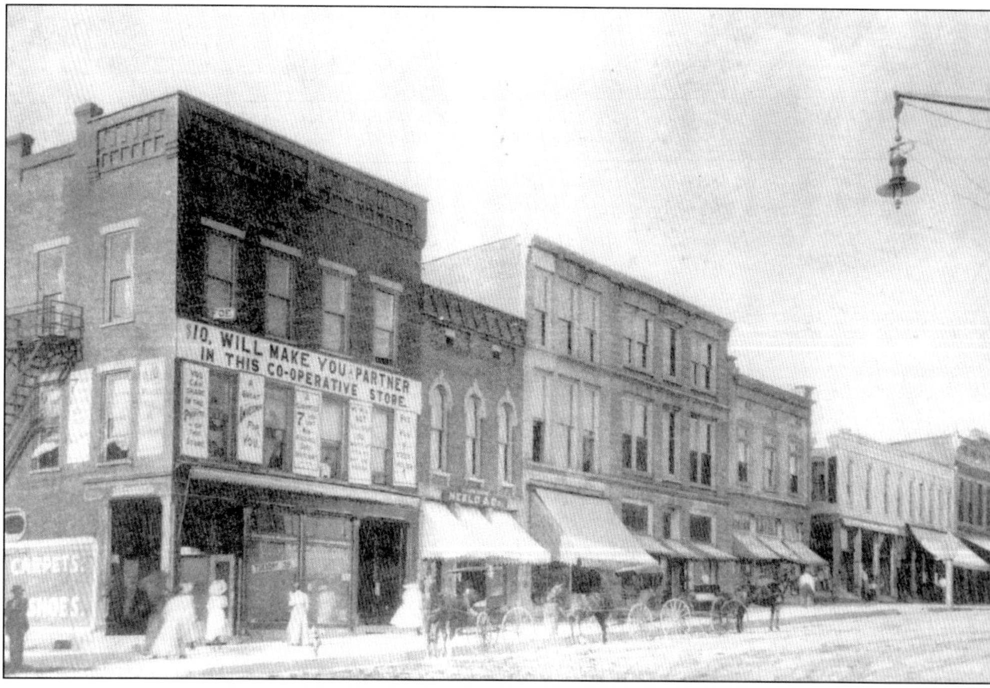

The square's north side is shown above and opposite in two postcard views from 1902. Above is the block from its west end. Below, an 1880s building, the Waldron "business block," was featured when a sidewalk sale was held, probably around 1900.

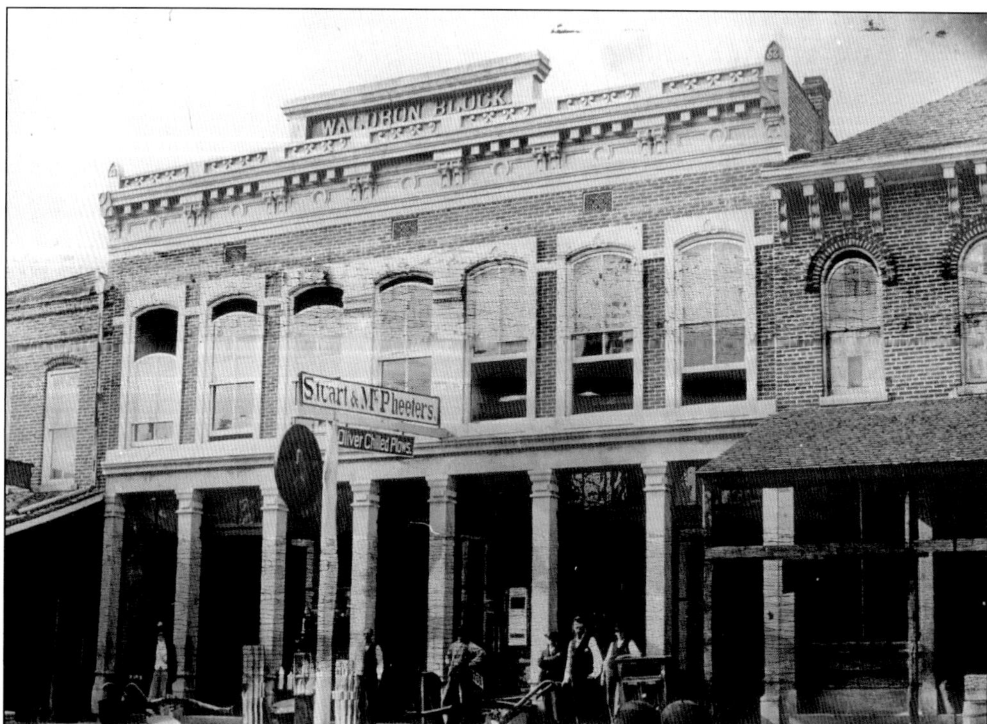

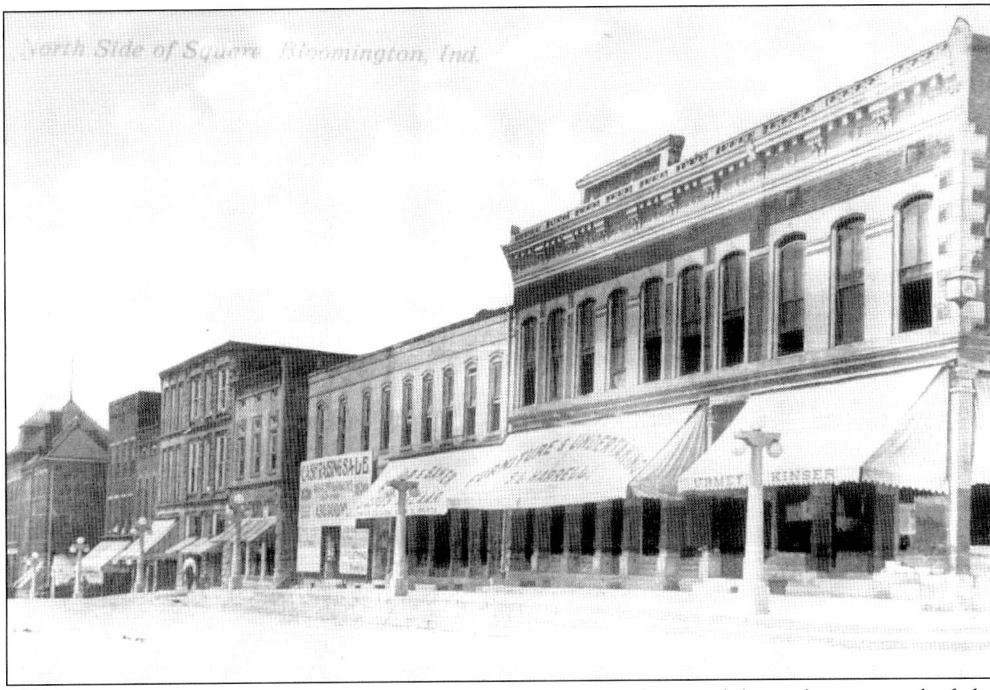

The Waldron Block, also shown below left, originally stood second from the east end of the square's north side. Before 1902, the corner building was given a new façade to match that of the original Waldron Block. Note the multi-gabled, three-story Bowles Hotel across North Walnut Street at the far or west end of the block.

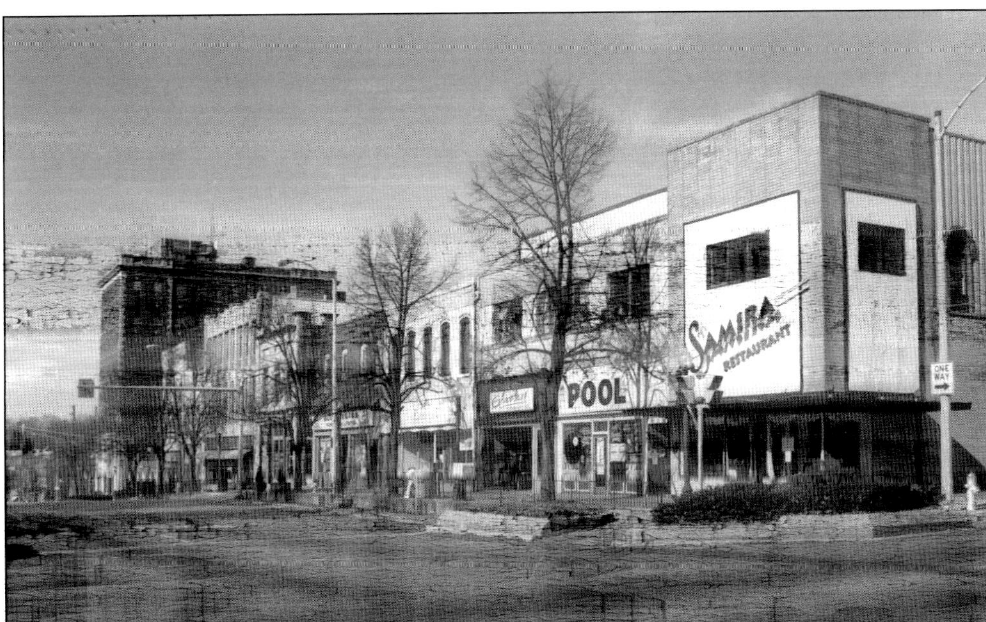

Most buildings on the square's north side were given new ground-floor façades or complete front façades. Exteriors of two buildings at the east end are quite recent. At right of photo, around the corner of the building, a 19th century, rounded window arch has been left visible.

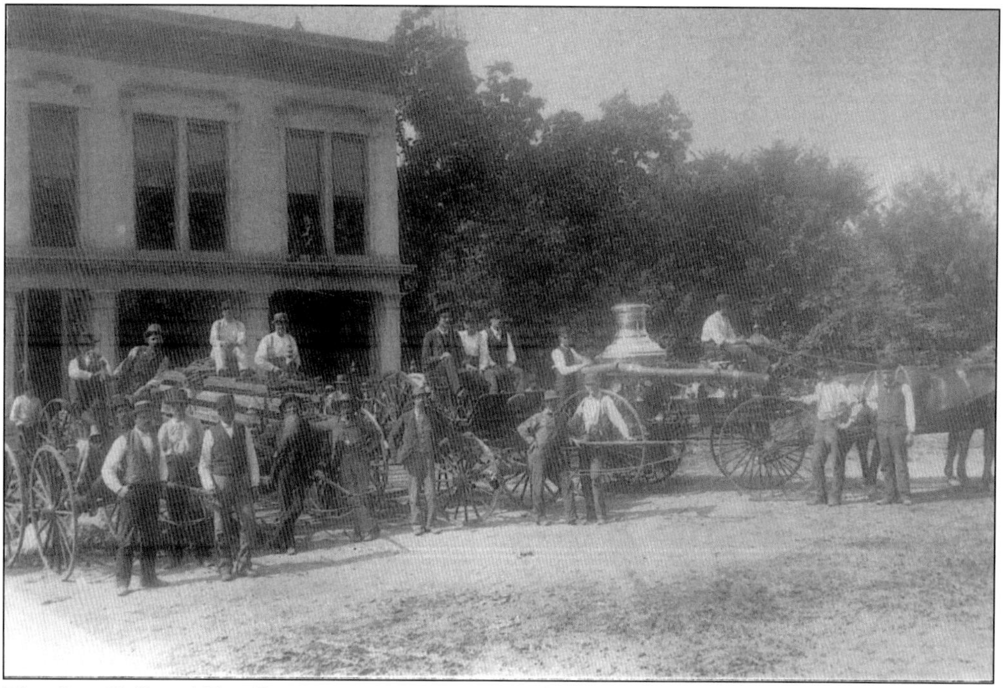

The City Hall and Fire Department, in 1891, were located in a two-story building on the east side of the courthouse square. The firefighters were volunteers until 1900, when the first paid department was formed with five men and two horses.

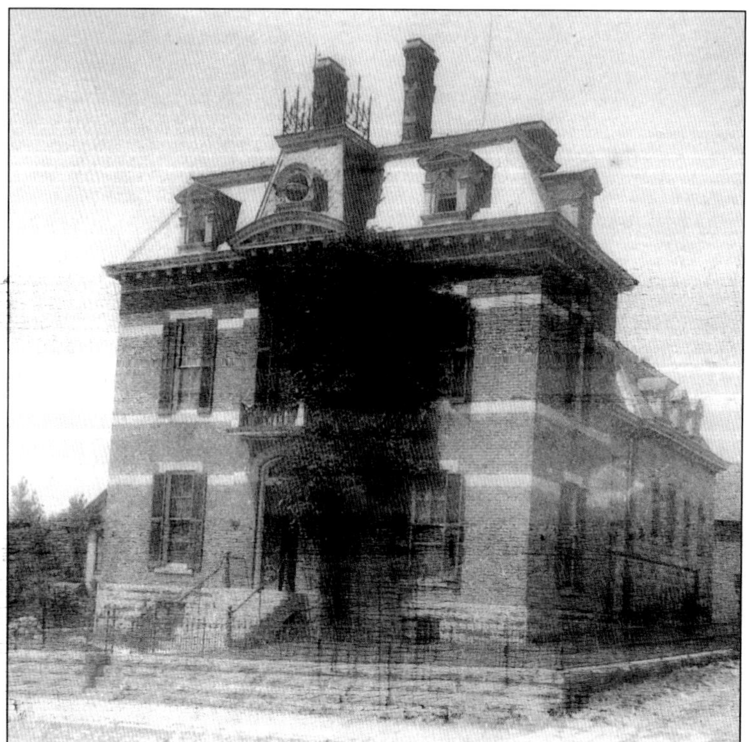

A magnificent 1880s building in Second Empire Style housed the Sheriff's residence and county jail. The building was located on Walnut Street between Fourth and Kirkwood. Just south is the site of the city hall of 1915, now the John Waldron Arts Center.

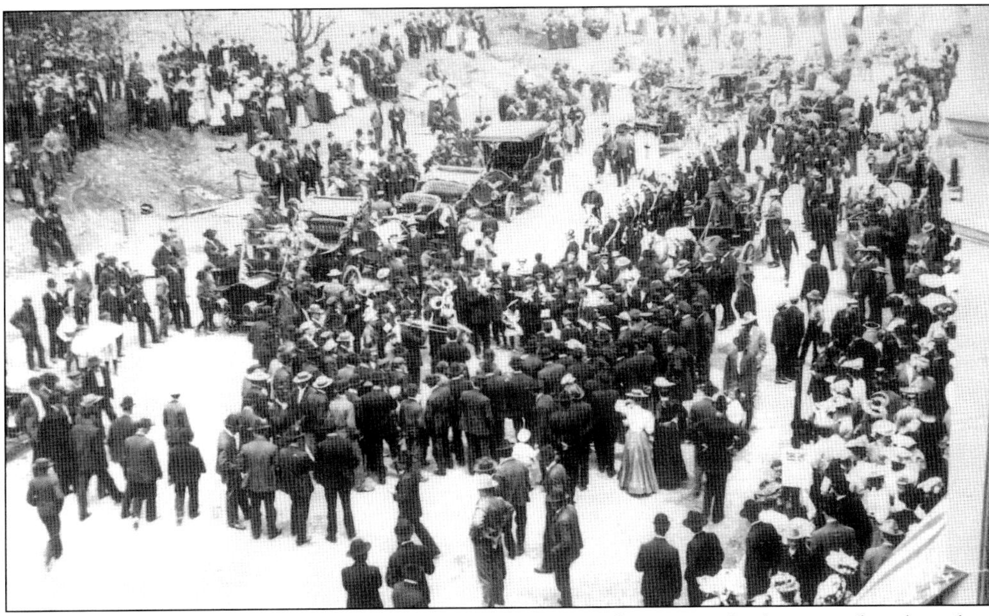

When the cornerstone of the third Monroe County courthouse was laid, a crowd gathered on the south side of the square (West Kirkwood Avenue). The courthouse, built 1907–1910, was designed in Beaux Arts style by the architectural firm of Wing and Mehurin of Indianapolis. Contractors Drake and Caldwell had recently built a resort hotel, the West Baden Springs in southern Indiana, which featured an enormous dome.

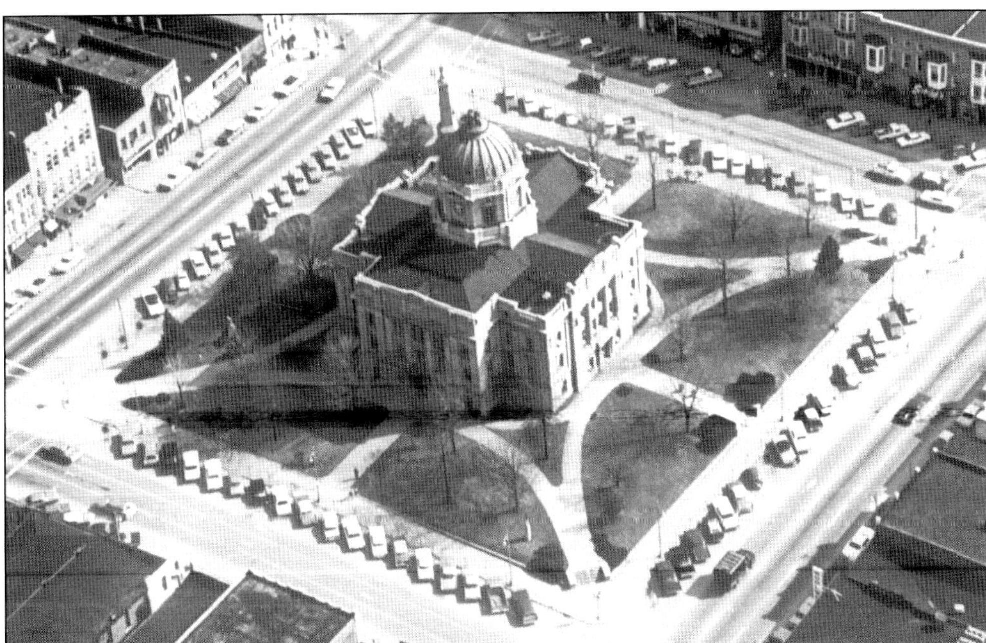

The courthouse was photographed from above during the 1950s with its northwest corner closest to the viewer. The finger-like obelisk of the War Memorial can be seen at the southwest corner of the square.

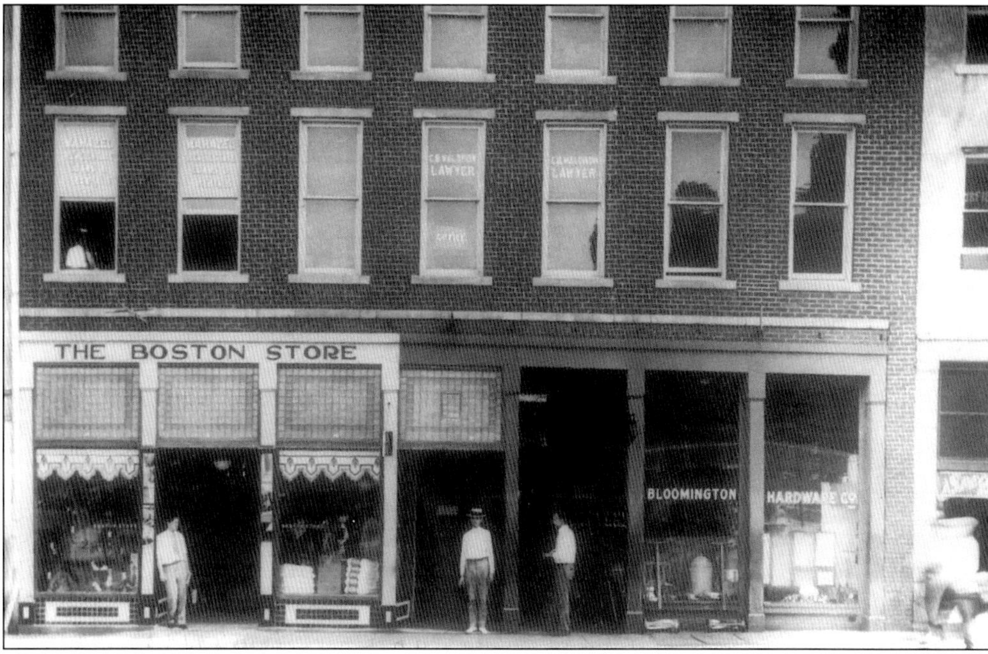

The ground floor at 103-105 West Kirkwood, on the south side of the square, was occupied by the Bloomington Hardware Company and Boston Store in 1930. The building was constructed as early as 1868 and remodeled in 1915. The Opera House once occupied the second floor.

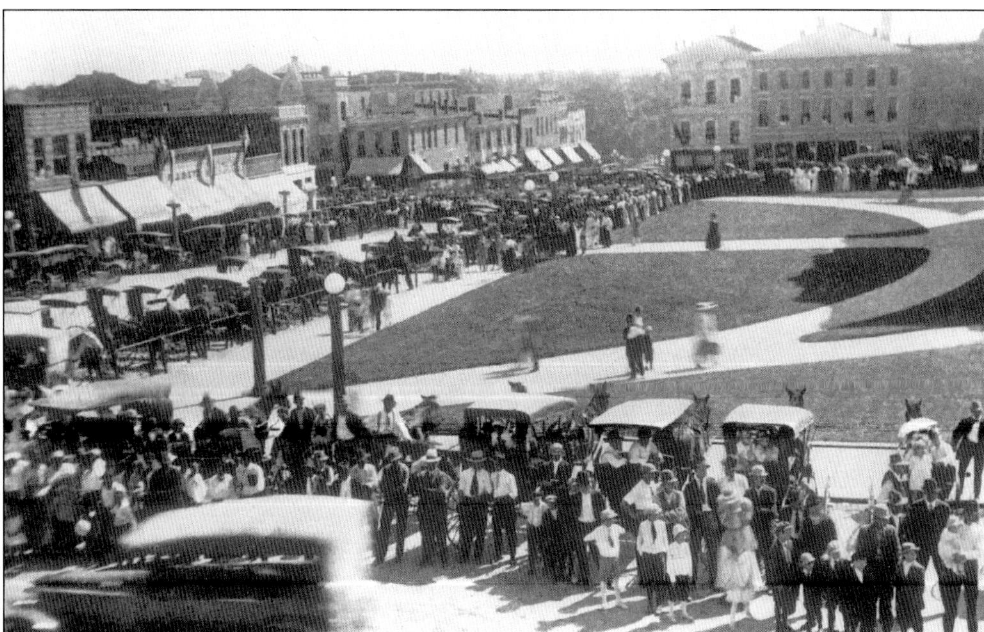
When the 1907 courthouse was built, trees and outbuildings associated with the previous courthouse were removed, making room for larger gatherings The crowd in the foreground, northeast corner of the square, may be waiting for the parade that can be seen passing at rear. Wagon horses tied to hitching rails date the photograph before or during World War I.

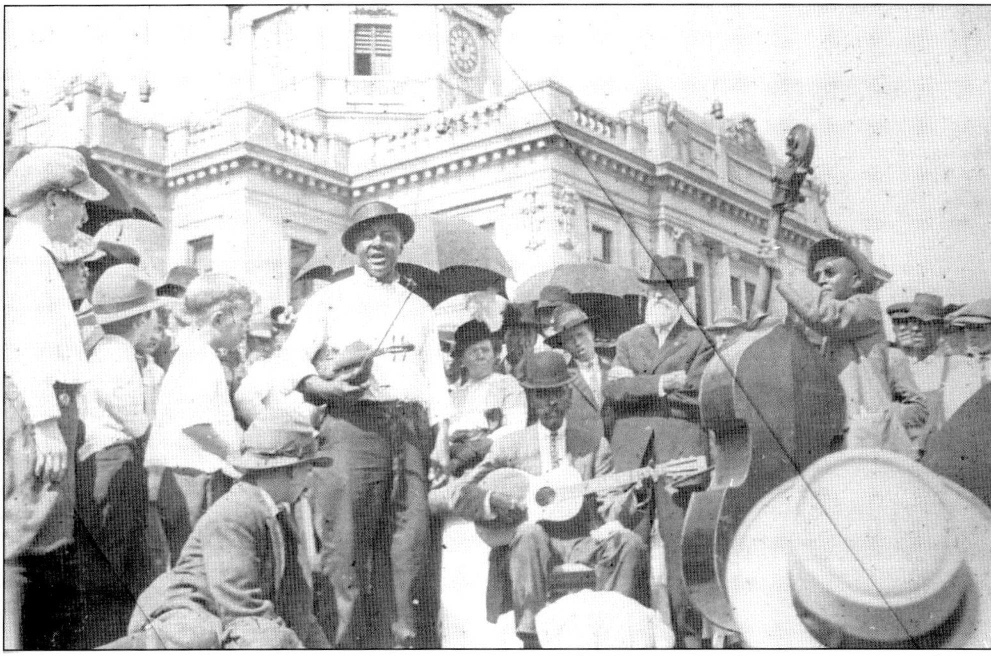

A small string band entertained children, townspeople, farmers, and an apparent Civil War veteran. This festive gathering was either the same as shown on previous page, or another around the same time period.

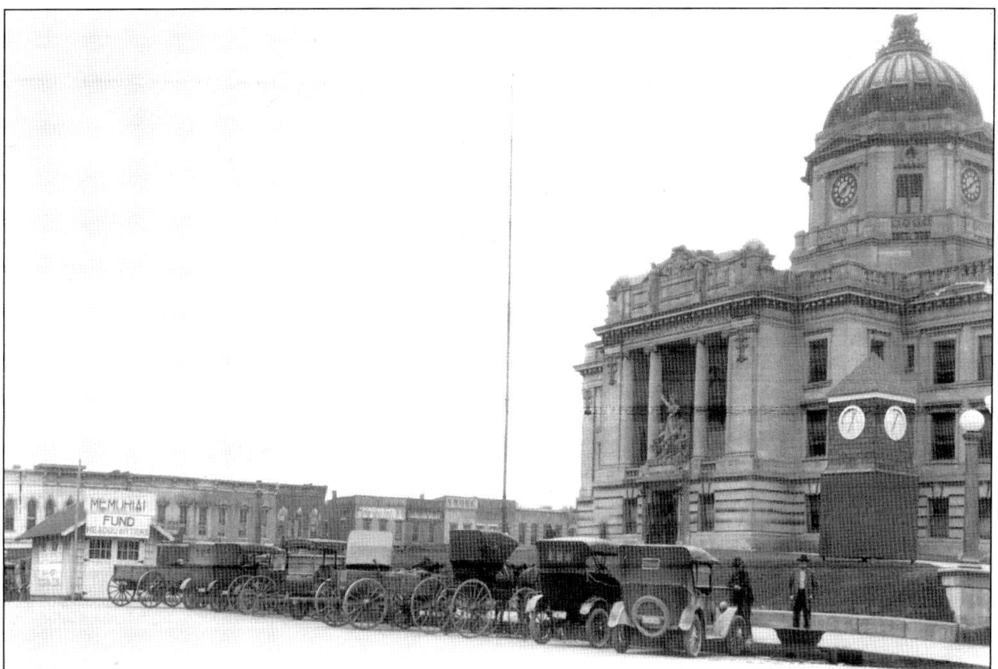

After the war, a somber mood was struck by the presence of a Memorial Fund kiosk (left of photo) on the south side of the square. Donations were being collected for a memorial to those who served in World War I.

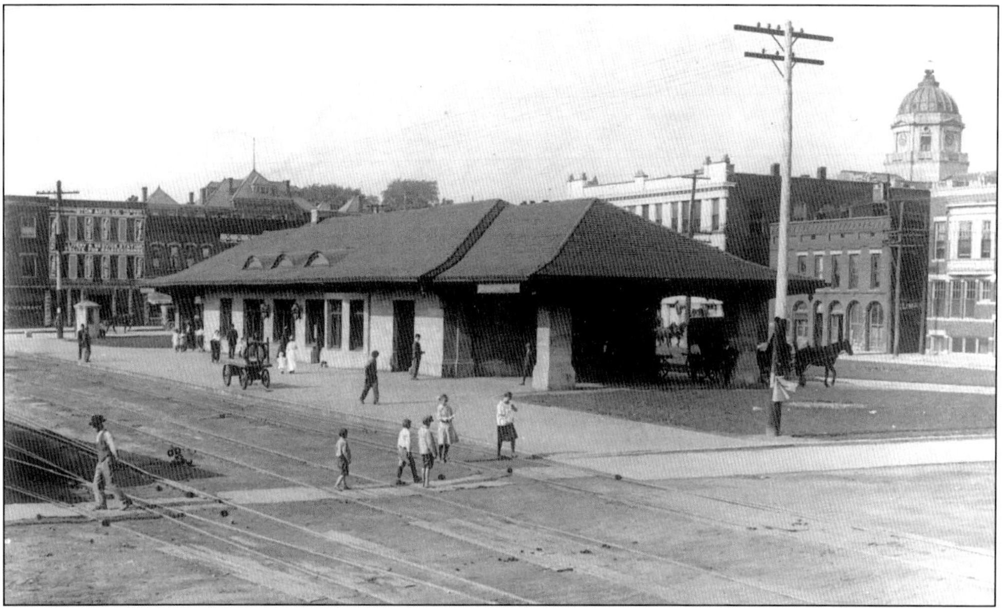

In downtown Bloomington after the turn of the century, "the new" was represented by the courthouse (1907), the Monon rail station (*c.* 1910; top), and the city hall (1915; lower left; now John Waldron Arts Center). Continuity was supplied by the fish-shaped copper weather vane atop the courthouse (lower right), which blacksmith Austin Seward had placed atop the previous courthouse in 1826.

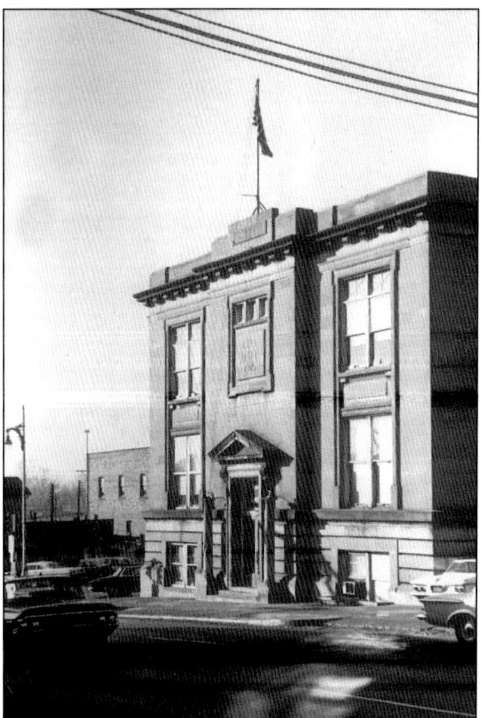

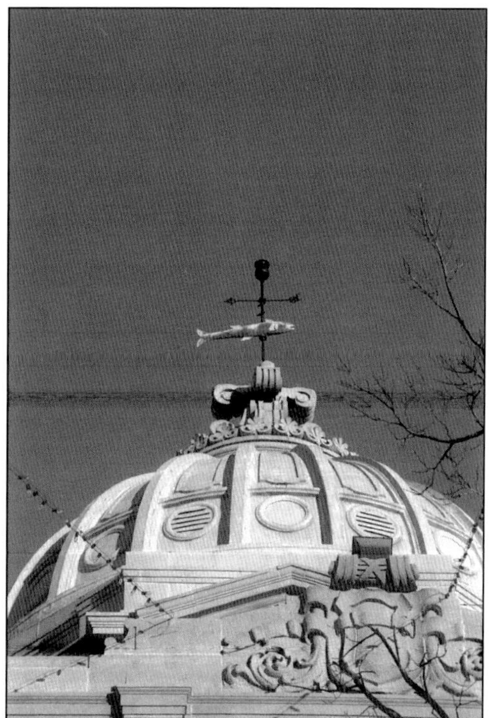

Four

In Step with the New Century

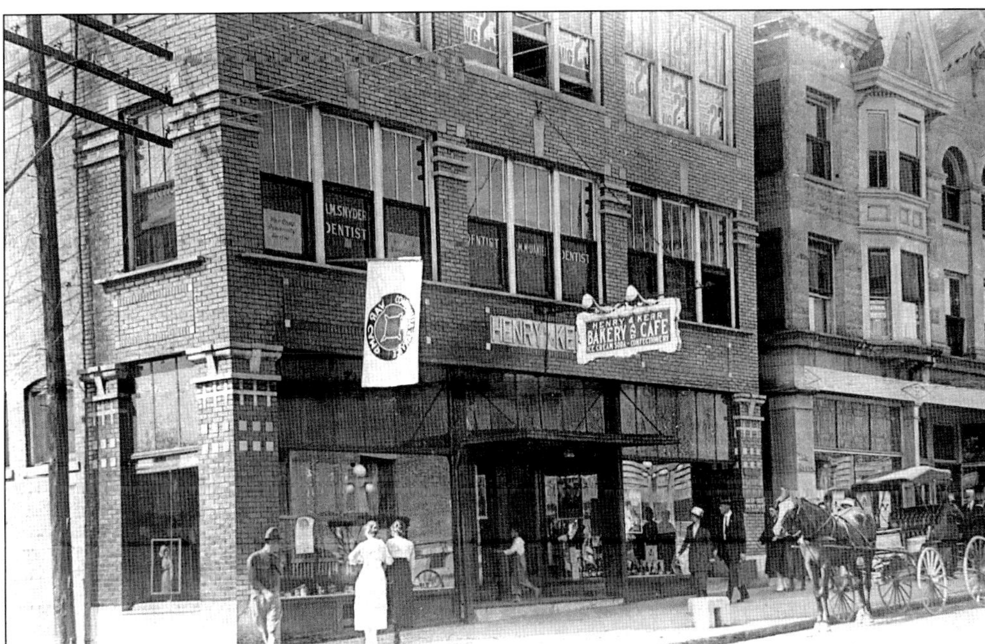

A soldier at left of photo, c. 1917, turns to admire two young women on East Kirkwood a half block from the square. The banner hanging from the building says "Service Committee—War Camp," a reference to Indiana University's service as a training camp during World War I.

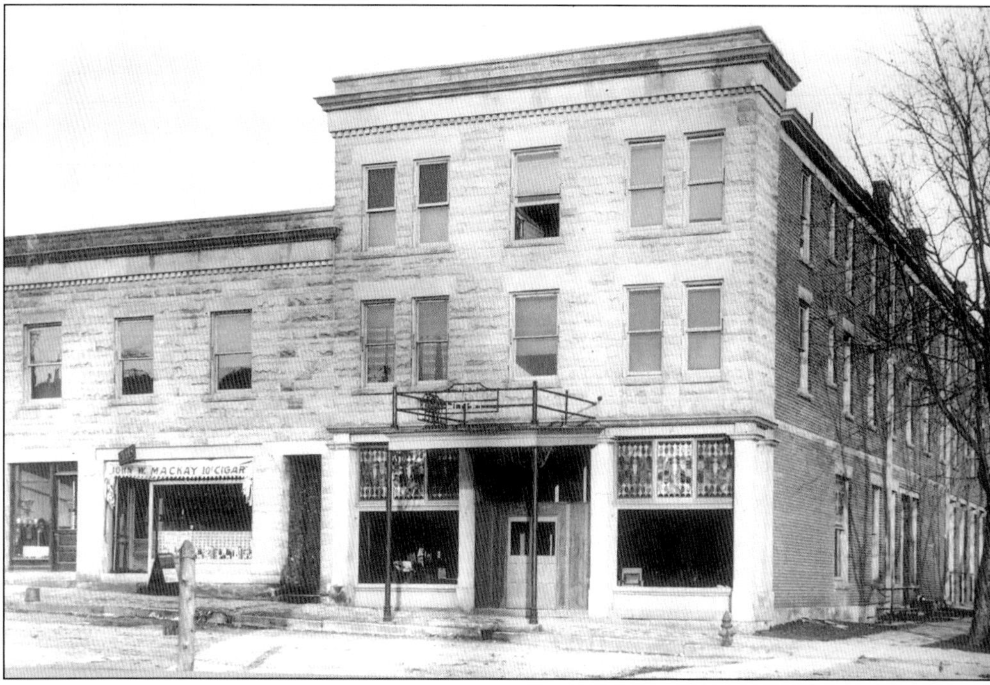

The Tourner Hotel (1916) was located on the northeast corner of West Fourth Street and South College Avenue.

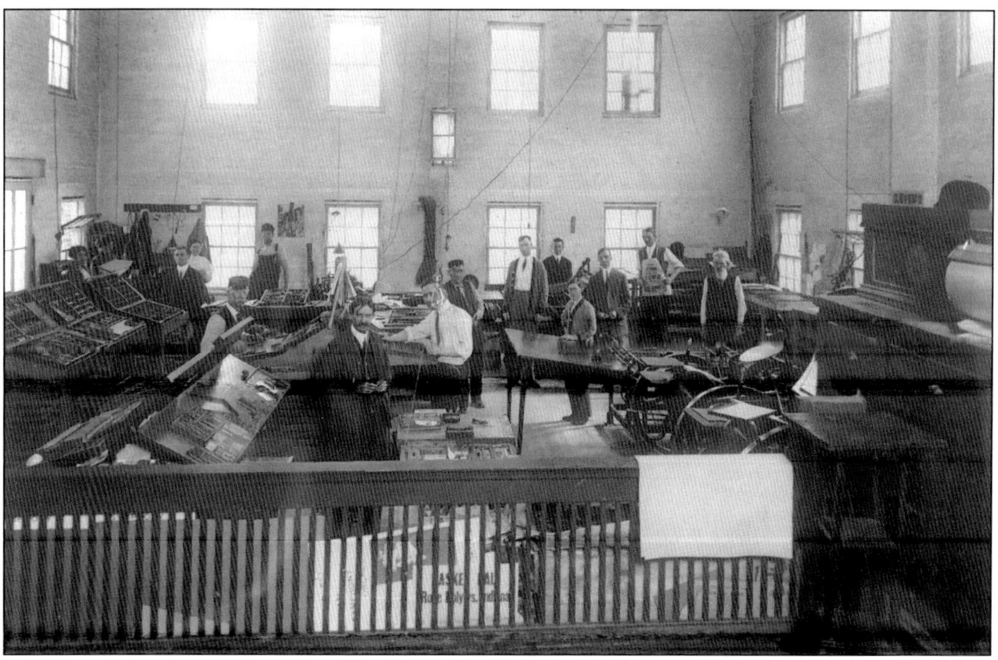

The World Courier Building is shown here and opposite soon after it was built around 1912. In the two-story pressroom below, the seated men at left appear to be engaged in hand setting type, which is stored in slanted bins on cabinets around the room.

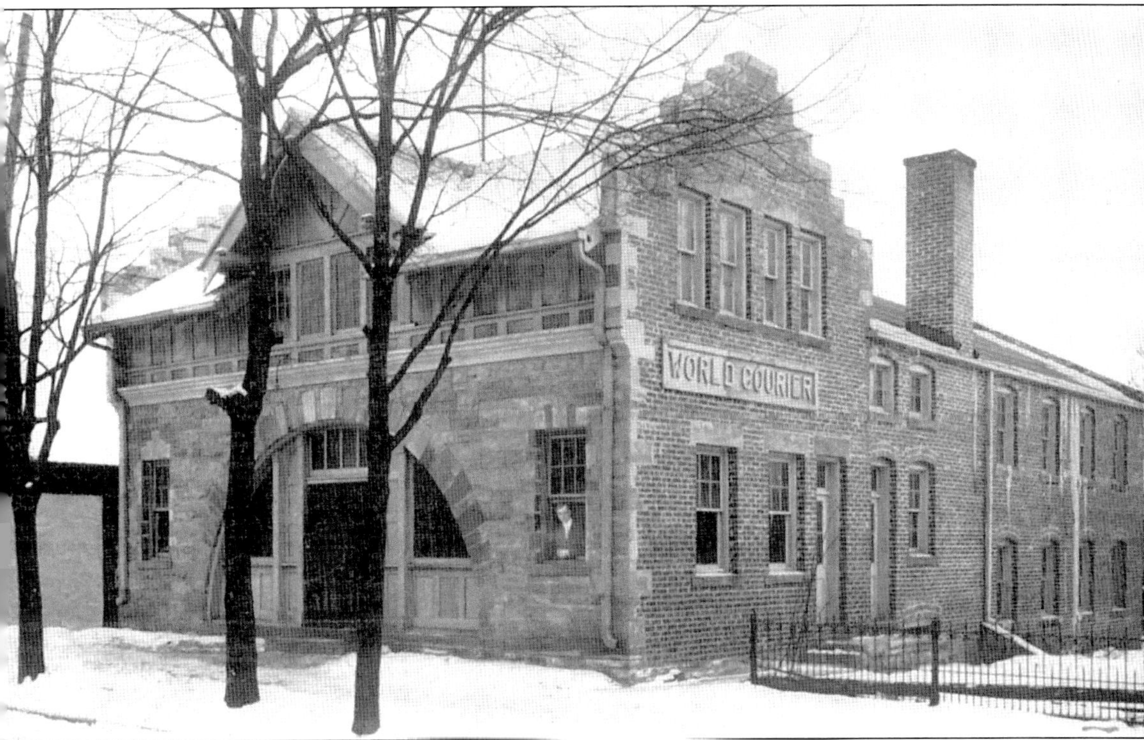

The *World Courier* was the product of mergers through the years. Between 1826 and 1912, Bloomington had 35 different newspapers. The *Courier* began publication in 1875, and the *Telephone* in 1877, a year after the invention for which it was named. Both the *Telephone* and the *World* were delivered daily when this 1912 Commercial Club publication showed off the *World's* parent office.

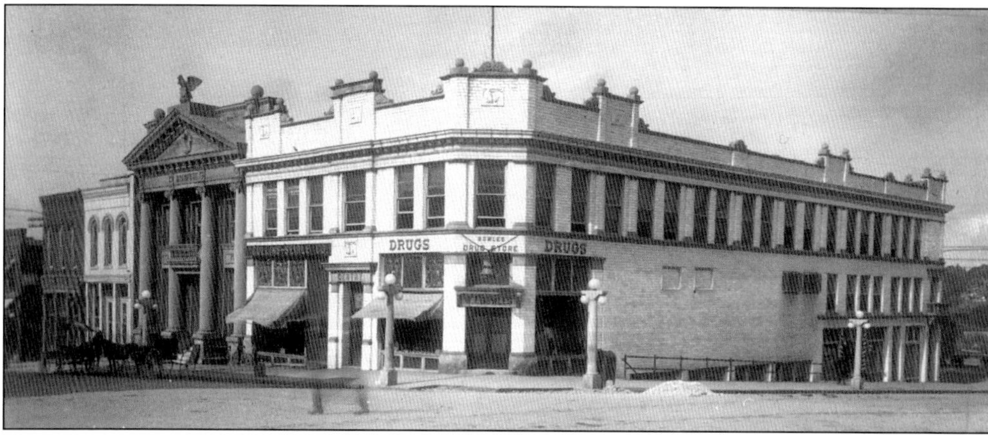

The southwest corner of West Kirkwood Avenue and South College Avenue, catercornered from the courthouse, was in demand for high-profile buildings through the years. Around 1910, the Gentry Building, housing the Bowles Drug Store, occupied the whole block from West Kirkwood to the alley behind it and had an ornate second façade facing the railroad station in back. South of the Gentry Building was the Bradfute Building, a neoclassical design with two-story limestone columns. The Gentry Building was demolished for construction of the Citizens Bank and Trust Company Building (1925), seen from West Kirkwood in the photo below.

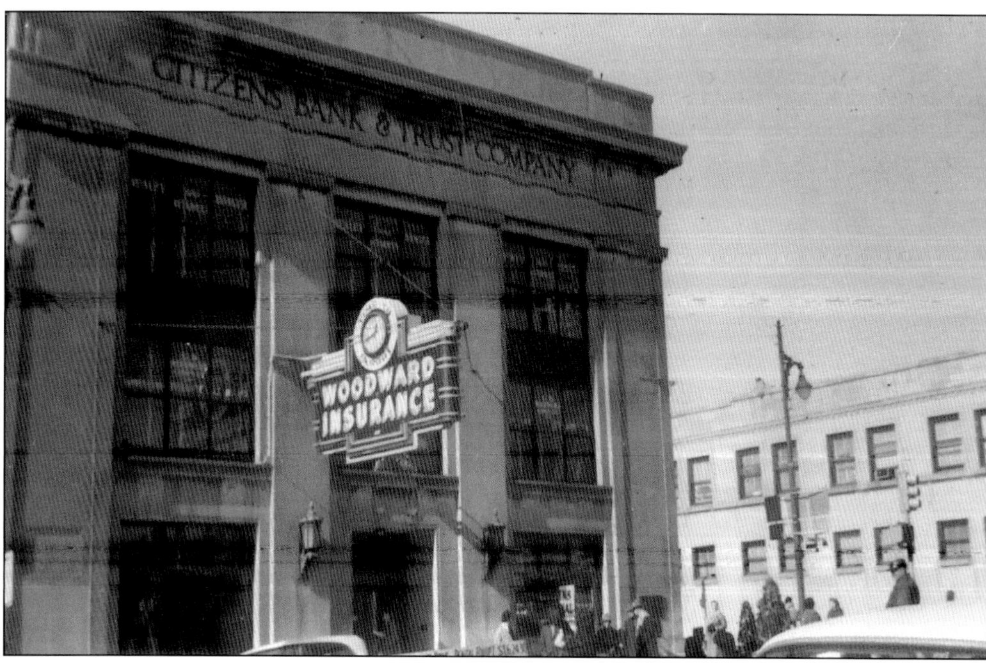

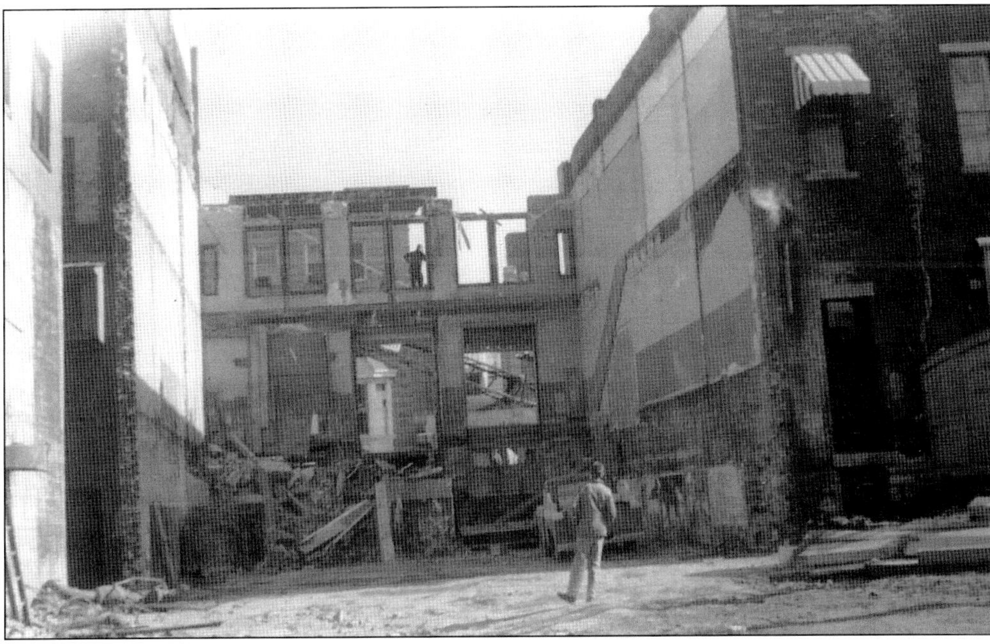

The Bradfute or Herald-Telephone Building was removed in 1962 in order to expand the Citizens Bank Building. The columns were located on the other side of the remaining wall at the front of the building, facing east toward South College. Money was collected to donate the columns to Indiana University, and they were placed at the Billy C. Hayes Track on Fee Lane behind Armstrong Stadium. During the 1960s, another building (below) replaced the 1925 Citizens Bank Building.

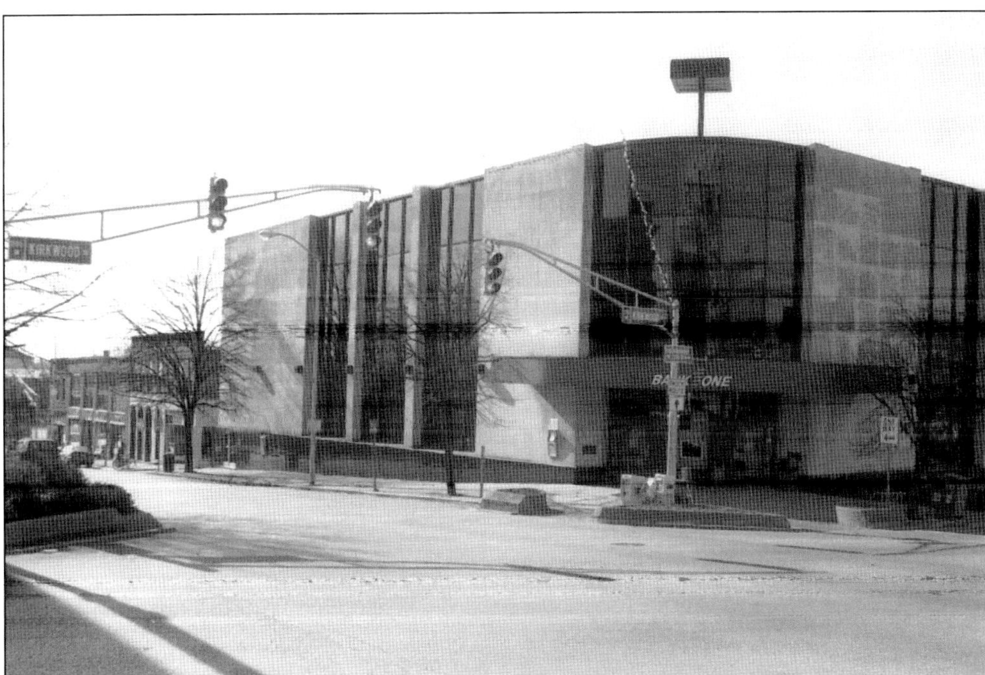

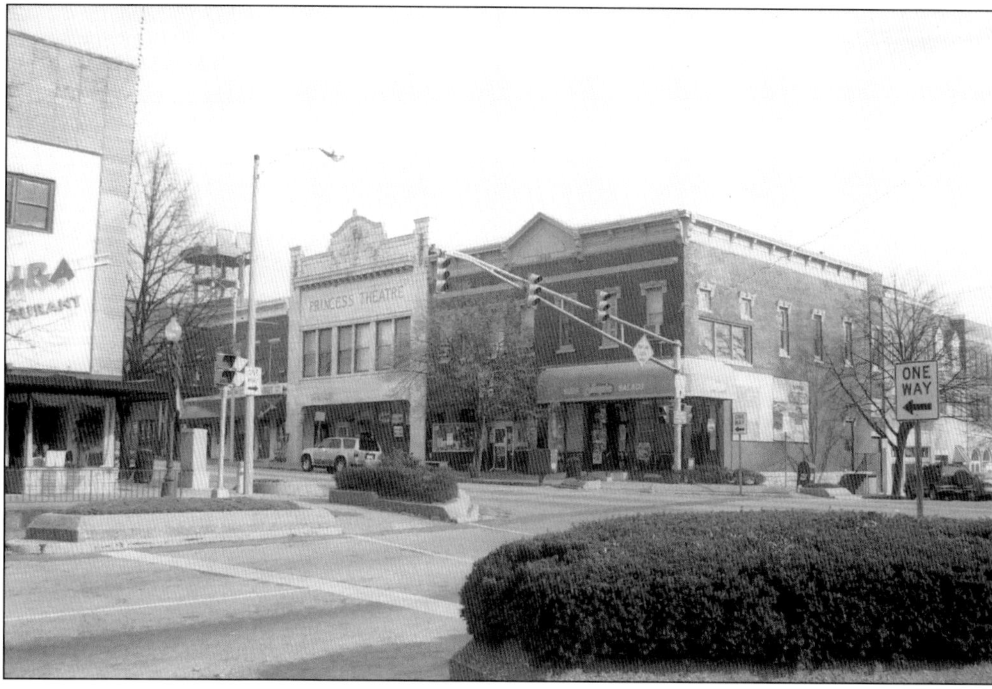

The Princess Theatre, originally the Wonderland on Sixth Street, was remodeled in 1923 to its present façade on Walnut with white-glazed and ornamental terra cotta tile. A part of the Princess that had opened onto Sixth Street later collapsed (below).

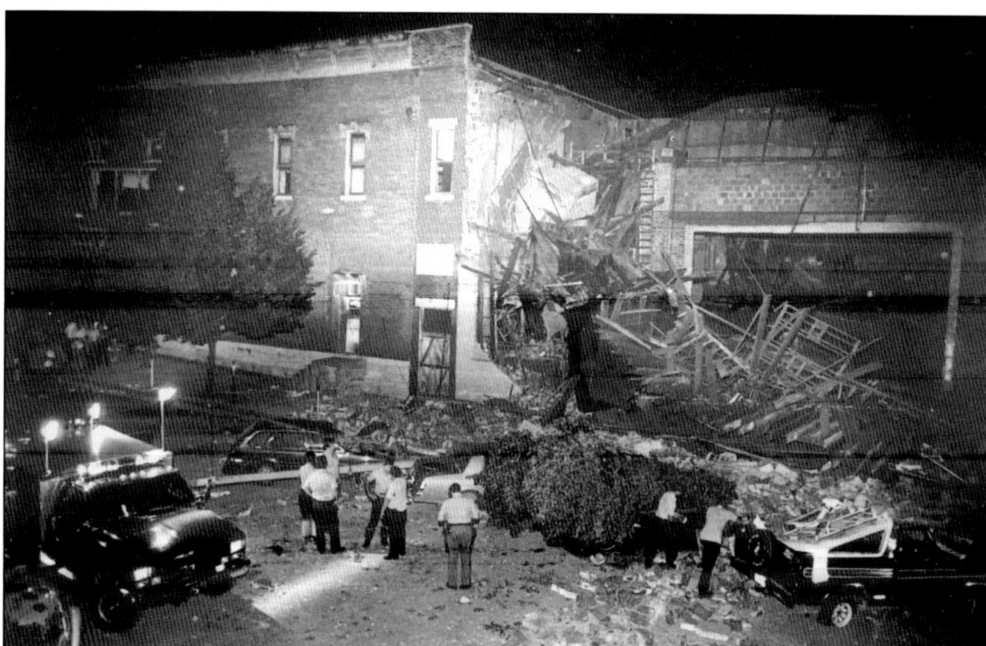

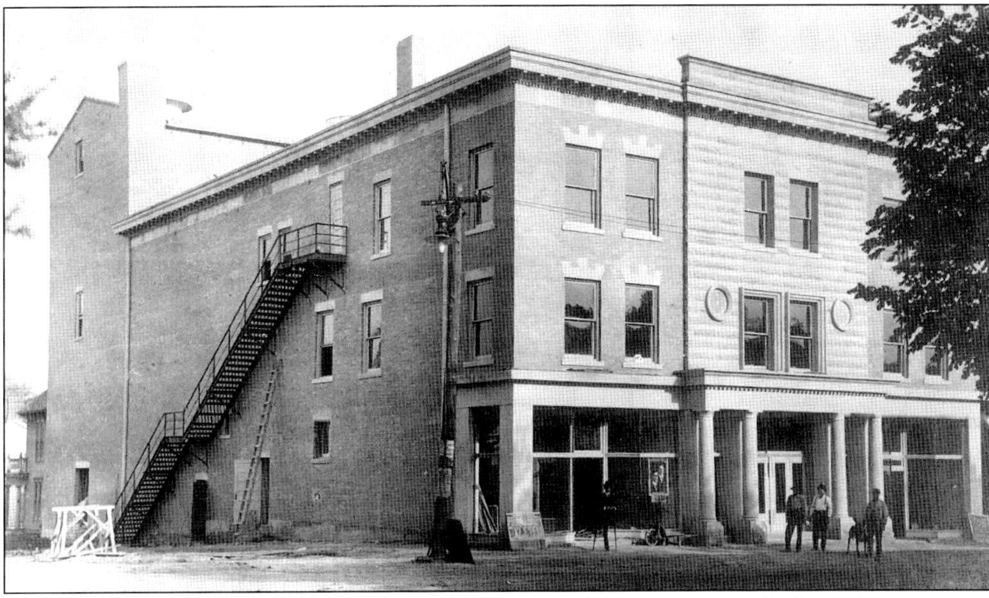

Variety entertainment first entered the 20th century in Bloomington with the 1907 opening of the Harris-Grand Theatre, located just a few doors north of the Princess. Proprietor Robert H. Harris, the nephew of Joel Chandler Harris and protégé of actor Edwin Booth, claimed that the Harris-Grand had the biggest stage between Indianapolis and Louisville. It featured live theater and university lecture series until 1940, when it converted to films only.

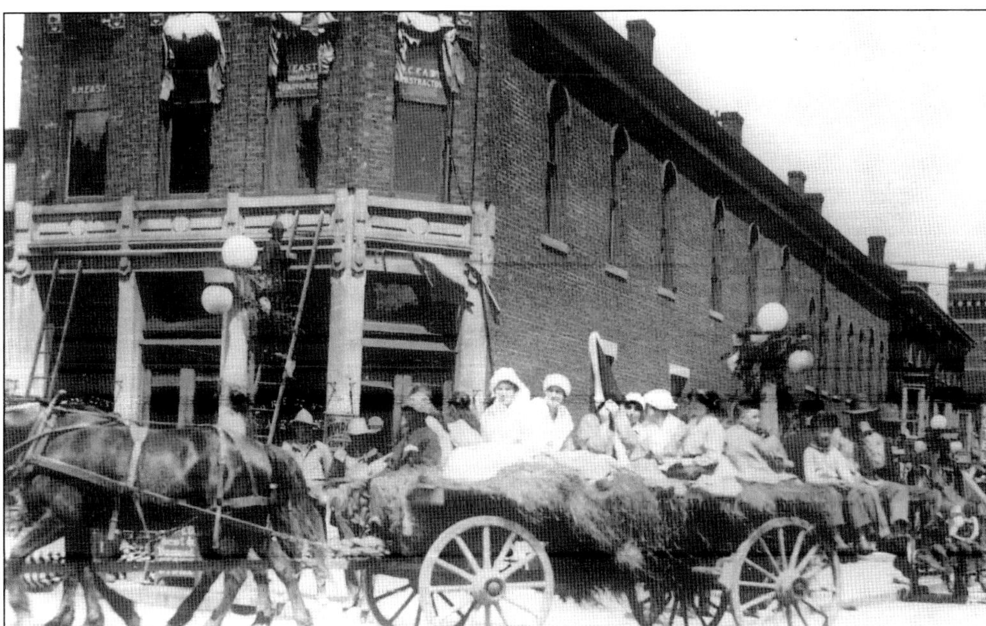

A once-in-a-lifetime event was the "Pageant of Bloomington and Indiana University," held on May 16, 17, and 18, 1916. Horse-drawn wagons formed part of the Pageant Parade, here passing the former Monroe County State Bank at the corner of East Kirkwood Avenue and North Walnut Street.

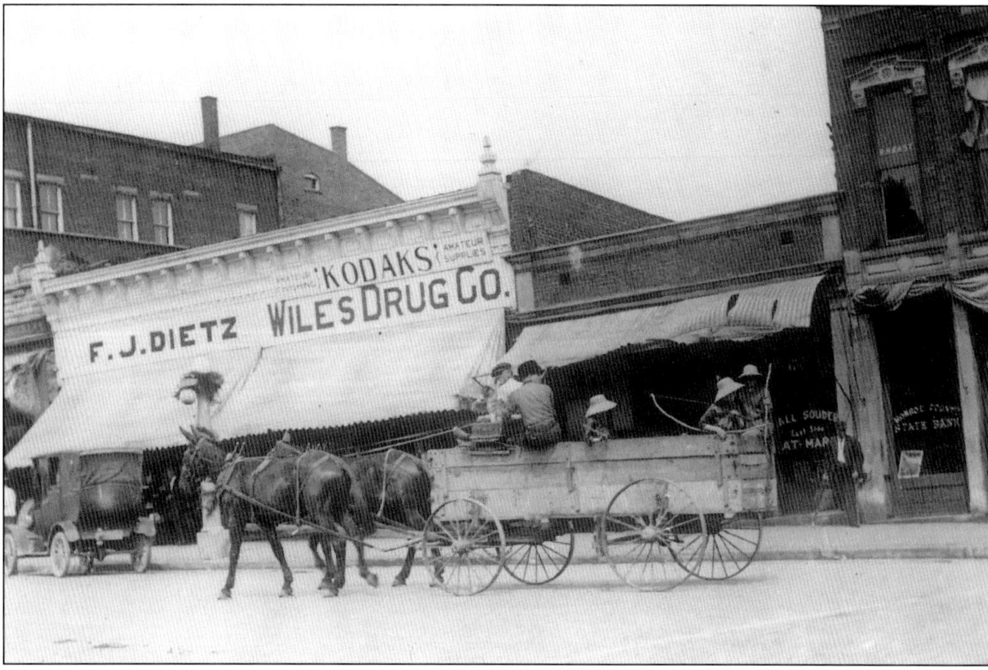

An automobile and a two-mule wagon passed the Wiles Drug Company as an apparent boy scout troop turned the corner (below) during the Pageant Parade. The Wiles Company had a Kodak dealership, which it advertised by creating a "lantern show" with glass slides made from photographs of both exotic and local scenes.

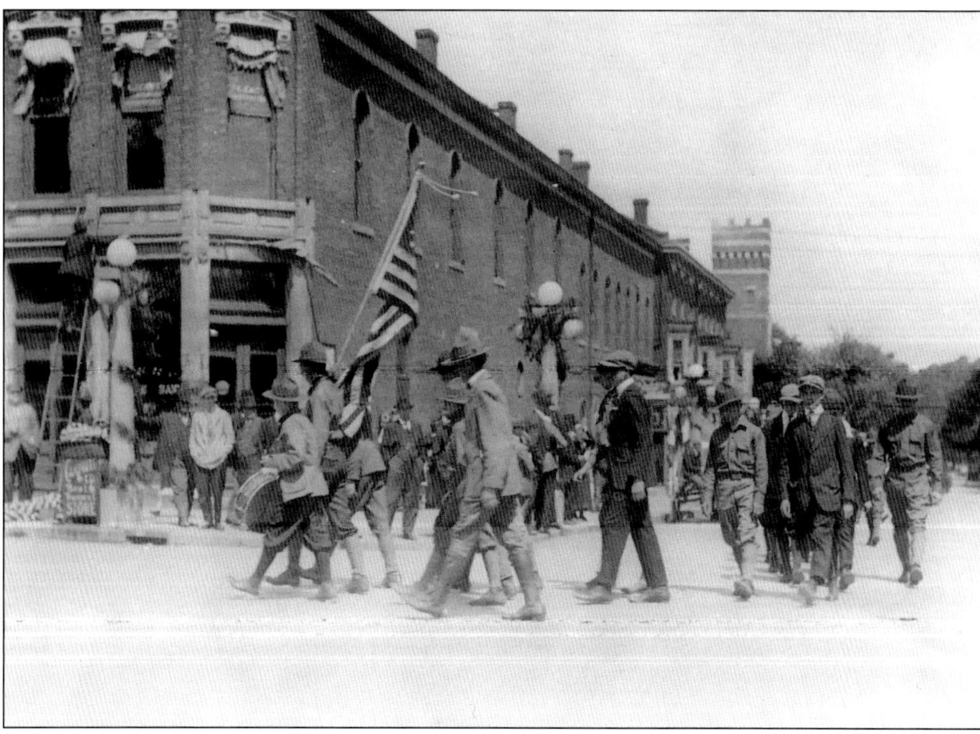

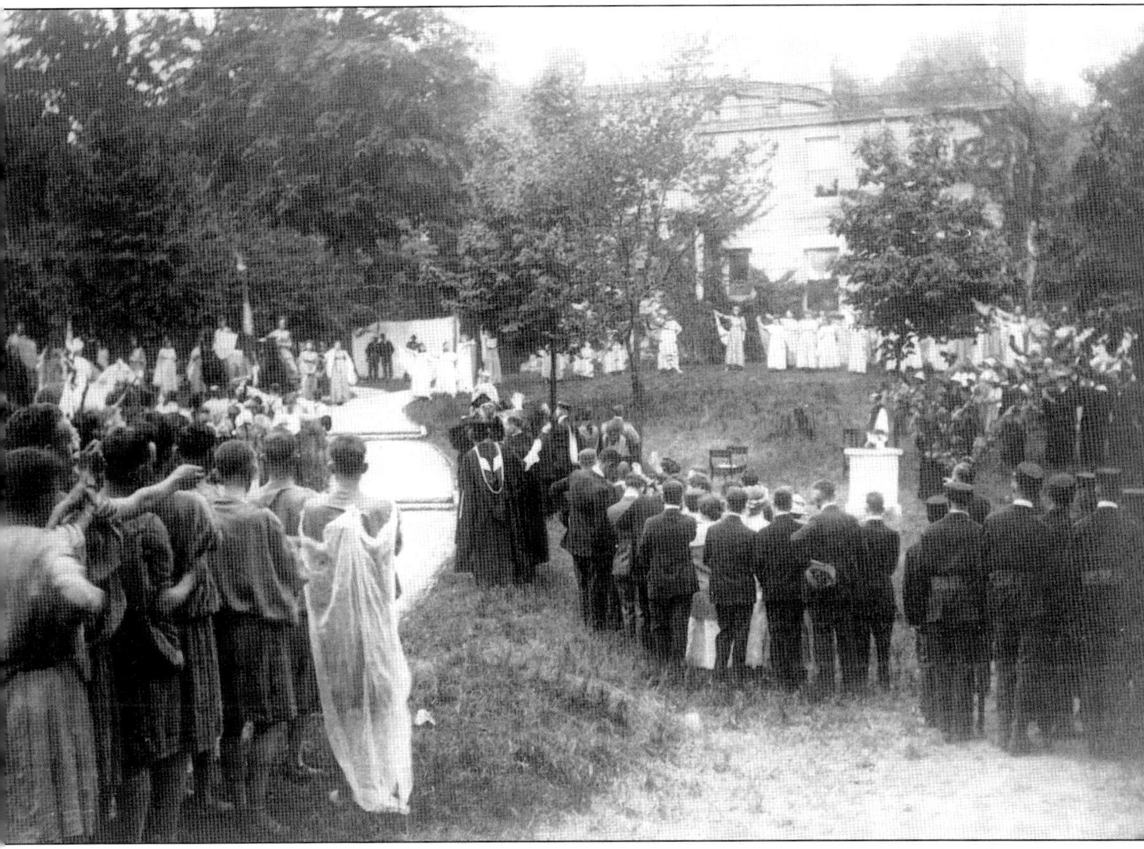

Students and townspeople both took roles in the Pageant of Bloomington and Indiana University. Scenes from pioneer history included depictions of the pioneer spirit in classical Greek garb and a reenactment of Bloomington's founding performed in supposedly local dialect. The pageant was enacted on campus near the Kirkwood Observatory.

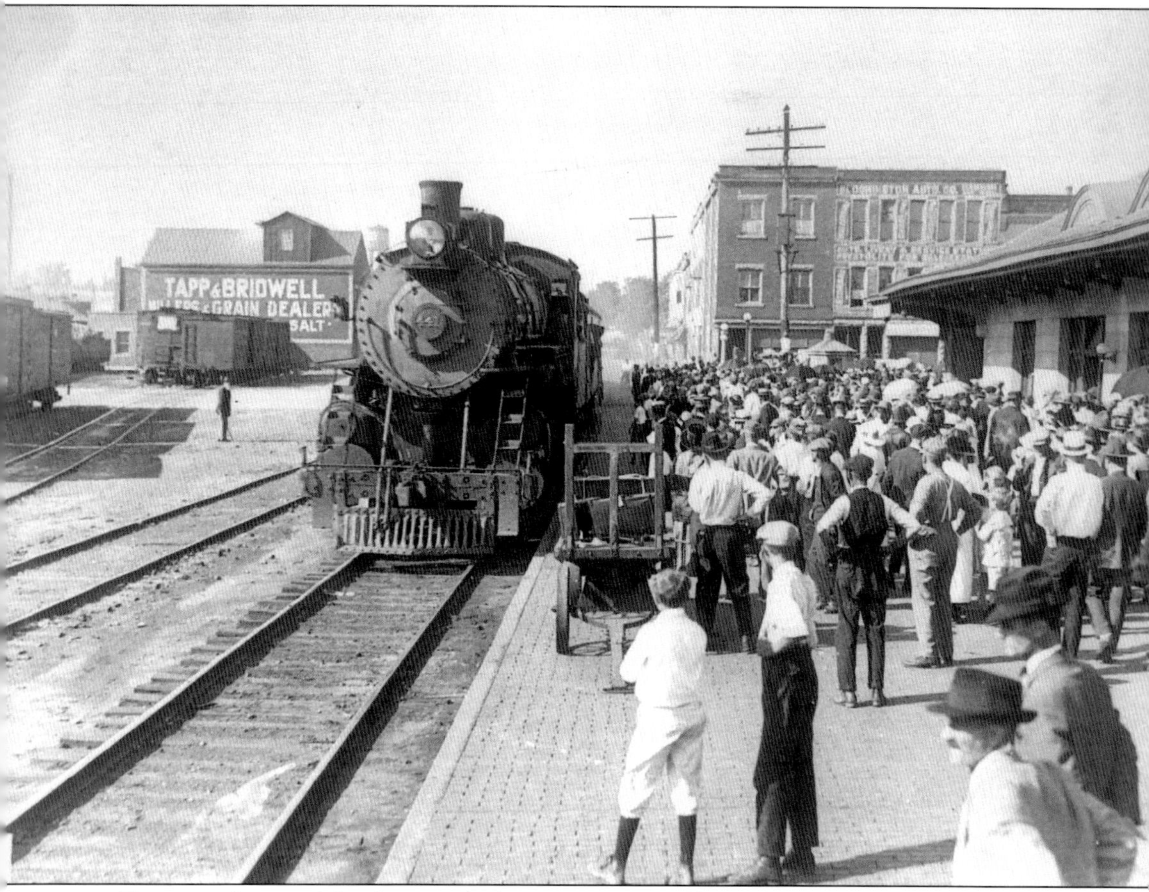

Townspeople waited for the arrival of trains carrying soldiers after the U.S. entered World War I in April 1917. The Selective Service Act soon followed the declaration of war and required men ages 21 to 30 to serve. The following year, the draft age was extended to ages 18 to 45. Indiana University was a federally supported Reserve Officers' Training Camp.

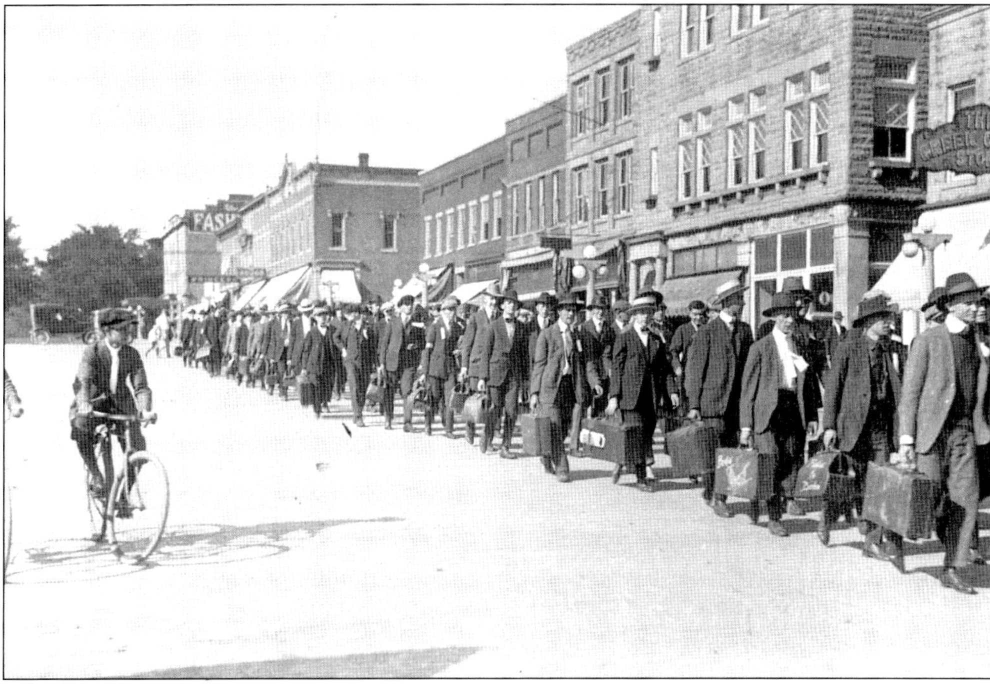

Newly-arrived soldiers marched from the train station to Indiana University carrying their valises. They may have been students from Midwestern and Southern universities who received prior training before coming to Bloomington. They were intended to form new units of troops from recruits who applied to IU's camp. Academically qualified recruits were able to enroll at IU.

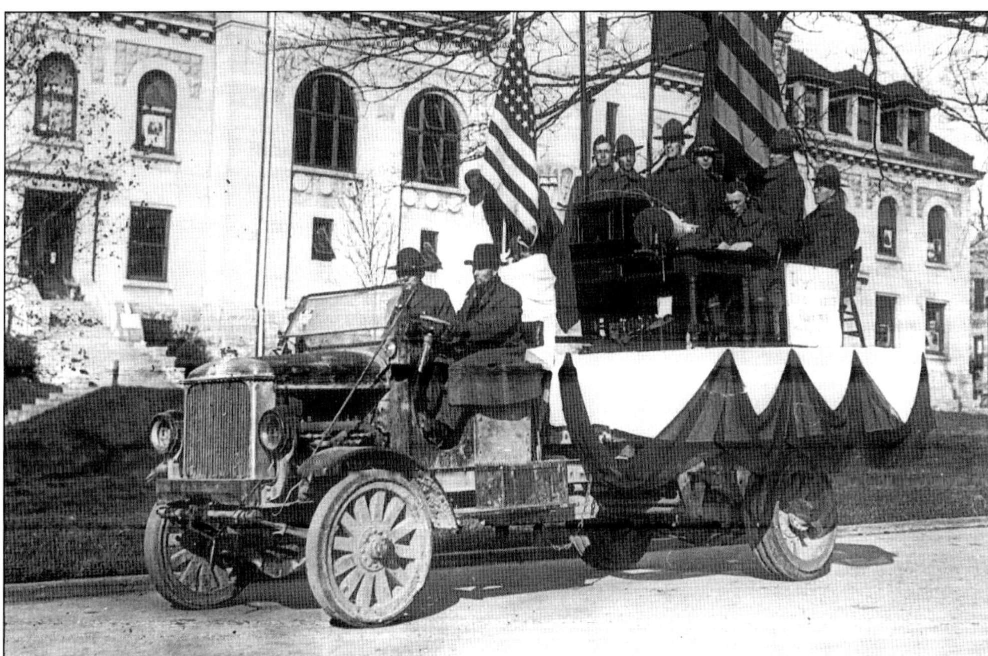

Some of Indiana University's trainees graduated from the Radio School. This float celebrated the Armistice, or laying down of arms, that occurred on November 11, 1918.

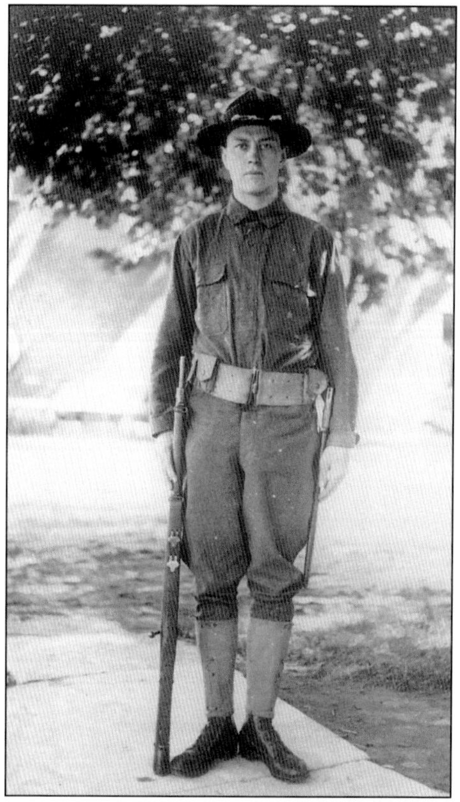

An unknown recruit in a new uniform posed with his rifle. Other new soldiers (below) learned to pitch their tents on the IU campus under the supervision of officers, small boys, and townspeople.

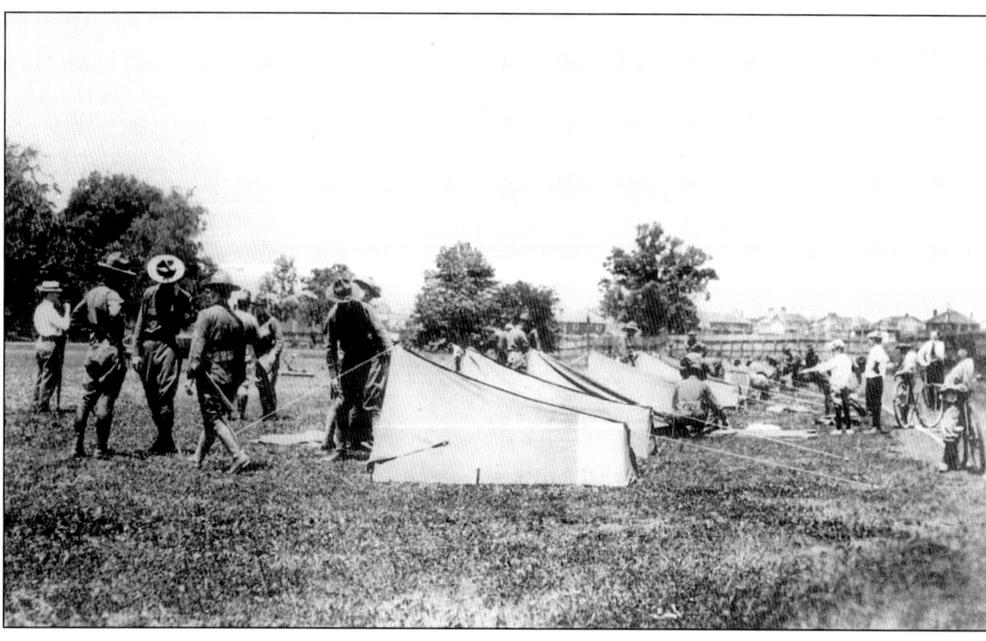

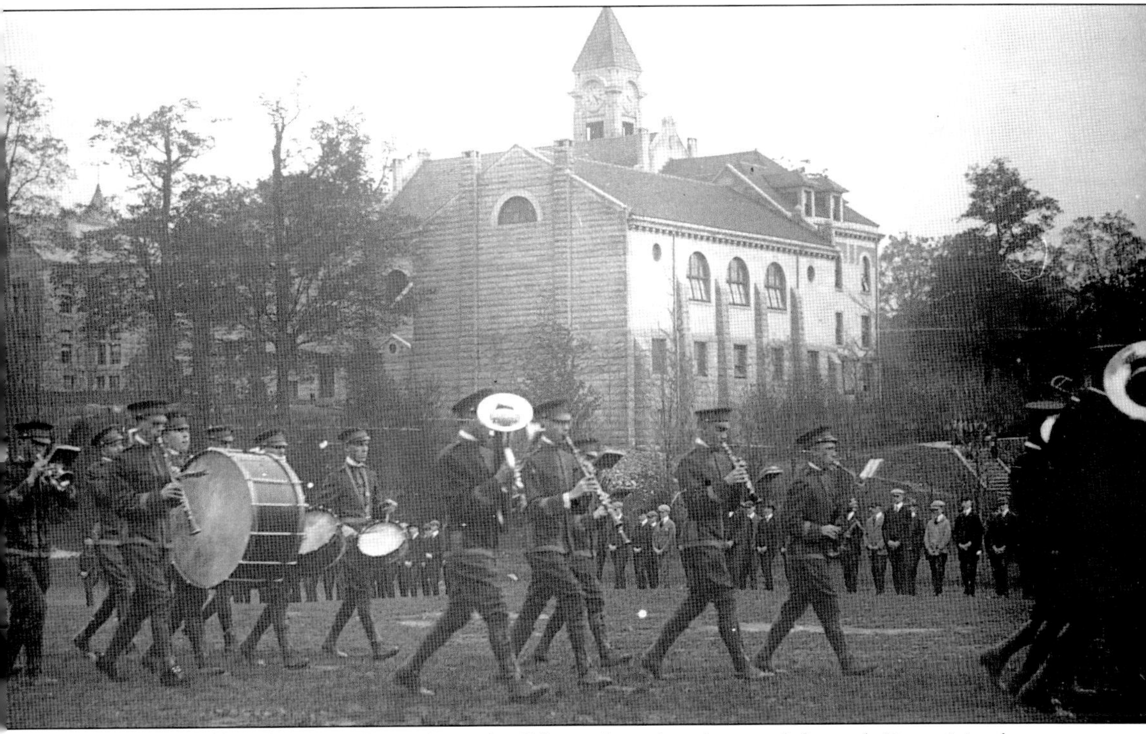

An unidentified band on parade, perhaps the IU marching band, passed through Dunn Meadow. The clock tower of the Student Building rises above the rooftops at top center of photo, which was made from a glass lantern slide in the Wiles Drug Company collection.

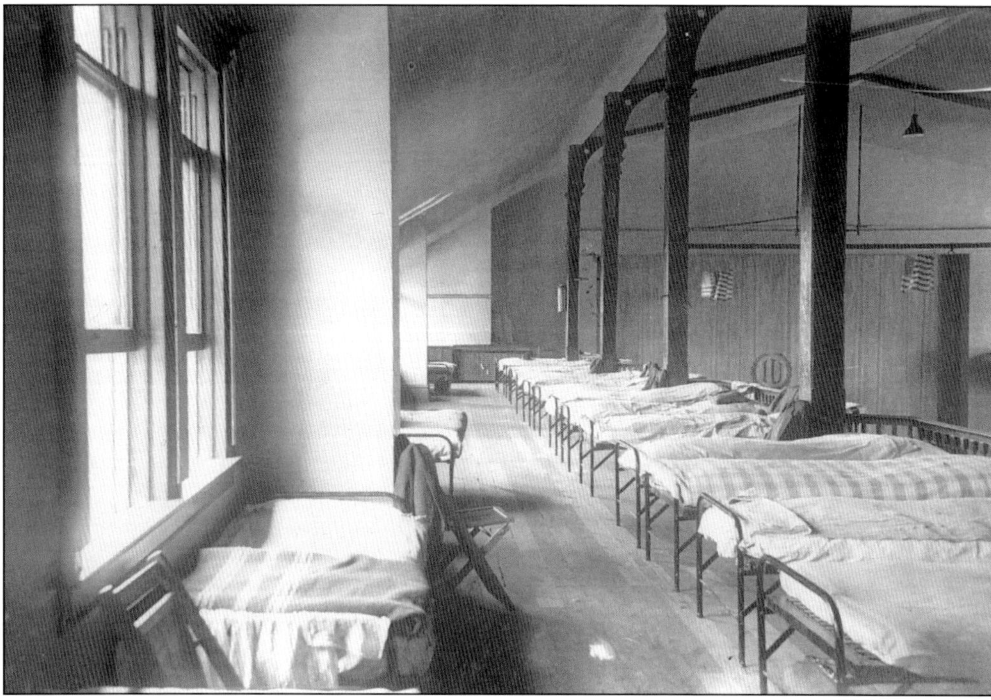

Assembly Hall on the IU campus was converted into barracks, then used as a hospital when a nationwide influenza epidemic broke out in September 1918. Below, troops stood at attention in downtown Bloomington.

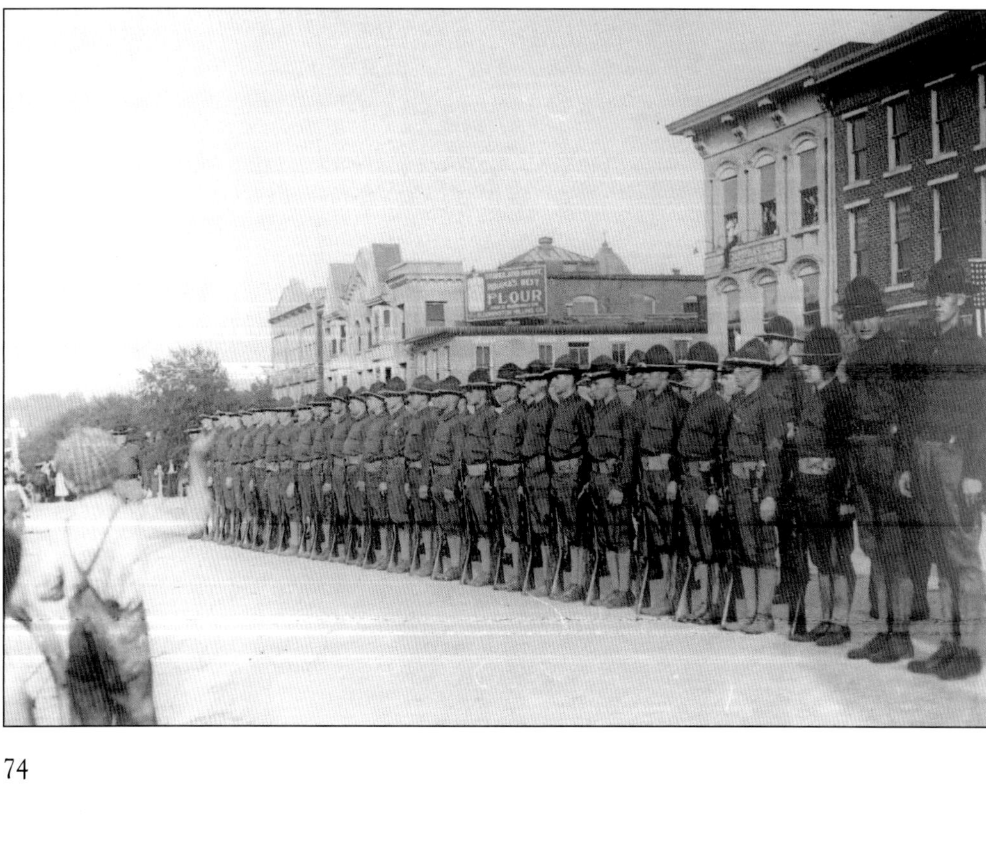

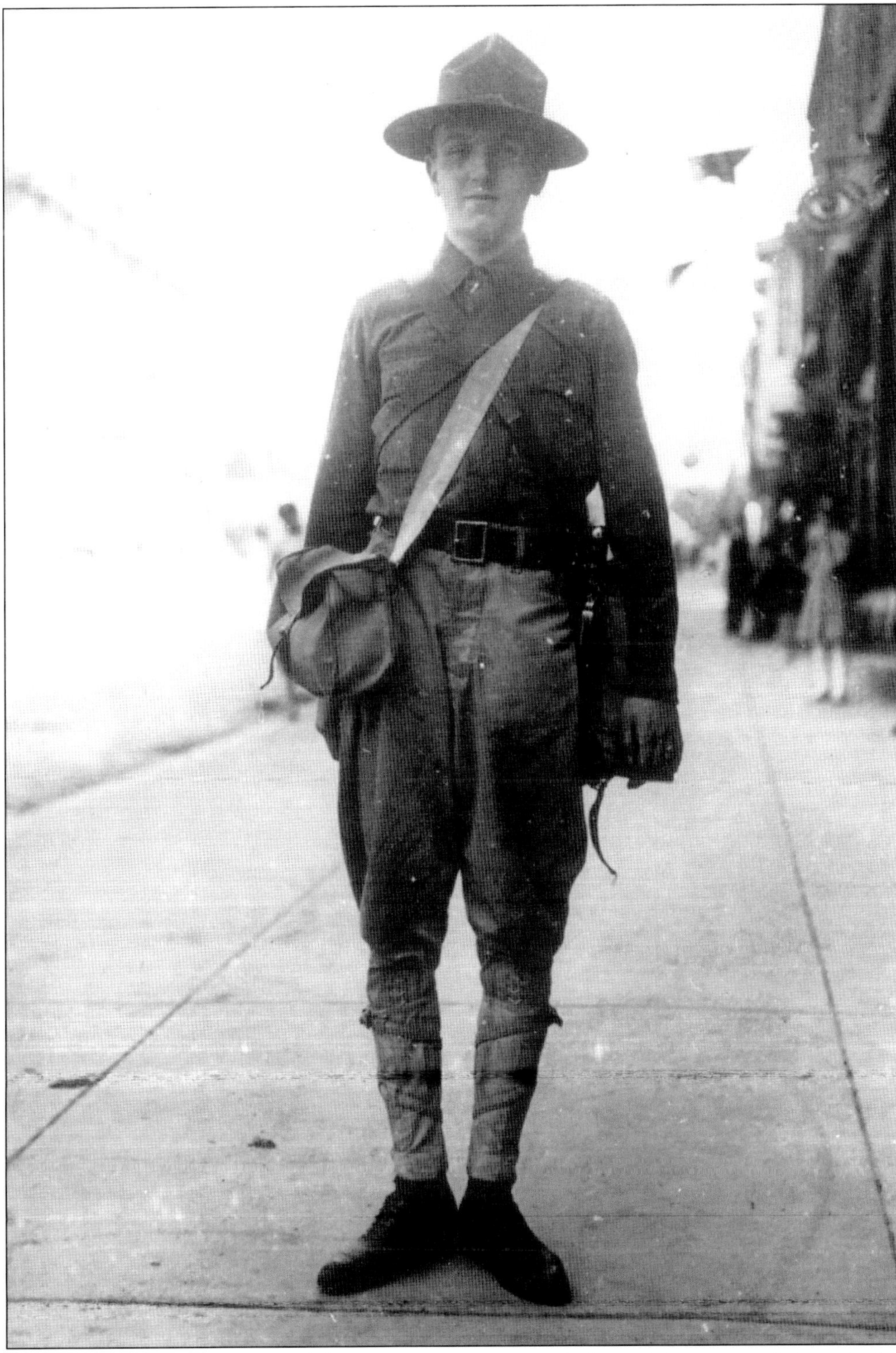

Another unknown recruit posed downtown while a young lady, at right center of photo in the distance, appeared to watch and wait.

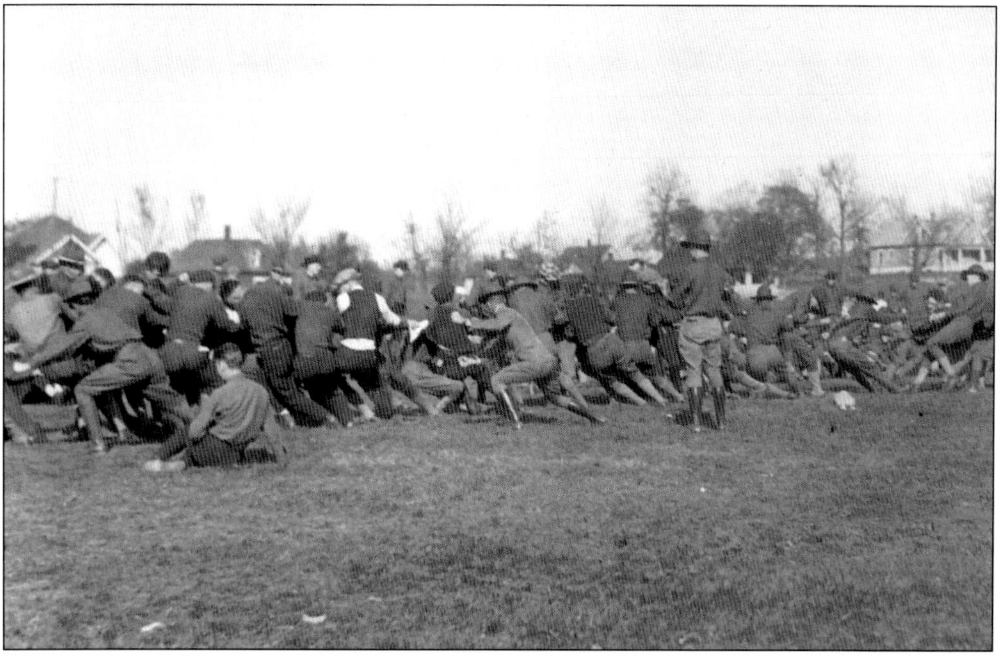

A trainees' tug-of-war on the IU campus was part of physical training.

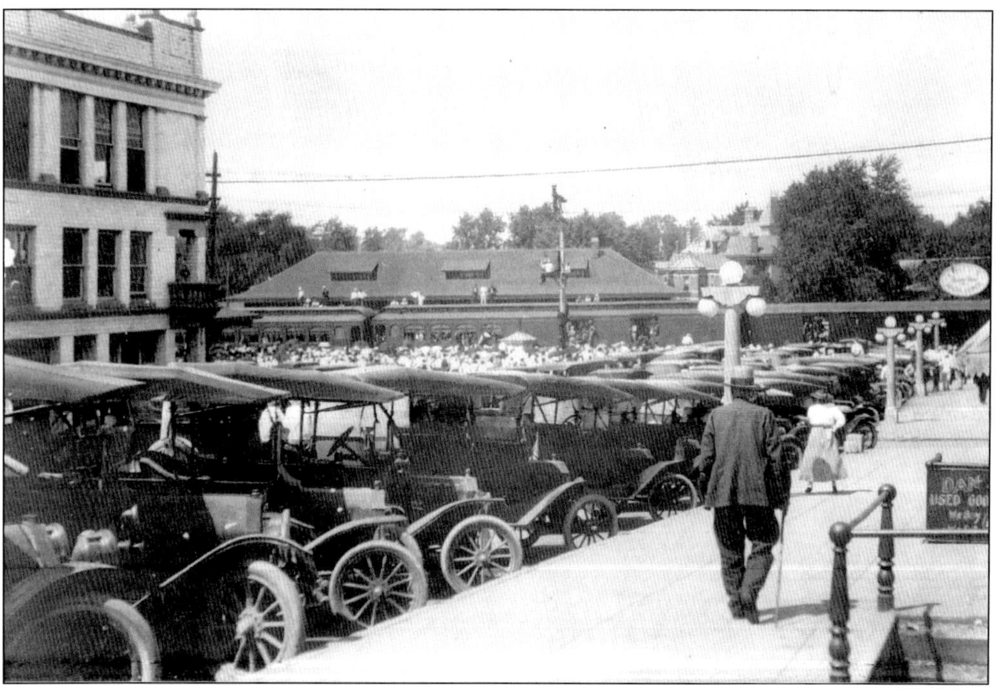

Spectators clung to the roof of the train station and filled its platform space as a troop train came through Bloomington during World War I. The Armistice brought an end to World War I in November 1918.

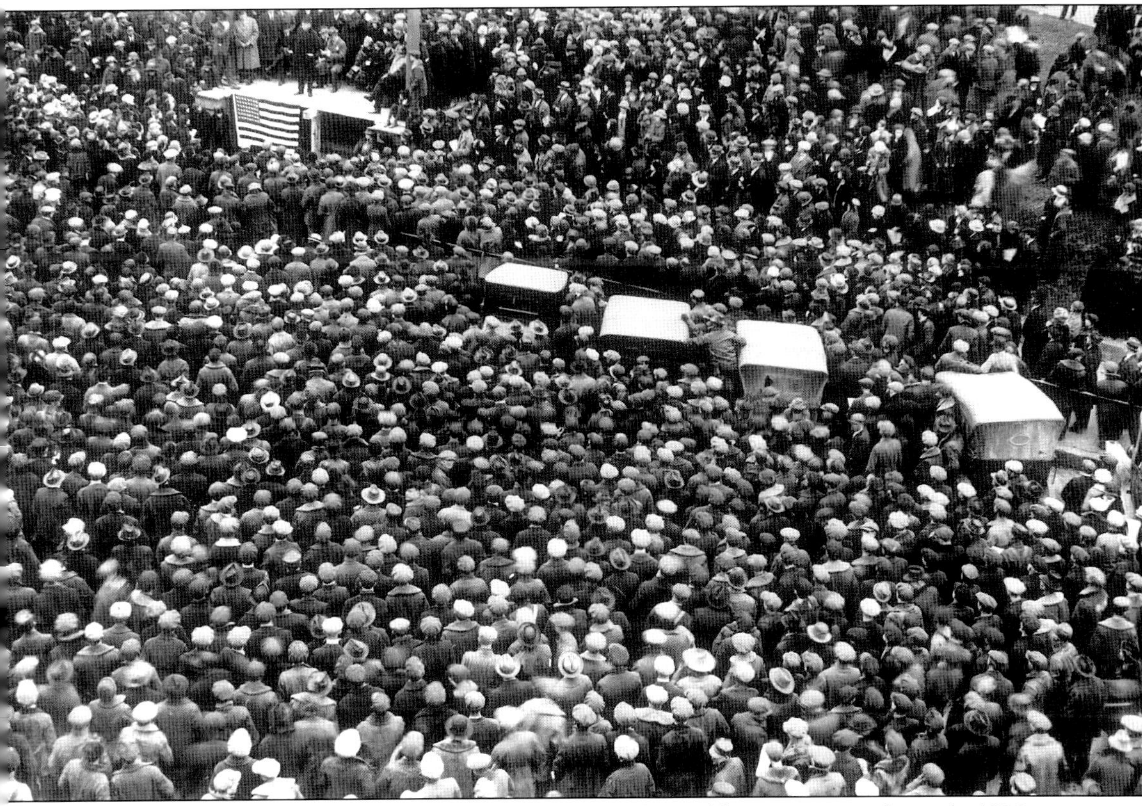

A speakers' platform stood on the courthouse lawn for this public meeting in the early 1920s. The controversial subject was Bloomington's water supply. Circa 1890, a town well on the courthouse square had served as public water until it was found to be too close to privies. Between 1890 and 1910, the city dammed various streams on Bloomington's west side and piped in water or brought it by wagon. All of these artificial lakes—the Twin Lakes, Weimer (or Wapehani) Lake, and Leonard Springs Lake—leaked because they were built over porous limestone formations. The public meeting was convened to call for damming Griffy Creek, which ran over shale, as a source of water.

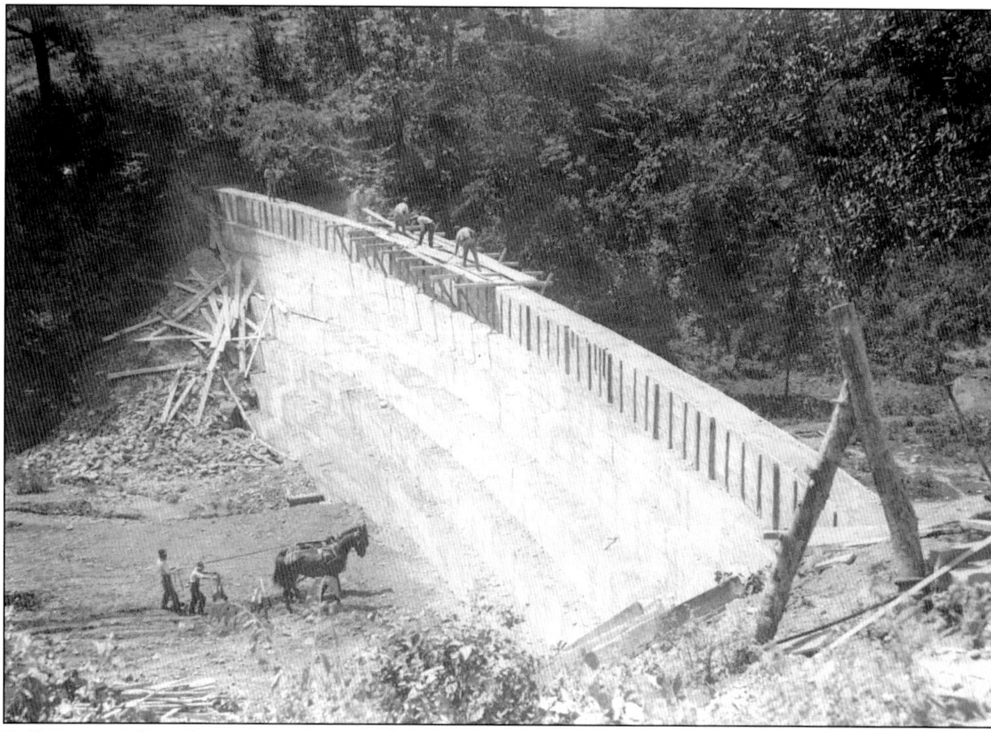

Following a drought in 1910–1911, the university dammed a stream to create a lake, pictured above and opposite, that is located near the IU golf course today. The university, which used 90,000 gallons a day, had been dependent on city water.

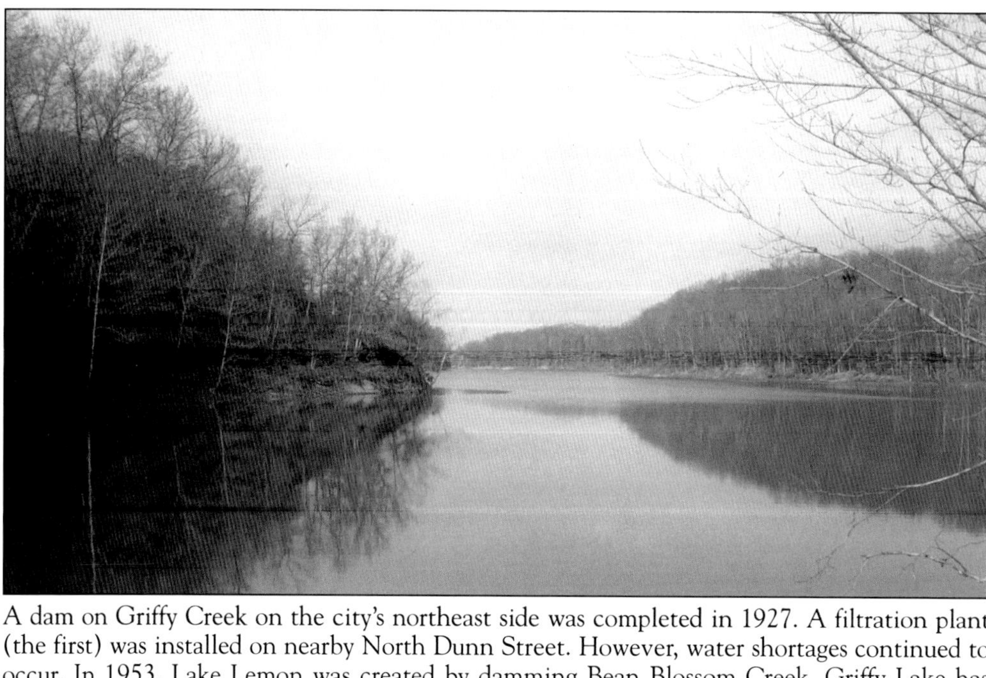

A dam on Griffy Creek on the city's northeast side was completed in 1927. A filtration plant (the first) was installed on nearby North Dunn Street. However, water shortages continued to occur. In 1953, Lake Lemon was created by damming Bean Blossom Creek. Griffy Lake has become a recreational area for students and townspeople.

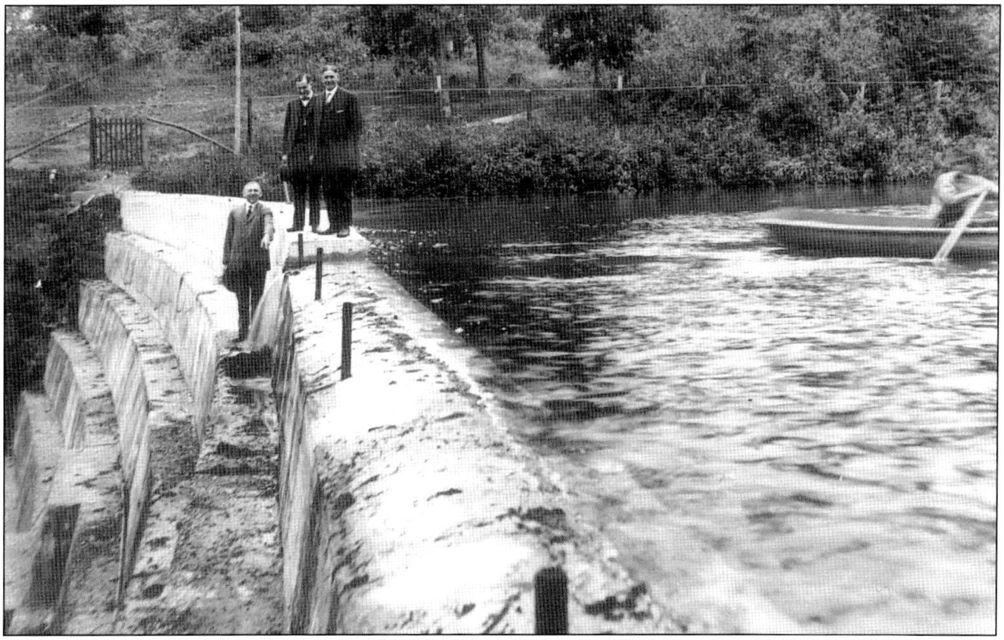

The university lake site had not been cleared before damming and cattle and hogs from nearby farms were grazing in the watershed. A report to President Bryan in 1913 recommended purchasing the rest of the watershed and trying to achieve storage capacity of 40 million gallons by extending and raising the dam. Eventually, IU again used city water to supplement its own plant. IU's consumption of city water rose from 48.8 to 170 million gallons per year between 1942 and 1950 as enrollment skyrocketed following World War II.

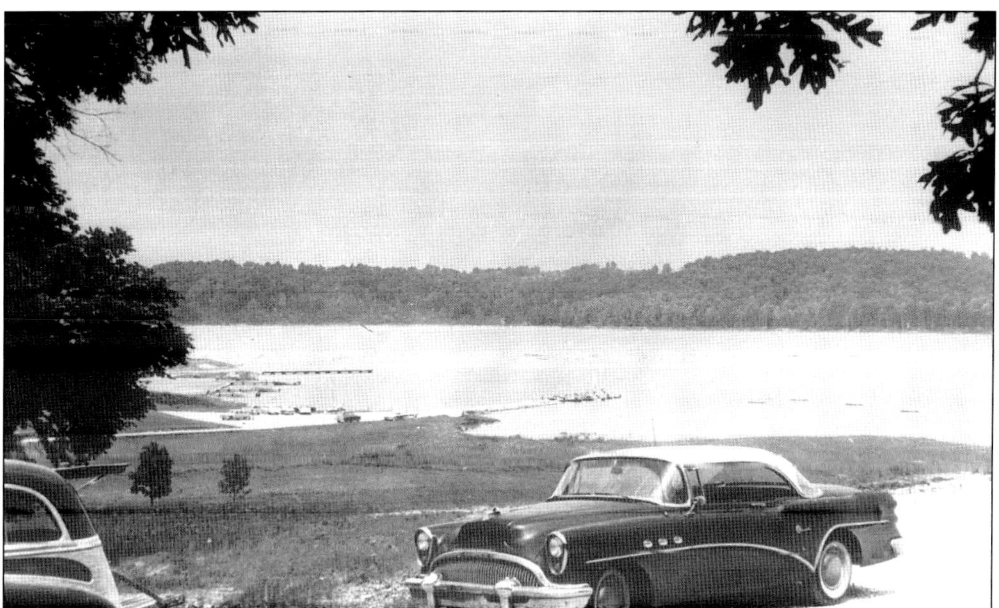

Lake Monroe, proposed in 1949, was intended as a flood-control project and recreational attraction rather than a source of city water. Completed in 1964 by the Army Corps of Engineers, Lake Monroe displaced farmers and the residents of several towns.

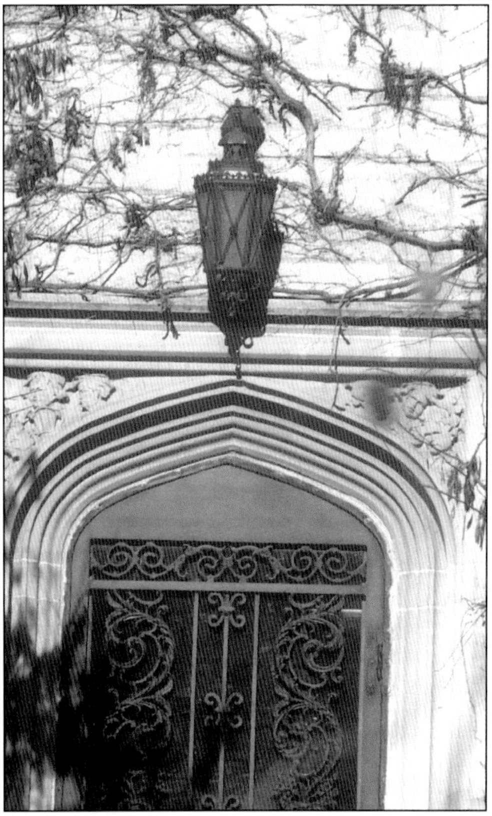

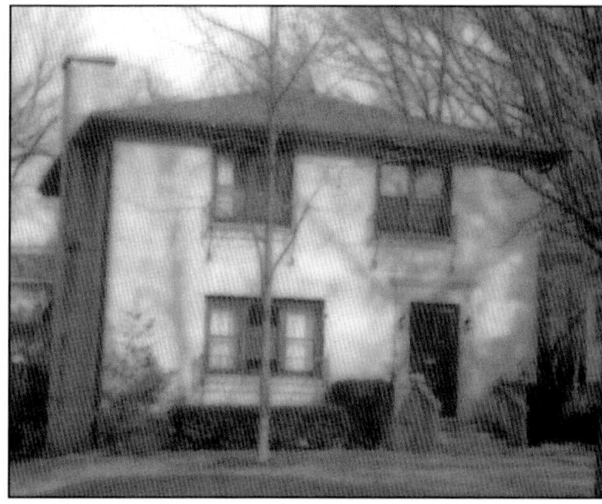

In the 1920s and 1930s, the Vinegar Hill neighborhood on Bloomington's southeast side filled in with houses such as these two on East First Street. The simple but elegant house above right was faced with smooth-finished limestone block and personalized with carvings of stylized flowers at the door and windows. The limestone-faced Cline-Hammer house (1928; photos above left and below) was built by quarry owner Kenneth Cline in loose imitation of Elizabethan-Jacobean architecture. Cline's children are depicted in portrait carvings over the entry door.

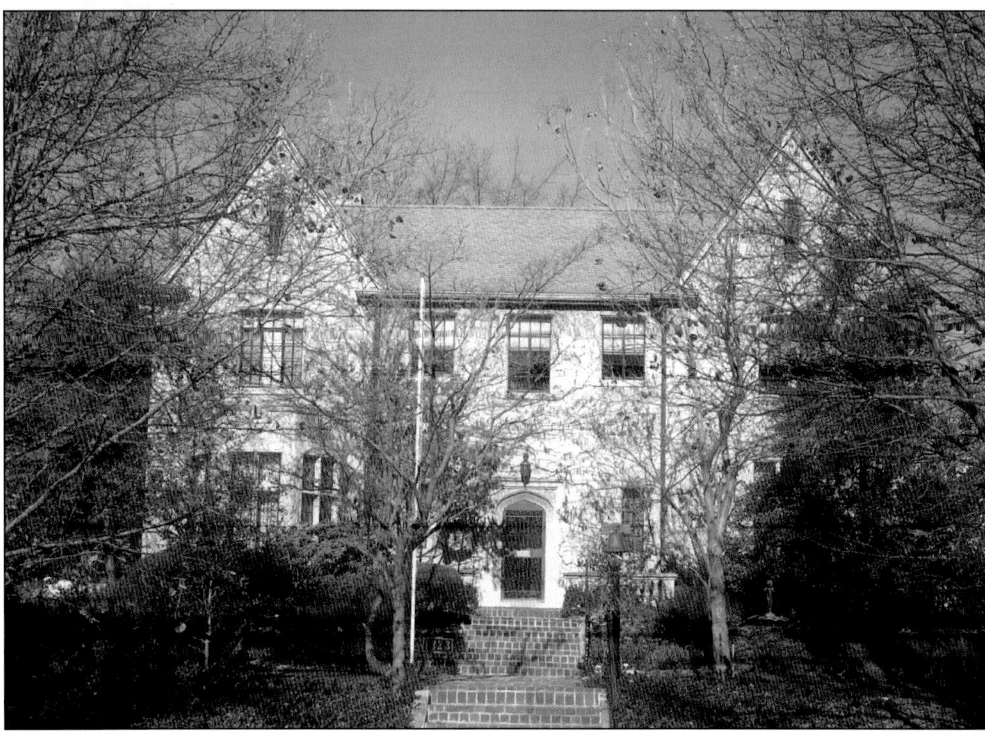

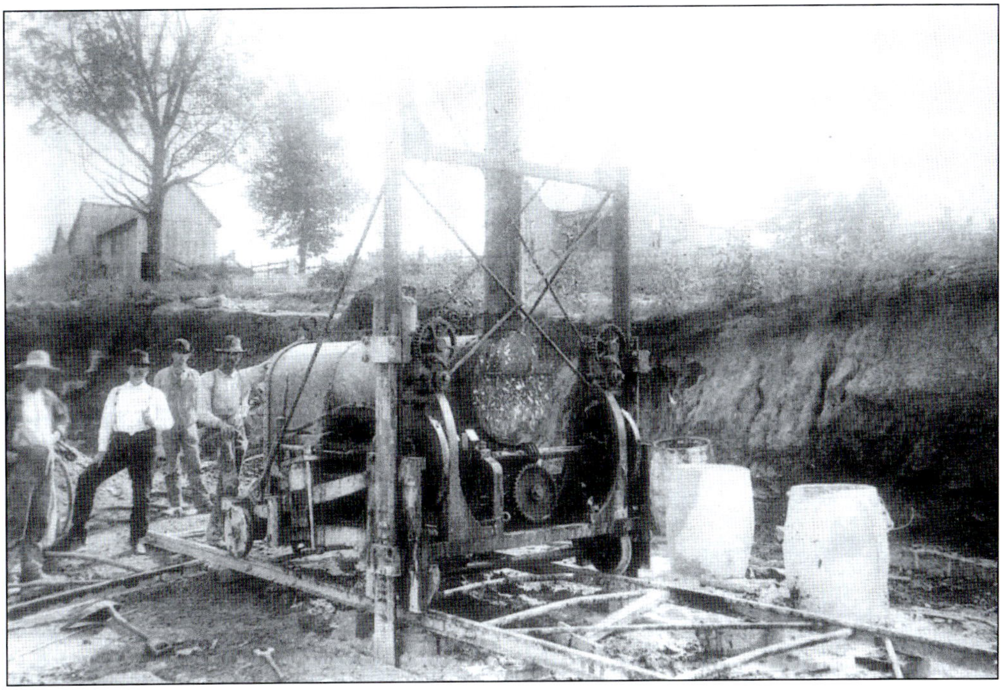

The limestone industry provided both building material and a source of wealth. When these quarry scenes were photographed *c.* 1891, steam power was the rule. By the 1920s, when the houses shown on the previous page were built, quarry and mill machinery was powered by electricity. Several limestone mills were located near Bloomington's downtown as late as the 1920s.

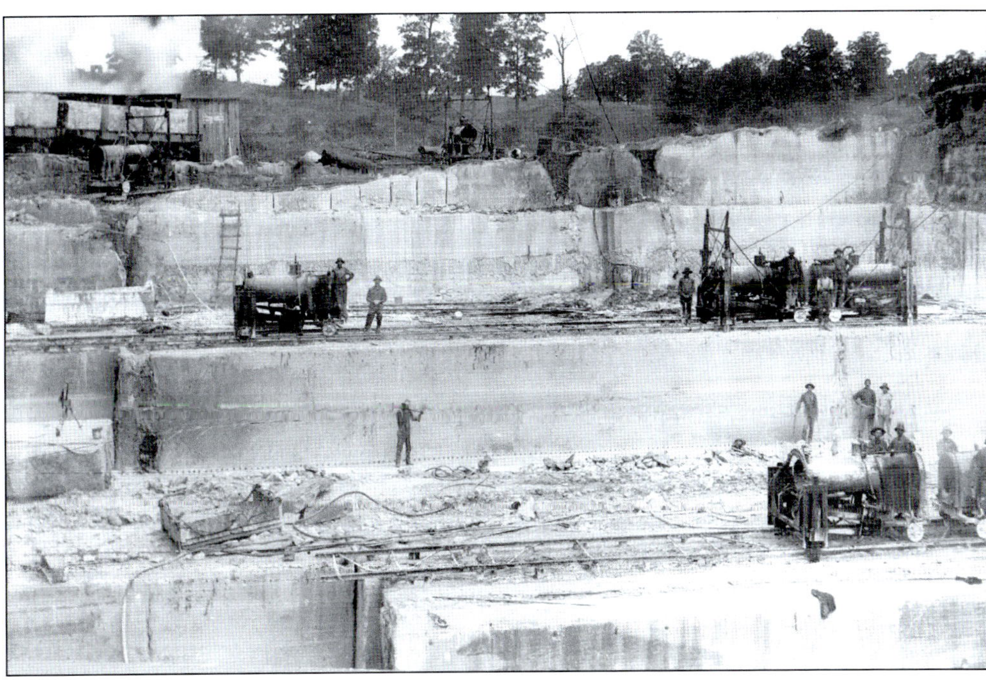

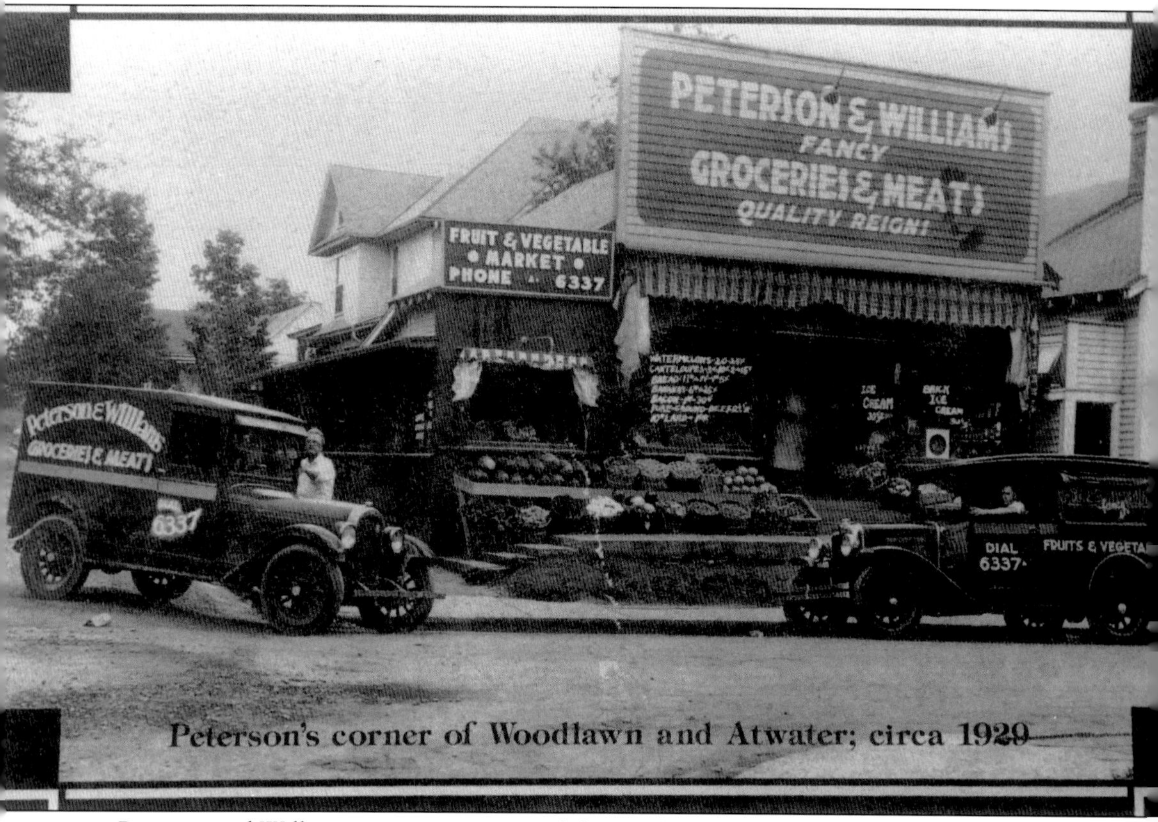

Peterson and Williams grocery store served the neighborhood of Elm Heights. Hunter, Second, Hawthorne, and Ballantine Streets, east and south of the grocery store and west of Vinegar Hill, had just been laid out.

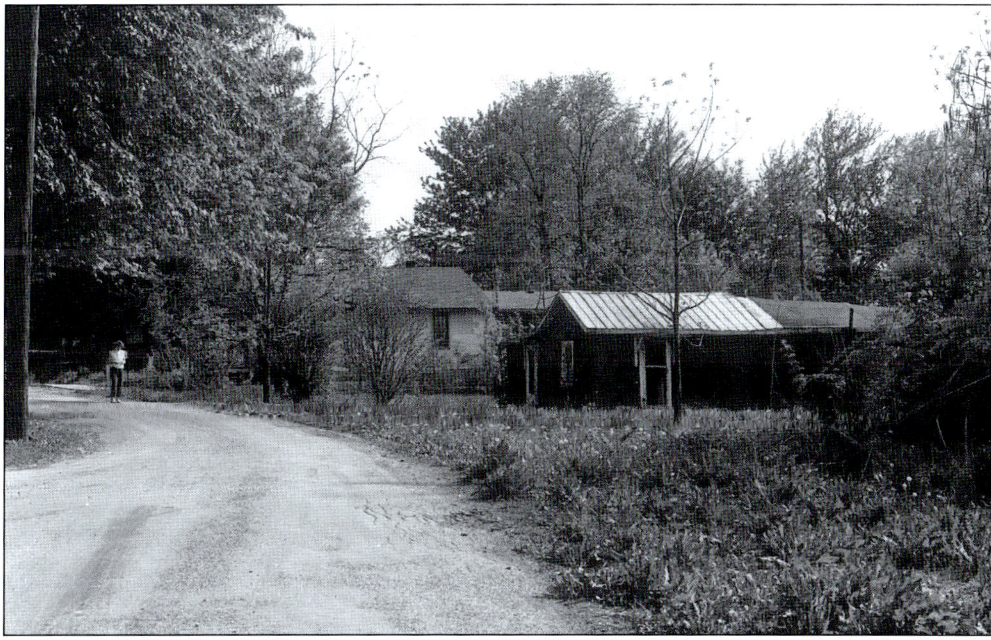

Streets north of the campus, such as East Fifteenth, kept an almost rural appearance until the 1960s. The Livingston Market (below), housed in a converted cottage with worn limestone stoop, was located at 707 East Thirteenth. Proprietors named Livingston had grocery stores at several addresses around Bloomington for many years.

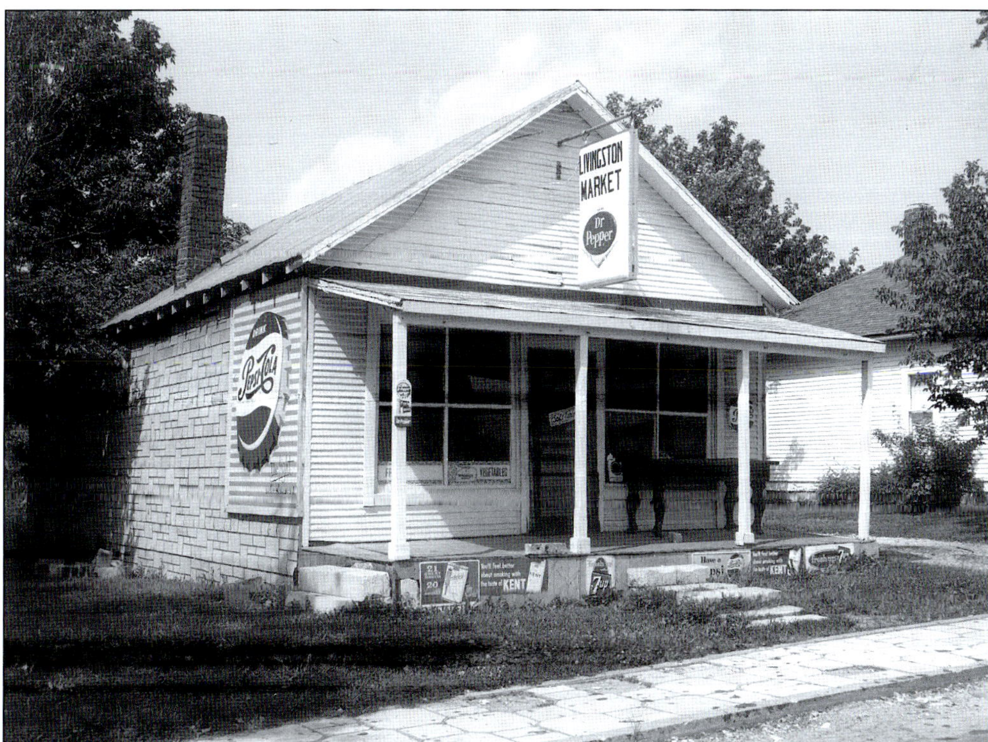

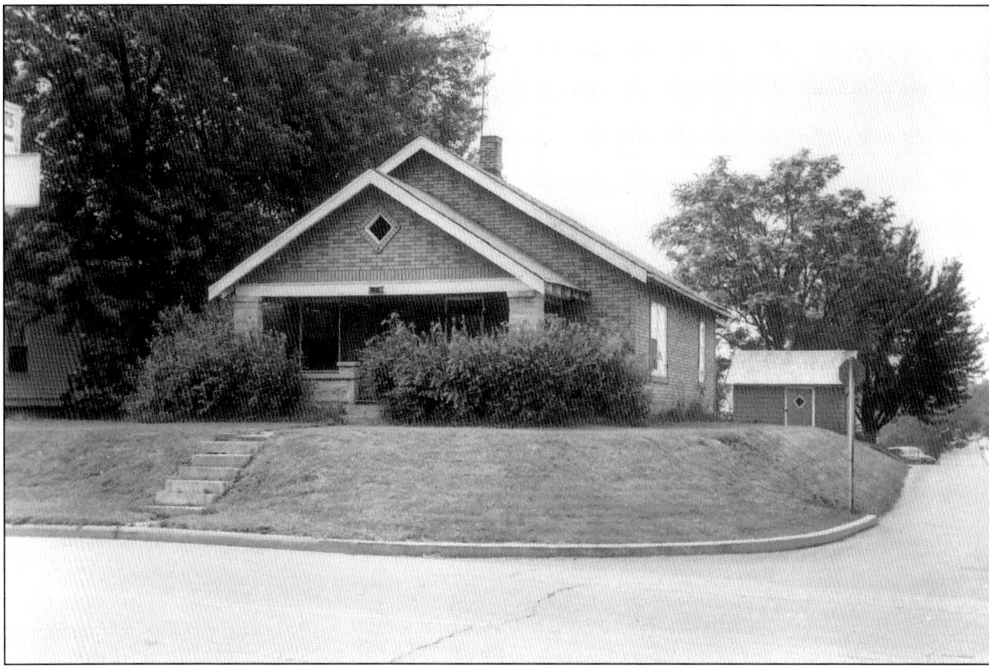

Low-slung "California bungalow" styling became popular in Bloomington *c.* 1918–1930. This house at an unidentified address, though modest, had a garage. The spacious bungalow porch was made of limestone blocks, a local touch for a nationally dominant style.

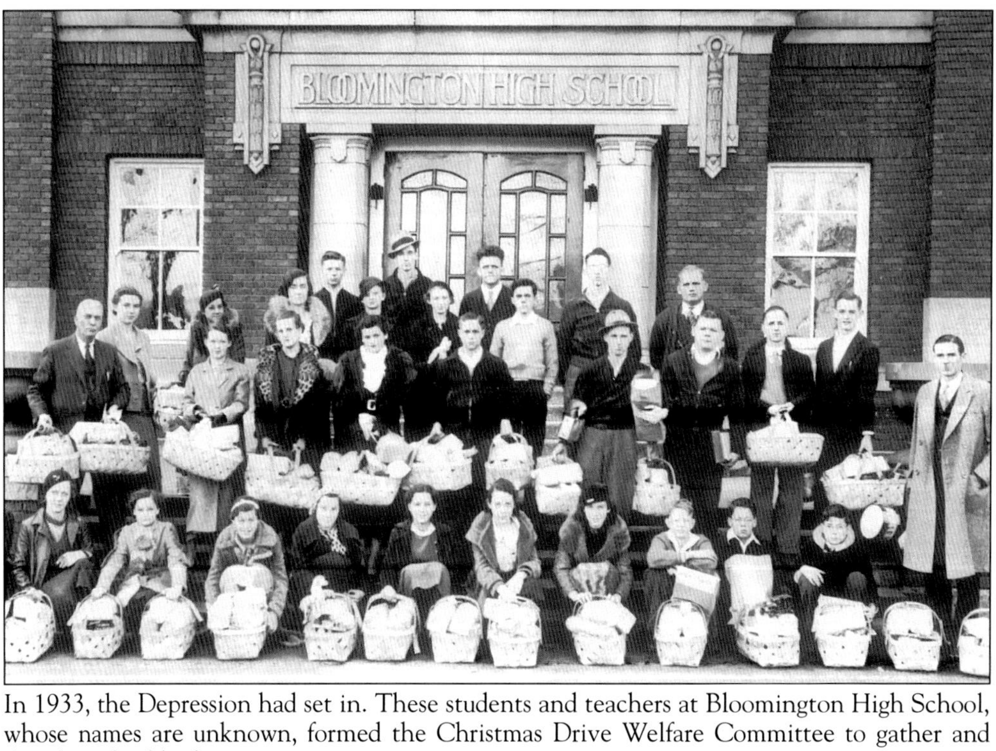

In 1933, the Depression had set in. These students and teachers at Bloomington High School, whose names are unknown, formed the Christmas Drive Welfare Committee to gather and distribute food baskets.

Indiana University underwent something of a building boom during the 1930s due to Federal programs intended to provide work and stimulate the economy. The Memorial Union building, completed in 1932, was added to in 1939. The date of 1820 carved above the Union's south entrance is that of IU's founding by act of the state legislature. The Administration Building (Bryan Hall), School of Music, and other major buildings were built 1931–1940.

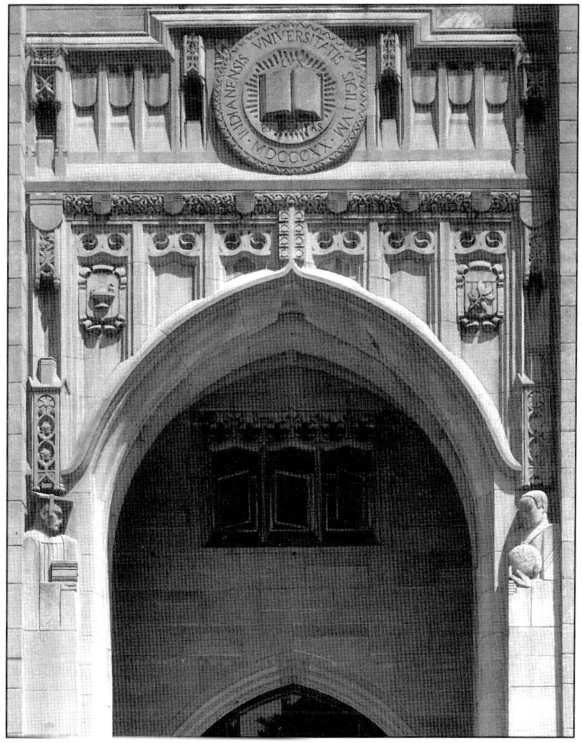

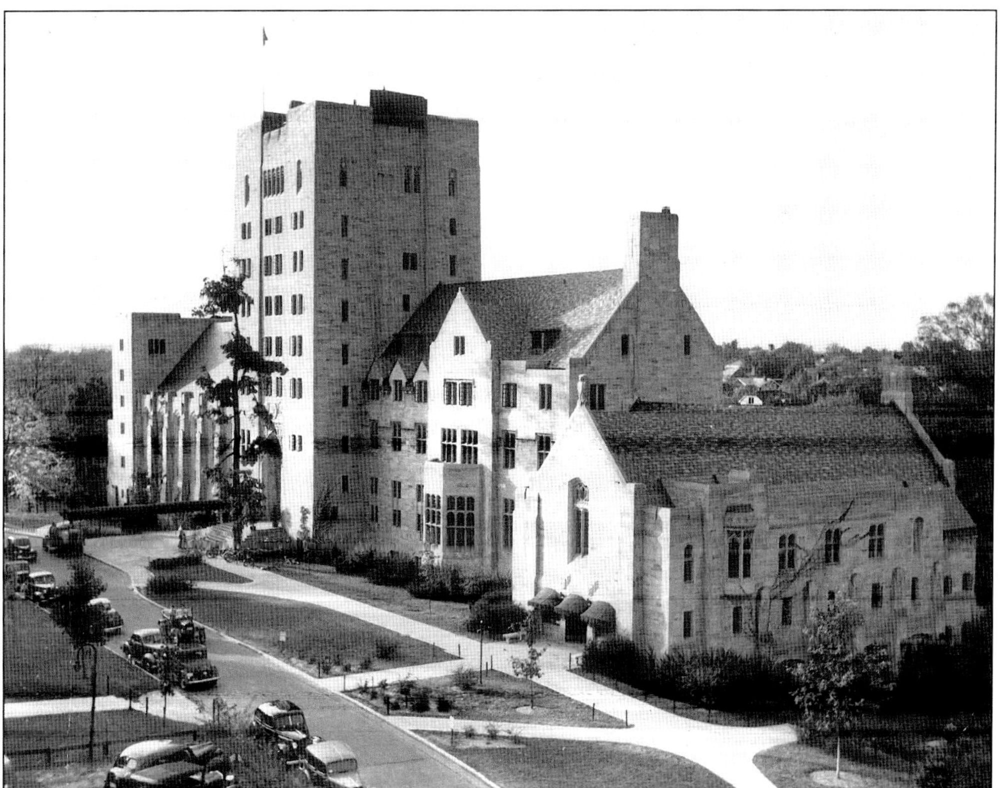

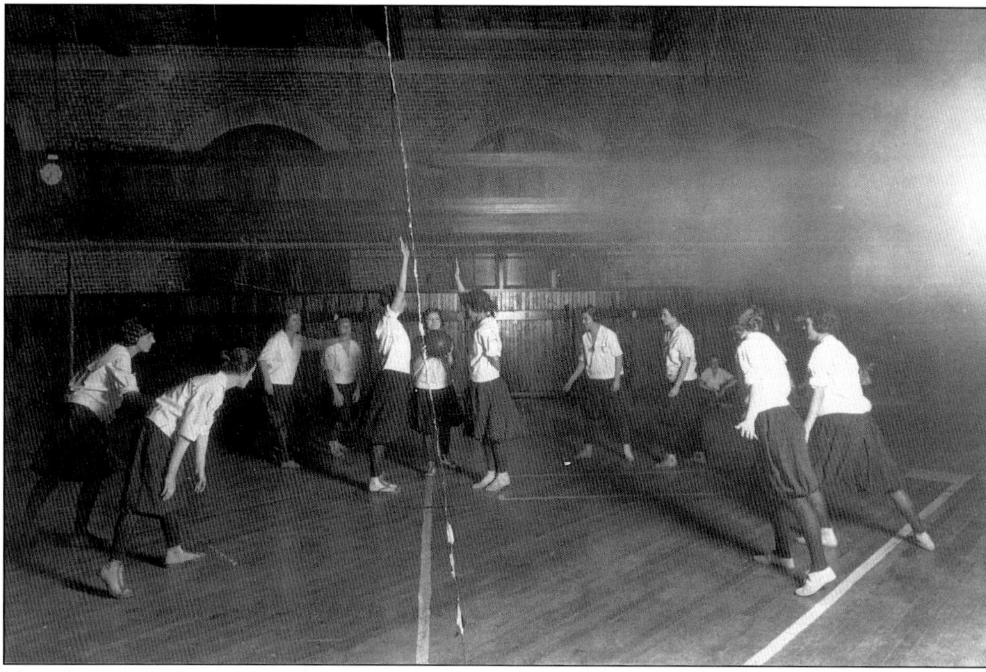

The freshman team won this 1922 Intramural Championship basketball game in 1922. Women's varsity athletics had their beginning 50 years later when Title IX, a 1972 federal legislative amendment, prohibited discrimination in educational programs or activities that receive federal financial assistance.

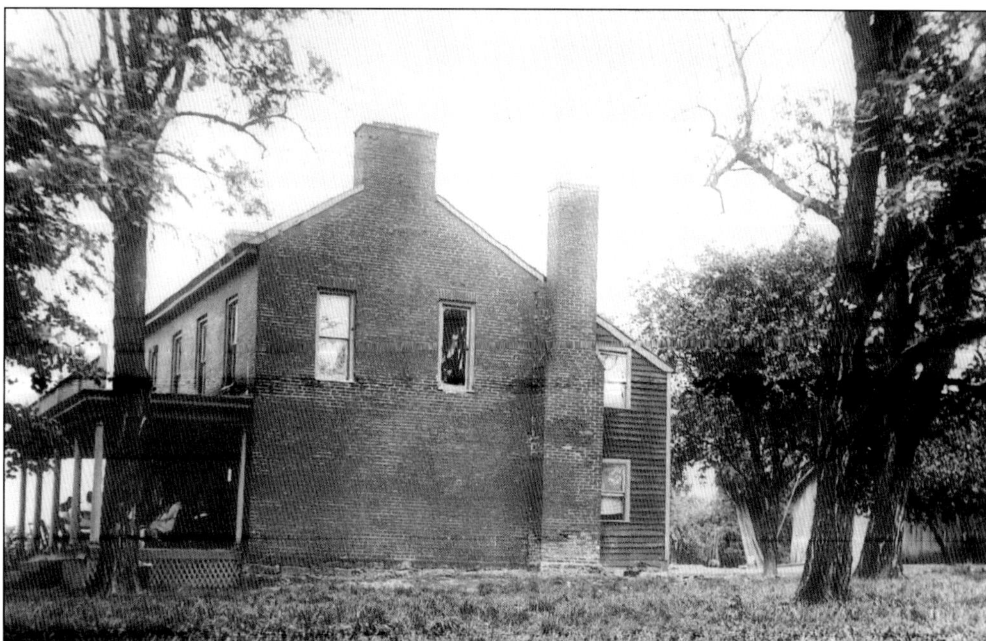

The Samuel Dunn house stood on East Seventh Street from 1824 to 1915, when it became the site of the Men's Gymnasium (1917). The gymnasium is now part of the Ora L. Wildermuth Intramural Center.

Five

STUDENT LIFE

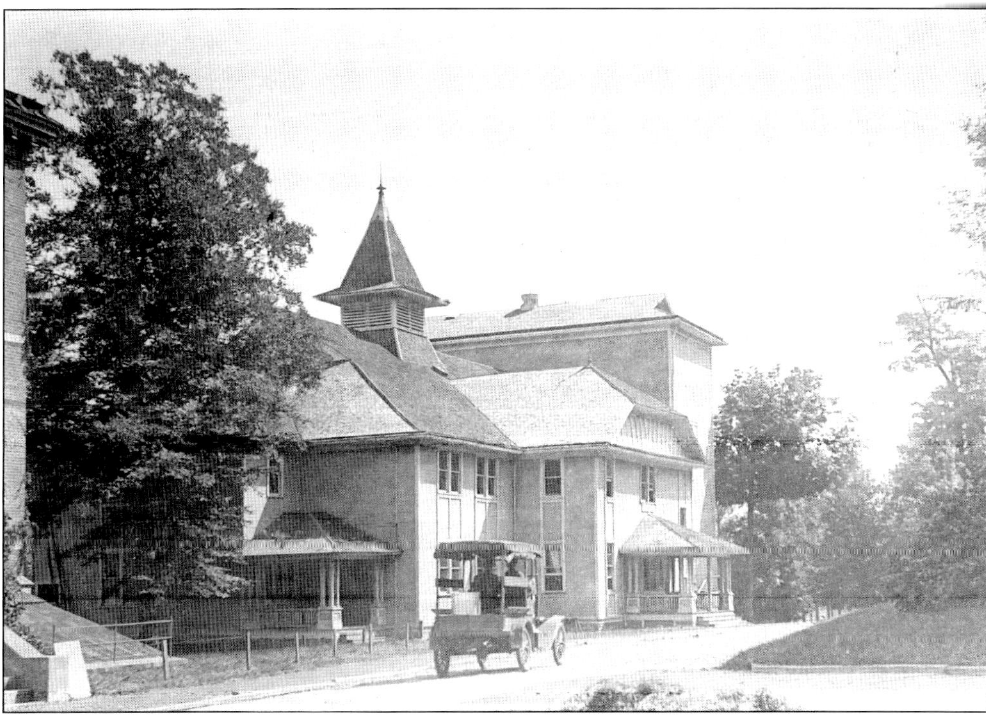

Assembly Hall served as both gymnasium and auditorium. The building received a three-story addition in 1914 (rear of building in photo) to enlarge the stage. Work was accomplished in time for a production of J.M. Barrie's *The Legend of Lenora.*

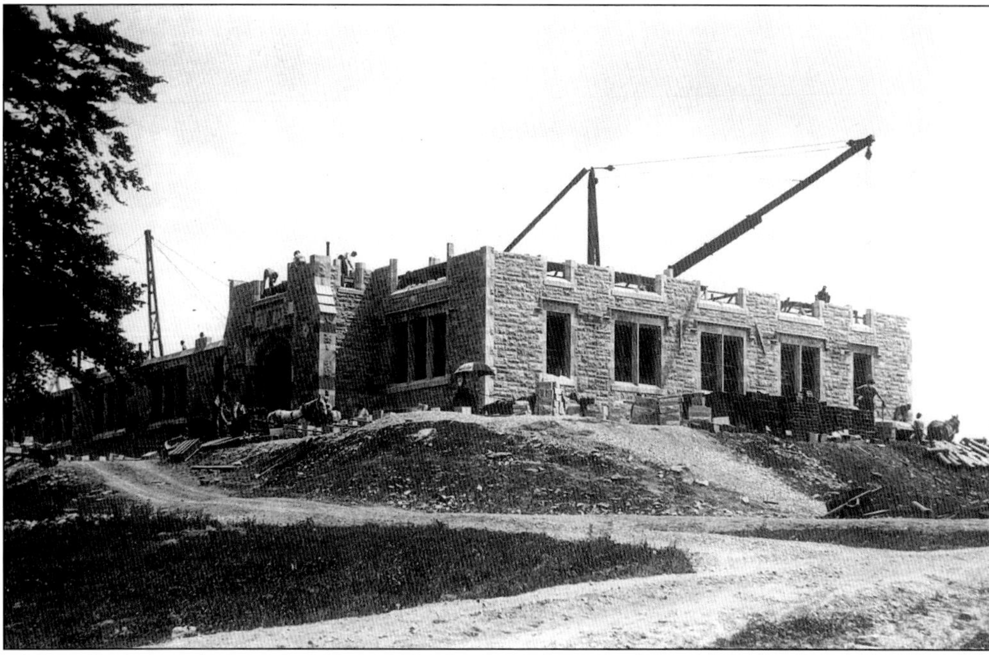

The Tudor Revival styling of the third Men's Gymnasium began to take shape *c.* 1917 with the help of men and horses or mules. Large derricks, one with a movable boom, rose above construction at the rear of the building. Walls were veneered in rock-faced limestone block.

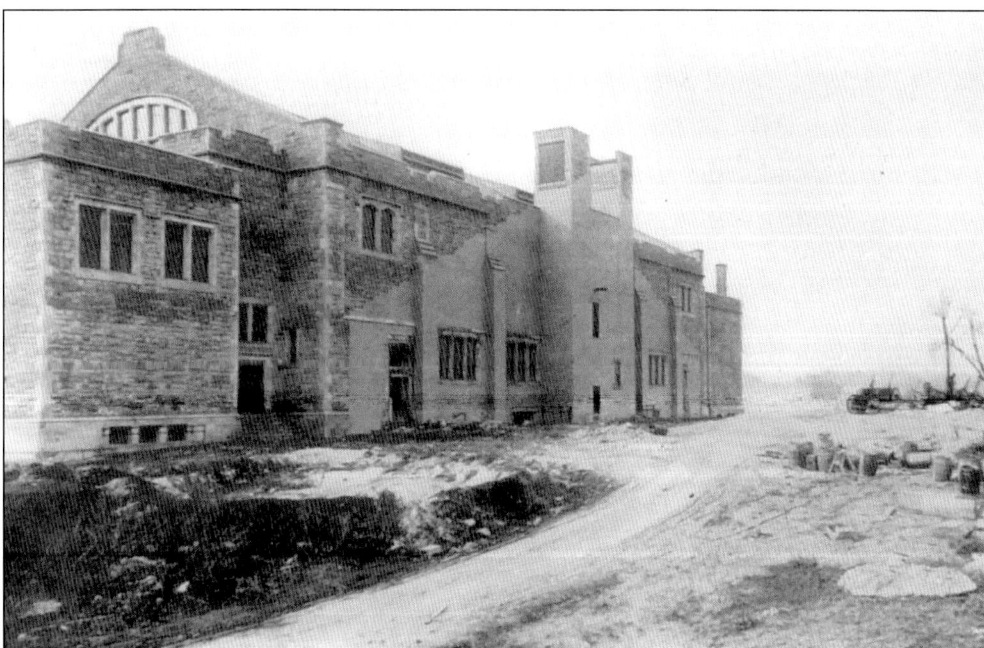

This Men's Gymnasium was completed in 1917. It included a swimming pool as well as a combined indoor track and basketball court. Varsity basketball was played here from 1917 to 1928, when the Field House was added.

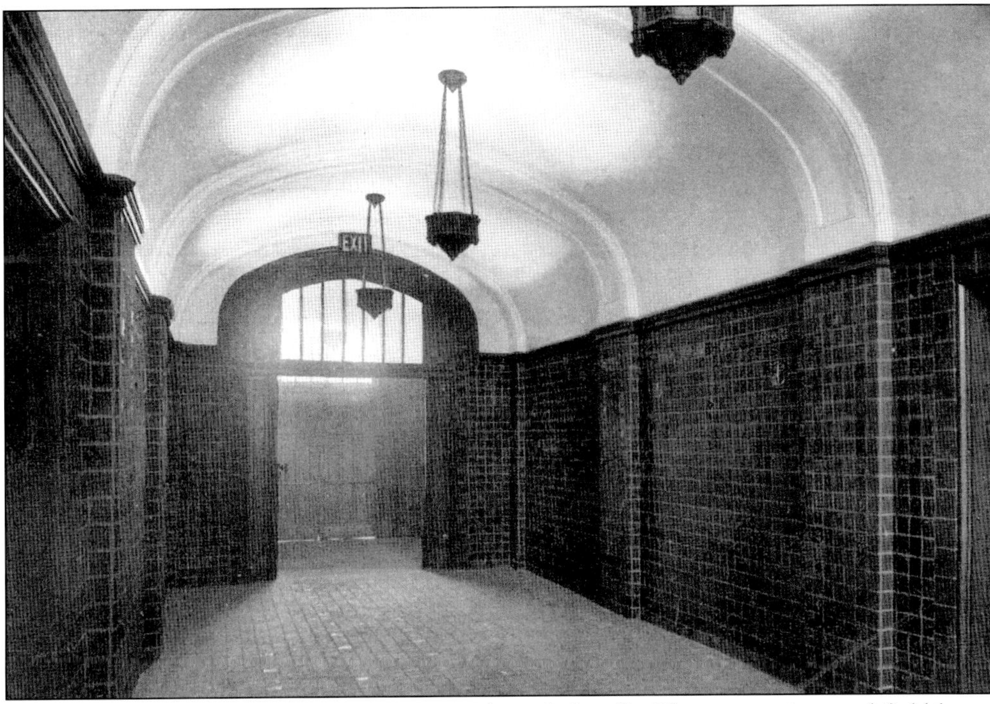

The interior of the third Men's Gymnasium has tiled walls. The gymnasium and field house became the Wildermuth Center. In 1961, a further addition on the north created the School of Health, Physical Education, and Recreation (HPER).

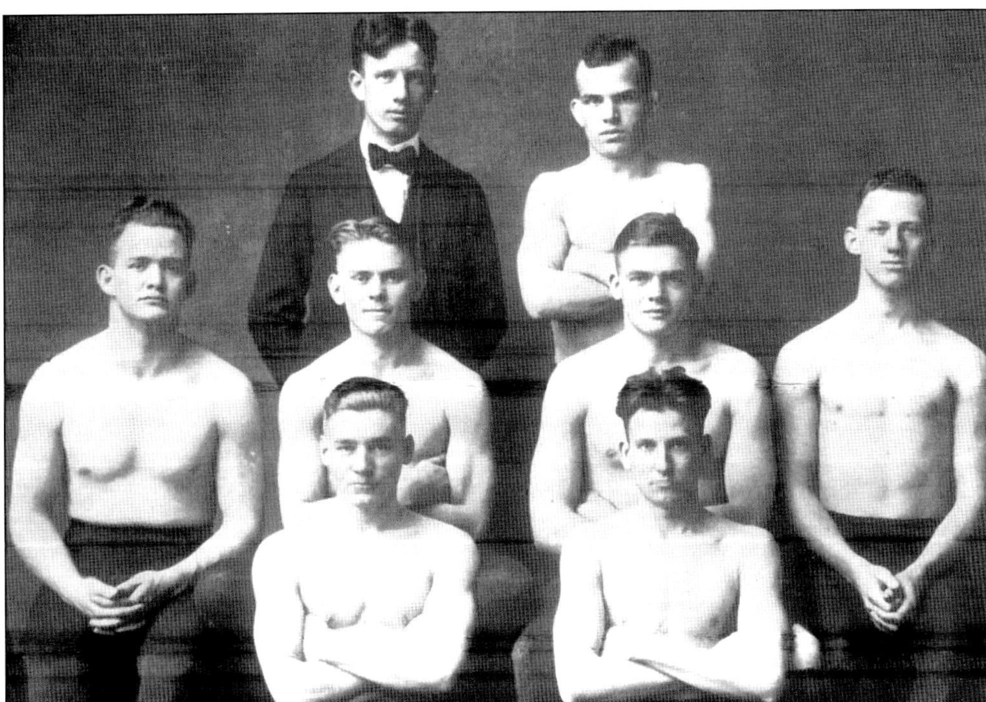

The IU men's wrestling team was captured for an appearance in the 1918 *Arbutus*.

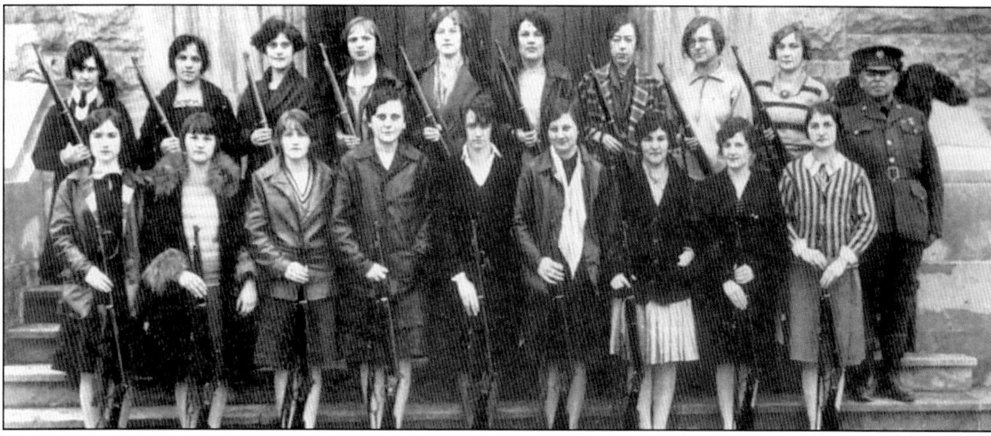

The "Coed Rifle Team," pictured here in the *Arbutus* of 1928, had its beginnings at least as early as World War I, when the women's team of "crack shots" was featured in the Bloomington newspaper.

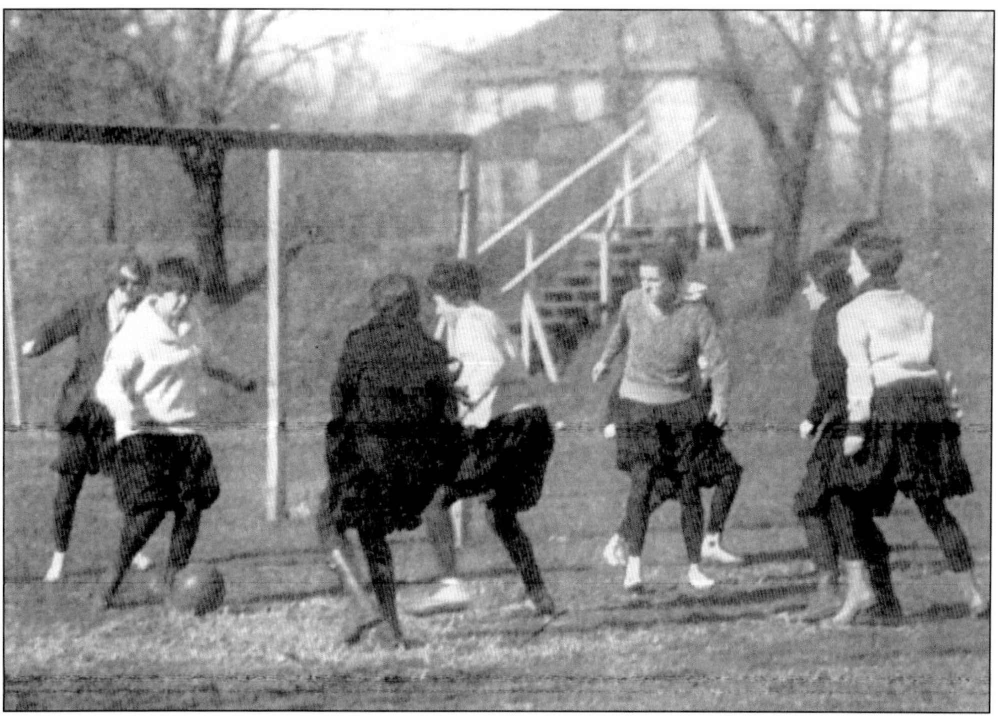

Women athletes played soccer in Dunn Meadow during the 1920s and 1930s. Action shots were featured in the 1920 *Arbutus*.

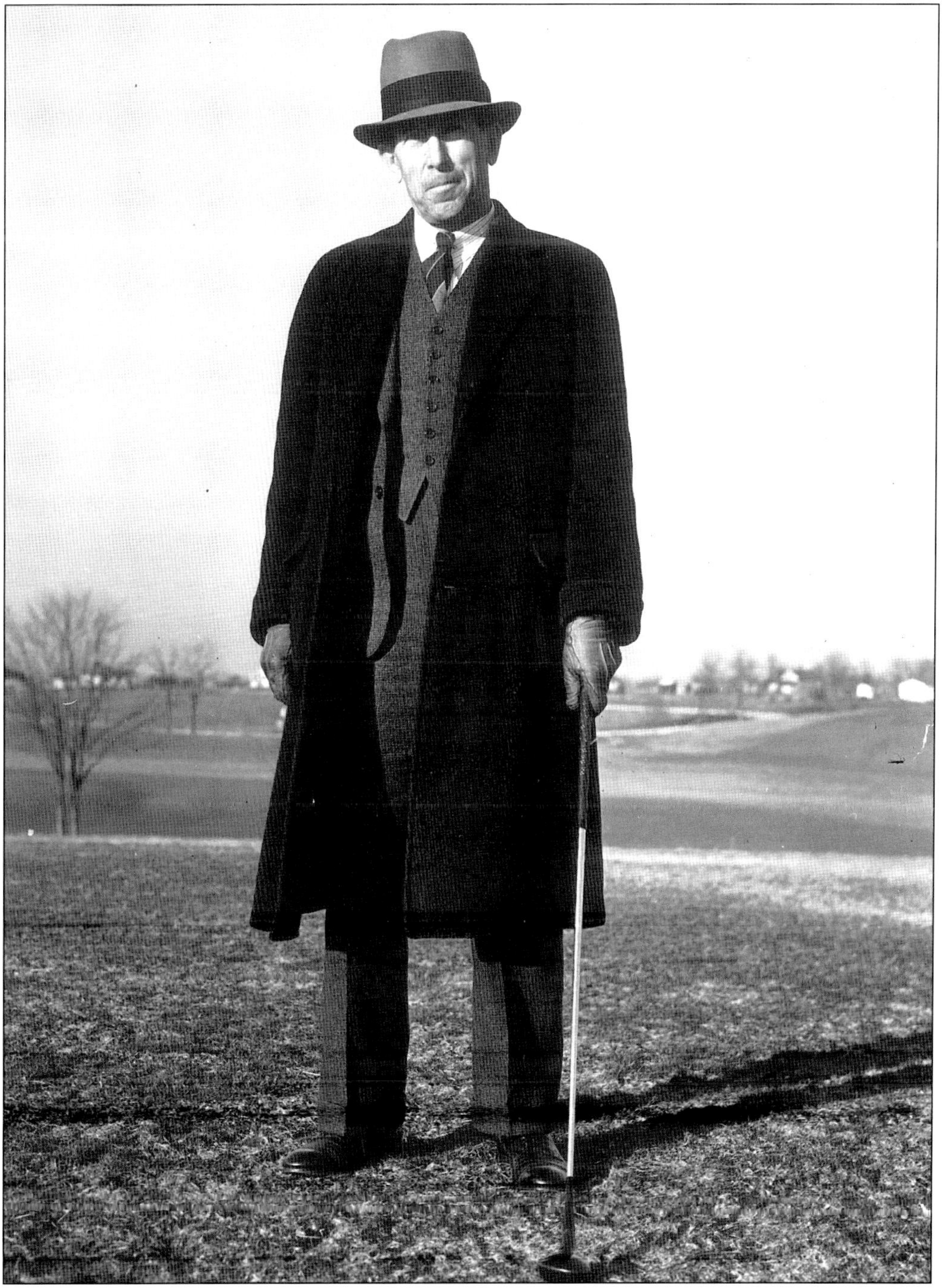

Hugh Willis, IU's first golf coach, served from 1934 to 1941. Willis was also a law professor from 1922 to 1942 and Acting Dean of the School of Law 1942–1943.

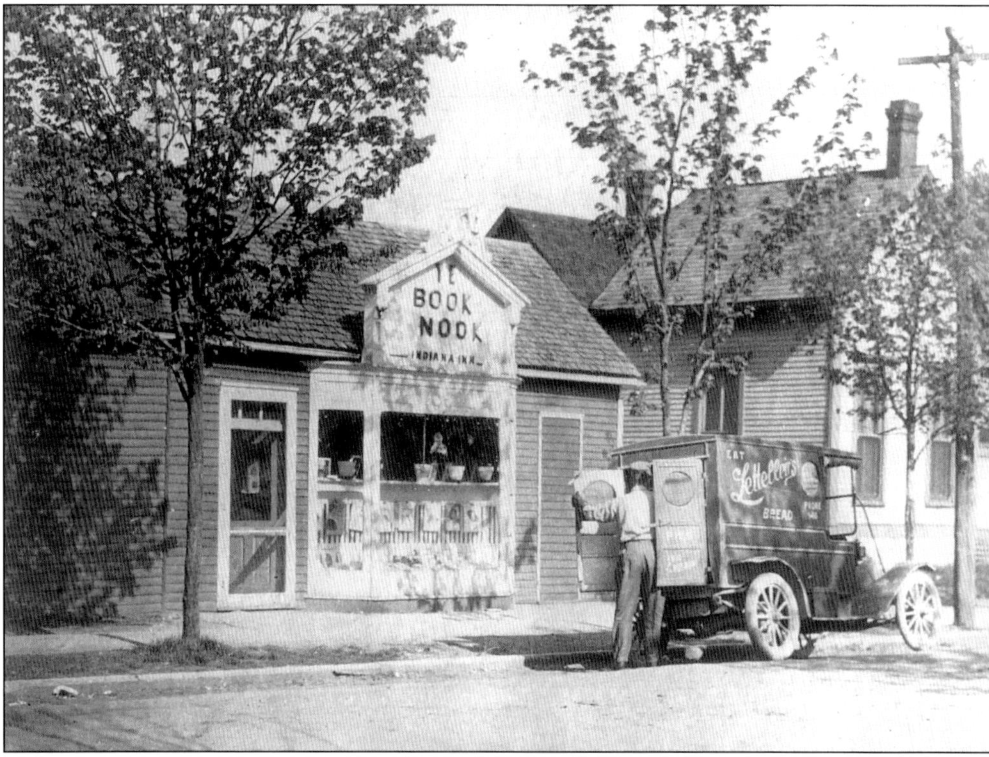

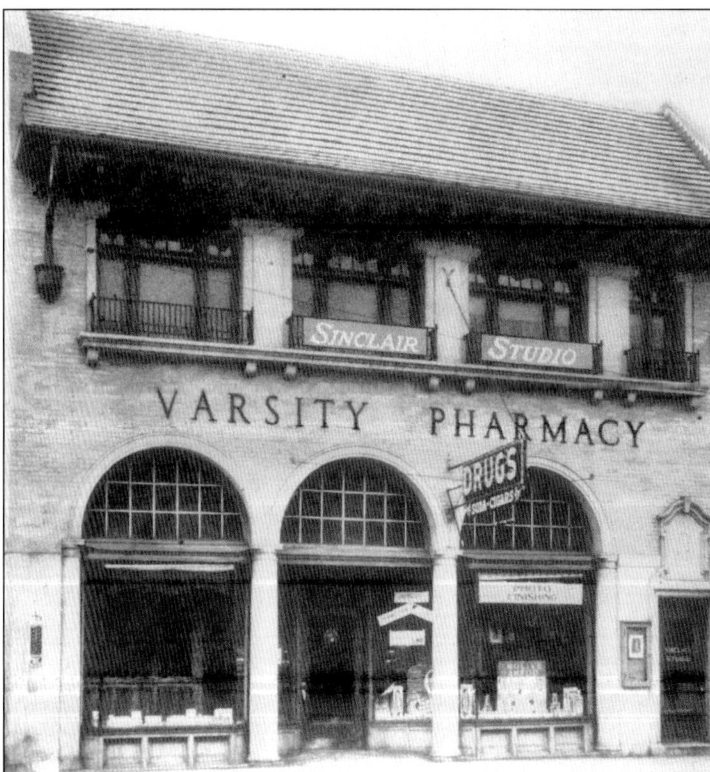

The original Book Nook, on Indiana Avenue, south of East Kirkwood, opened around 1907 to sell school supplies. The original building was torn down around 1914 for a new Book Nook (opposite page), designed by architect John Nichols.

Next door to the Book Nook, the Varsity Pharmacy (*c.* 1920) still stands, although it is no longer a pharmacy. Designs like the Varsity's fanciful Spanish Colonial and the eclectic styling of the new Book Nook (opposite) lent a touch of the exotic to neighborhood shopping streets in the 1920s.

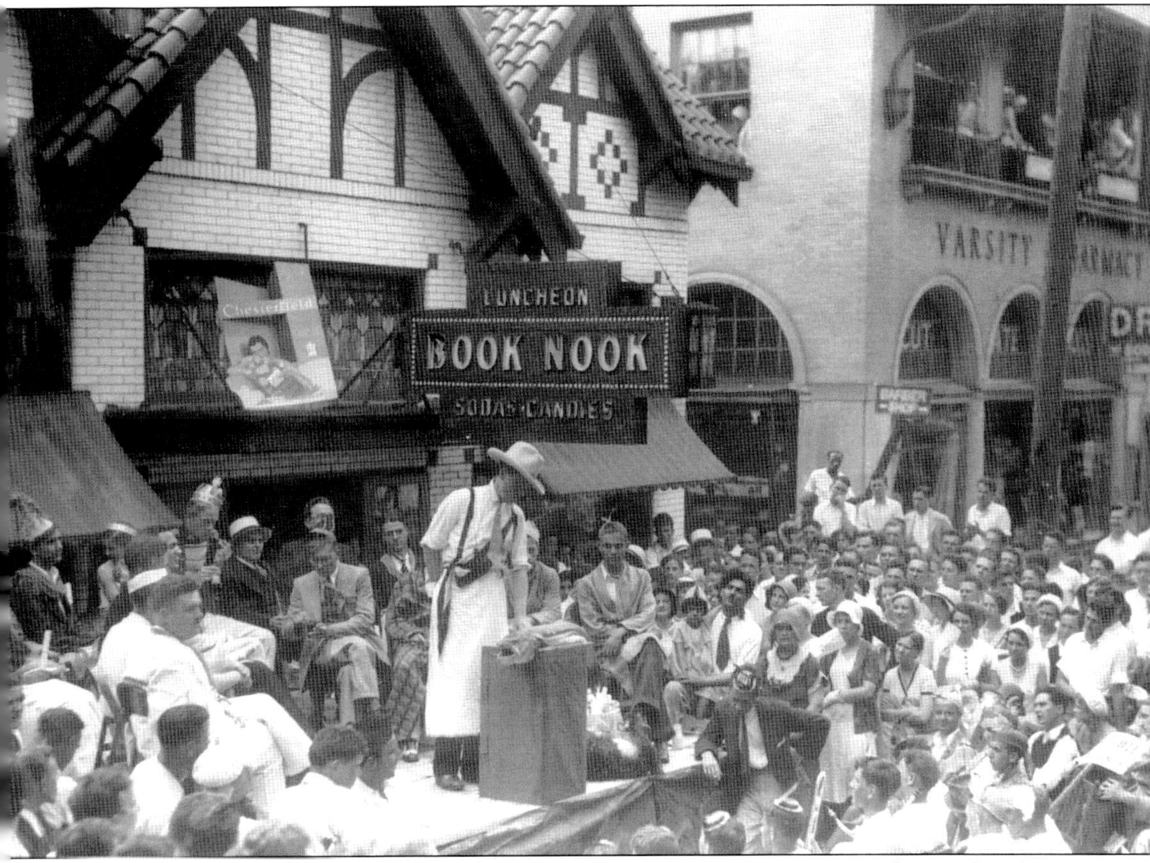

The Book Nook soon entered student life and legend. It was run by George Poolitsan, then by Poolitsan's cousins Peter, George, and Harry Costas of Chicago. In four years between 1927 and 1931, Pete Costas sponsored the "Book Nook Commencement," a mock graduation ceremony in costume. Herman B Wells, later President (1938–1962) and University Chancellor (1962–2000) of Indiana University, was a popular young economics instructor when he attended the last mock commencement in 1931. Dressed in a white suit, Wells sits on the platform at left.

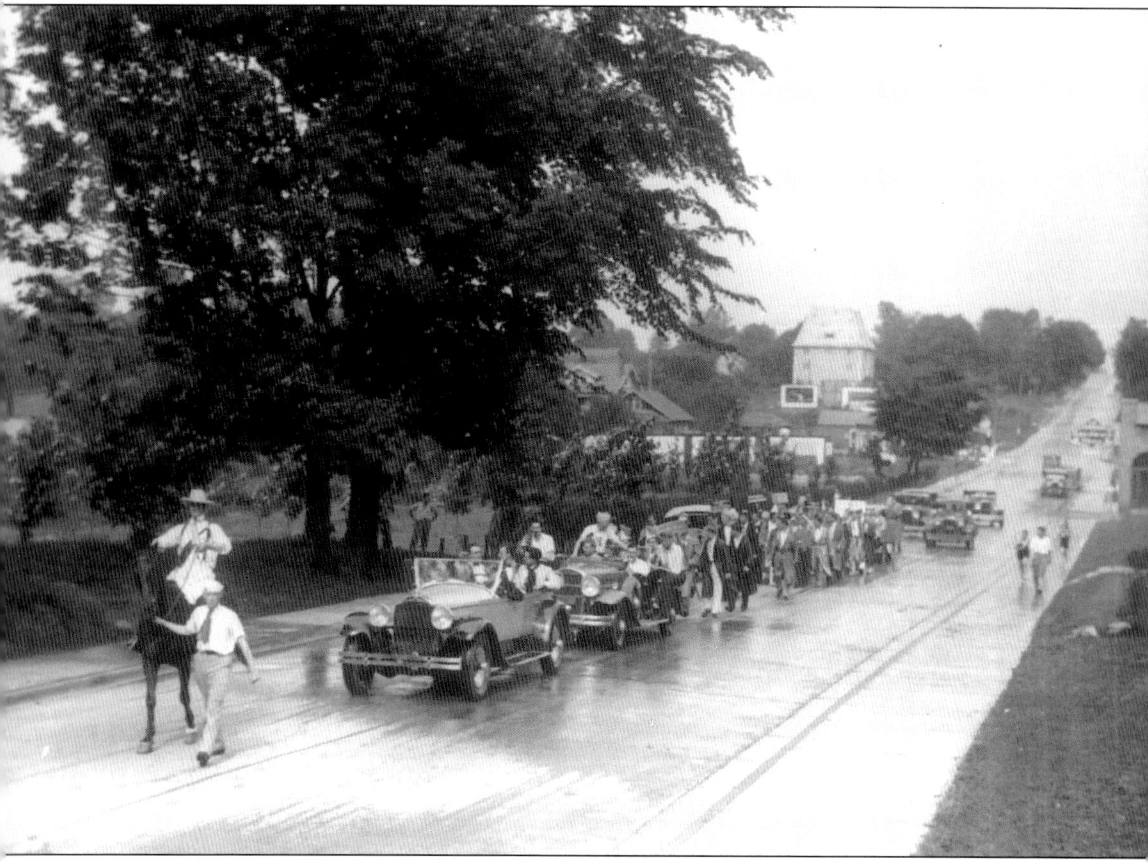

A rain shower on Third Street near the Music School did not cancel the parade that was part of the Book Nook Commencement. The Book Nook Commencements ended in 1931. The next year, Pete Costas moved the Book Nook to another building down the street at Indiana and Kirkwood. The old Book Nook, again run by the Poolitsan family, became the Gables.

John Versal Collins and Edwina Bearss were king and queen of the last Book Nook Commencement, June 2, 1931.

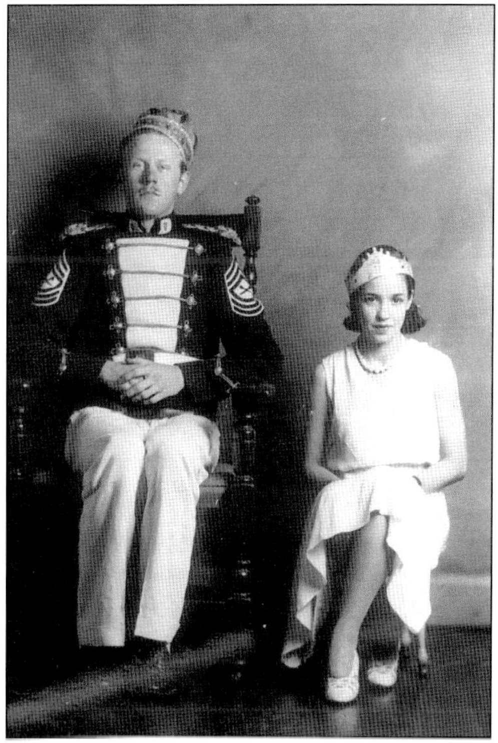

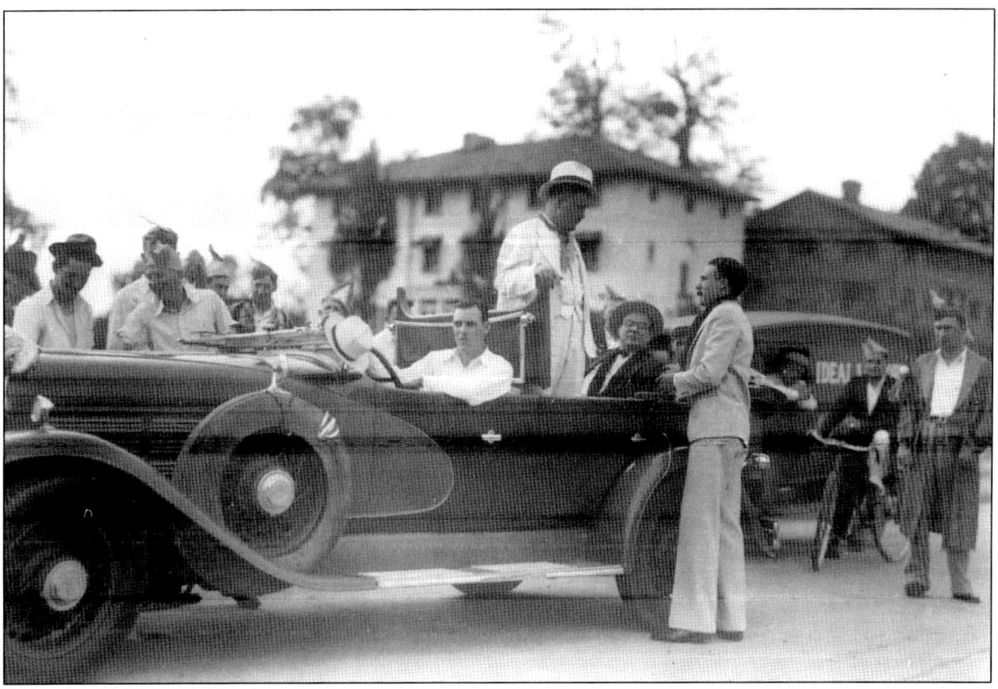

Herman B Wells, standing in the back of the convertible, chats with Pete Costas, watched by costumed parade participants and a passing truck driver. Seated beside Wells is Ward Gray Biddle, who managed the IU Book Store and the Indiana Memorial Union. Biddle held several high university offices.

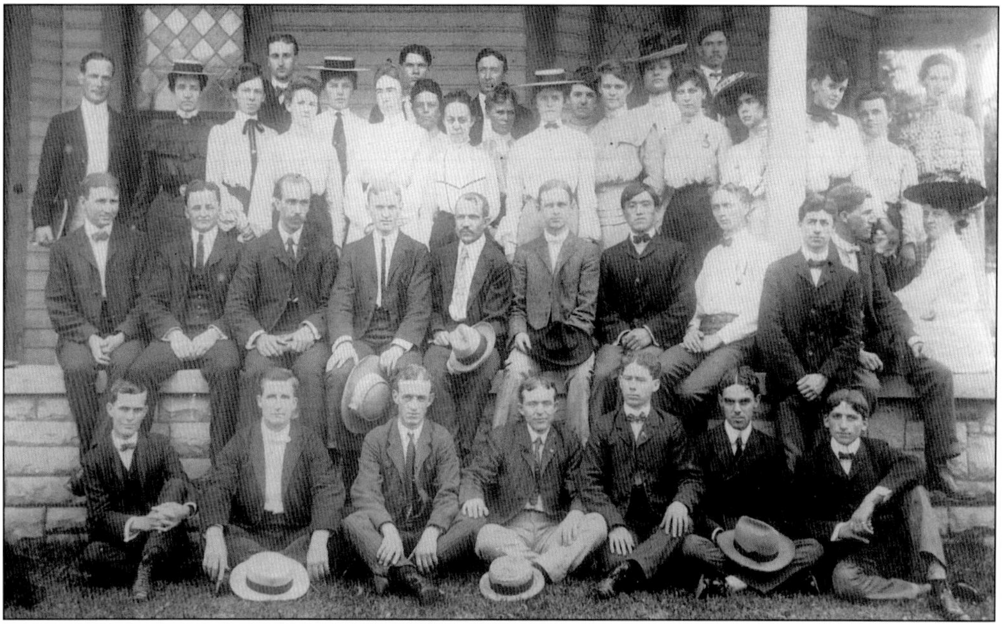

From as early as 1838 until the early 1900s, some students ate at "boarding clubs," or eating clubs, in private homes near campus. Their rooming house was often at a different location. Students, who paid a fixed fee for meals, organized a few of these clubs themselves. One club is said to have had a vegetarian menu. This large group and its location are unidentified.

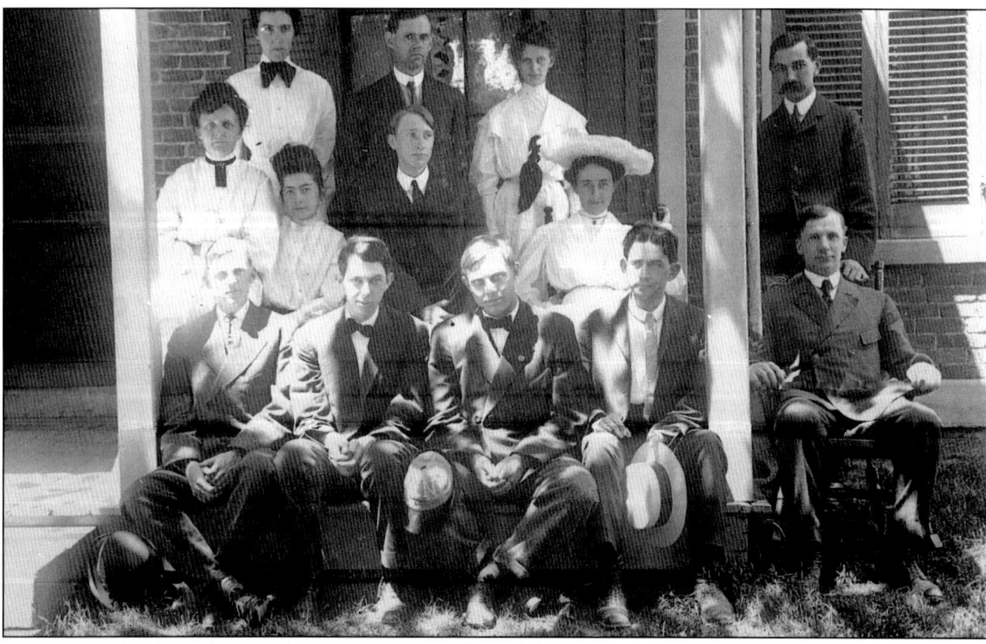

Students who boarded with Miss Nina Hall and her sisters at 414 West Kirkwood Avenue pose in 1905. Standing, back row, are Flora C. Broaddus, John E. Darby, Leona L. Turner, Prof. Charles Zeleny. Middle row: Miss Drysdale, Etelka J. Roukenbach, Horace Lawrence Durbanow, Ivy L. Chamness. Front row: Charles A. Albers, Raymond Wile, Will Aydelotte, Arthur M. Banta, Frank W. Thomas.

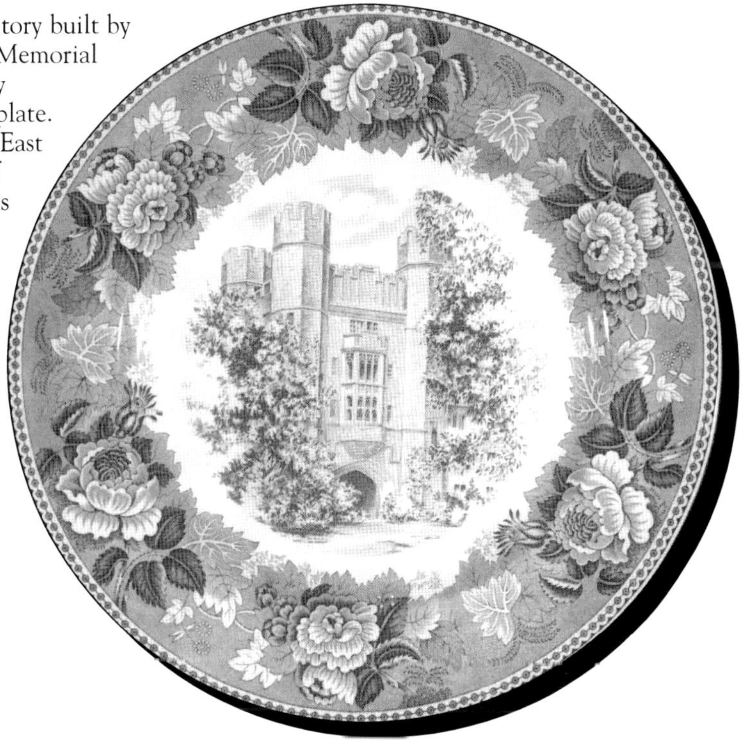

The first women's dormitory built by Indiana University was Memorial Hall (1925), a dormitory commemorated on this plate. Memorial Hall, at 1021 East Third Street, was one of four women's dormitories in the Agnes E. Wells Quadrangle, completed in 1940. Buildings in the quadrangle now serve as IU offices and classrooms.

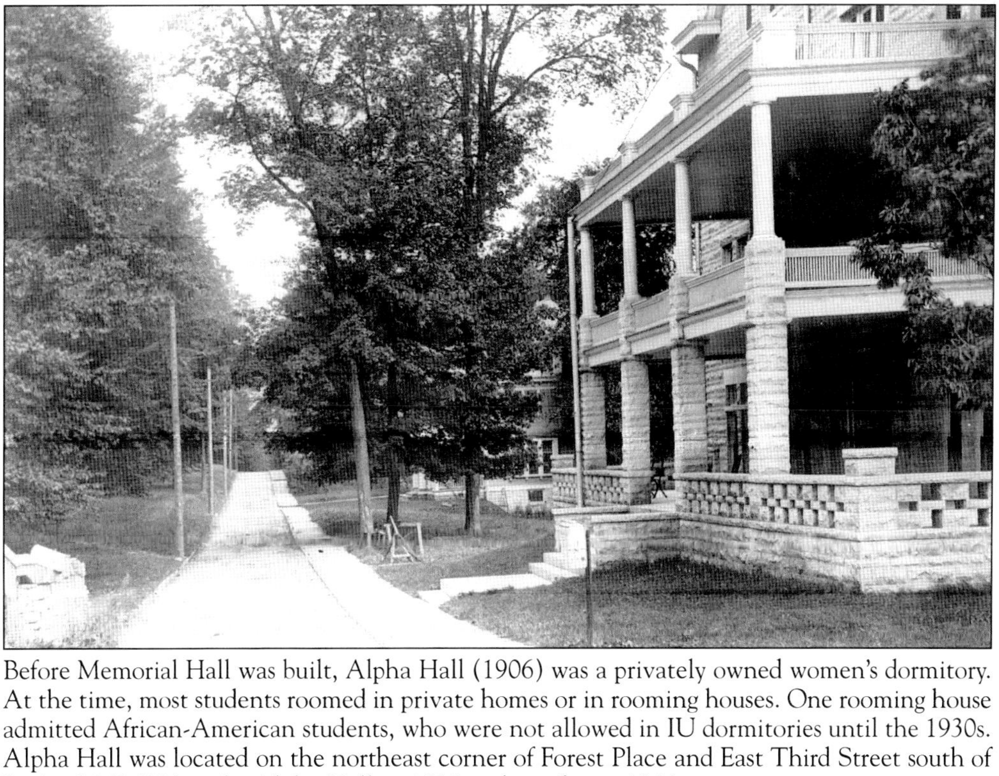

Before Memorial Hall was built, Alpha Hall (1906) was a privately owned women's dormitory. At the time, most students roomed in private homes or in rooming houses. One rooming house admitted African-American students, who were not allowed in IU dormitories until the 1930s. Alpha Hall was located on the northeast corner of Forest Place and East Third Street south of Jordan Hall. IU bought Alpha Hall in 1936 and razed it in 1961.

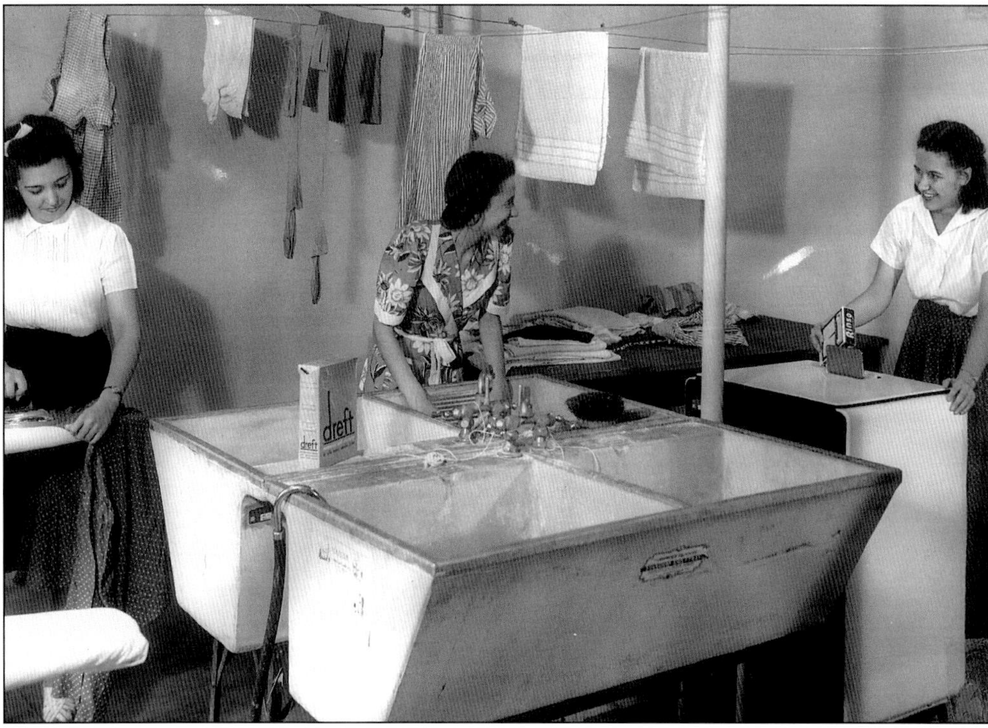

For a residence hall bulletin published in 1941, these student residents in Sycamore Hall demonstrated use of the laundry room, while others (below) moved along the cafeteria line at Morrison (then Beech) Hall. With Memorial and Goodbody halls, these two dormitories (1940) completed the Agnes E. Wells Quadrangle.

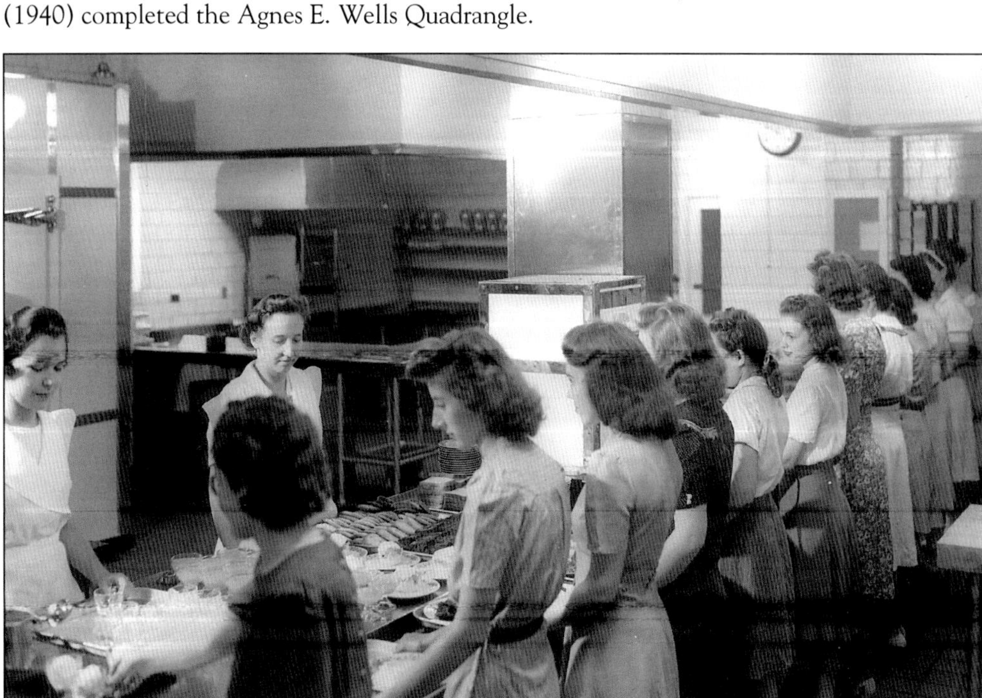

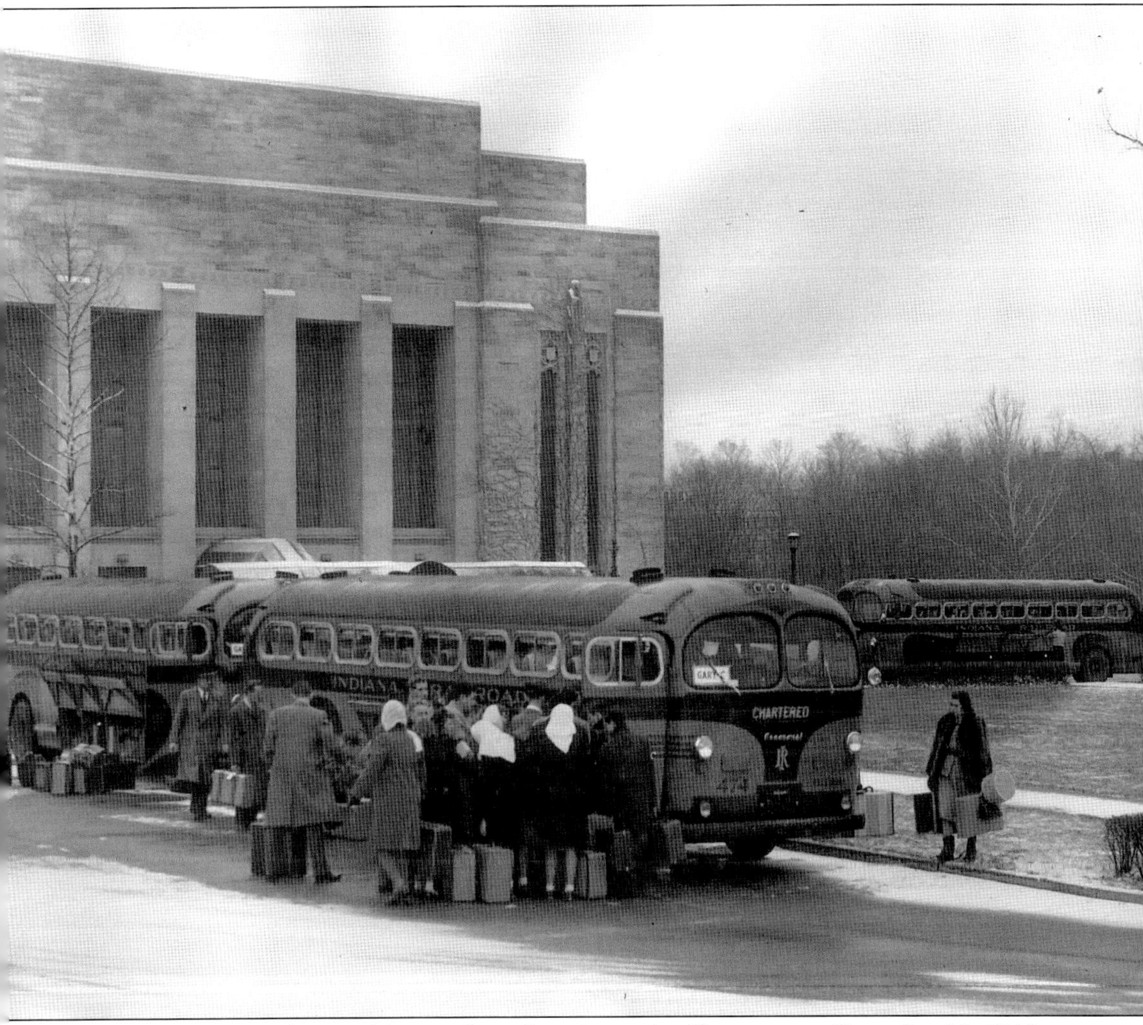

Students lined up for chartered buses taking them home for Christmas on December 20, 1946. The buses were parked in front of the recently completed IU Auditorium (1941), an Art Moderne building with a distinguished interior including murals by Thomas Hart Benton. Showalter Fountain would not take its place in front of the auditorium until 1961.

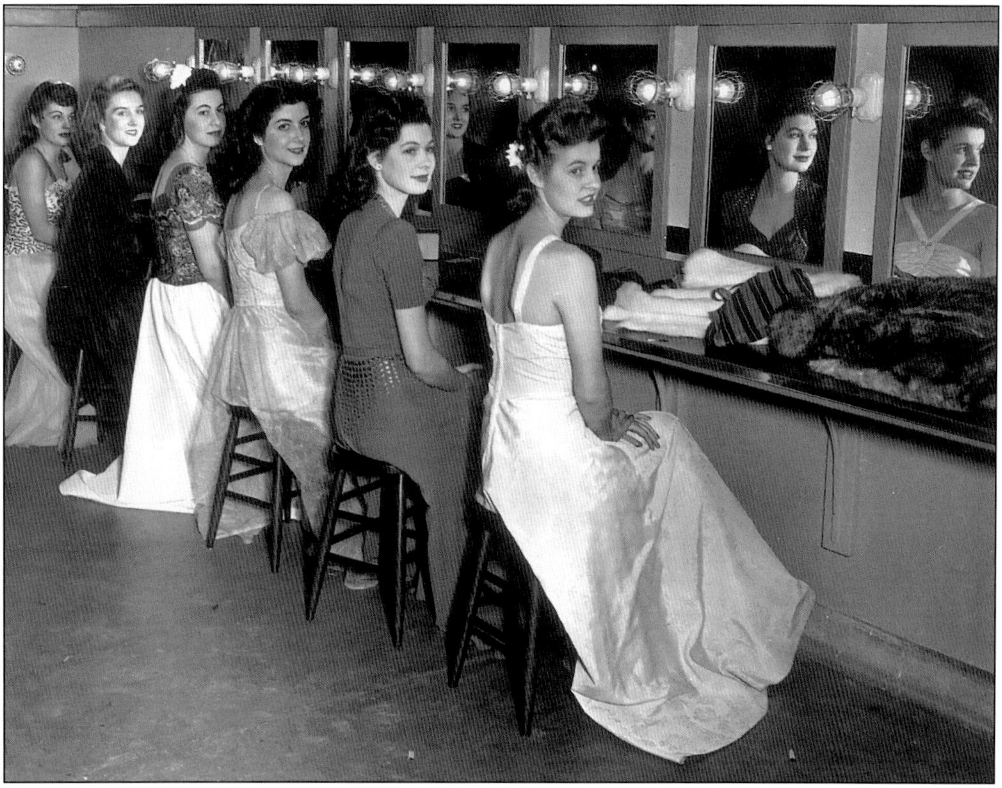

Contestants posed during a campus beauty contest on January 9, 1942, shortly after the United States entered World War II.

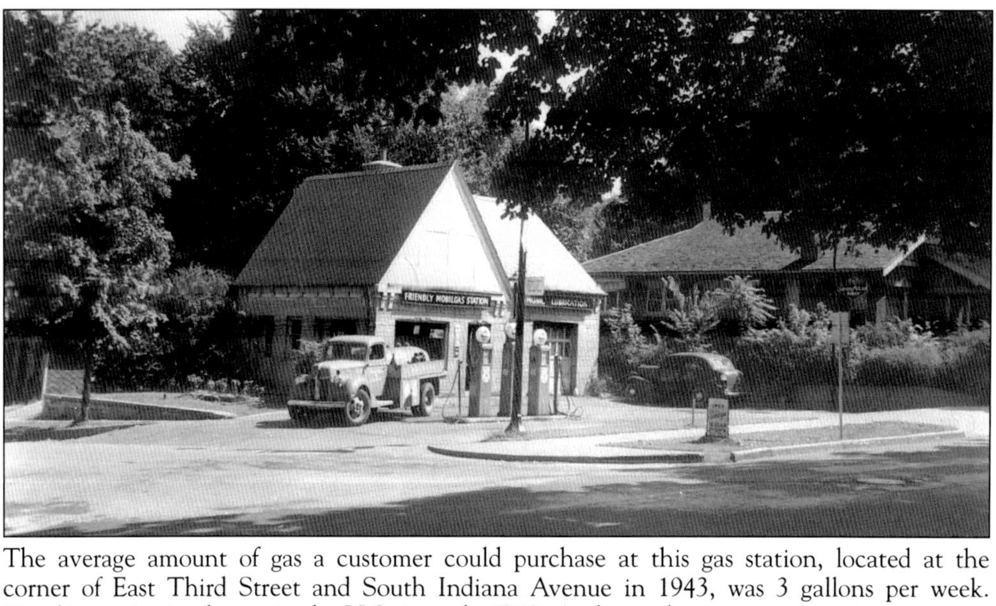

The average amount of gas a customer could purchase at this gas station, located at the corner of East Third Street and South Indiana Avenue in 1943, was 3 gallons per week. Gasoline rationing began in the U.S. in early 1942. At first voluntary, gas rationing was soon made mandatory. By December 1942, each of the 48 states had passed a rationing law. After January 1, 1942, no new automobiles were produced until July 1, 1945.

Dorothy Ullrich of Des Moines, Iowa, was one of many American women who enrolled at the Naval Women's Reserve School, a training school for naval storekeepers held for 16 weeks *c.* 1944 on the IU campus. Ullrich shakes hands with Commander H.G. Mosler.

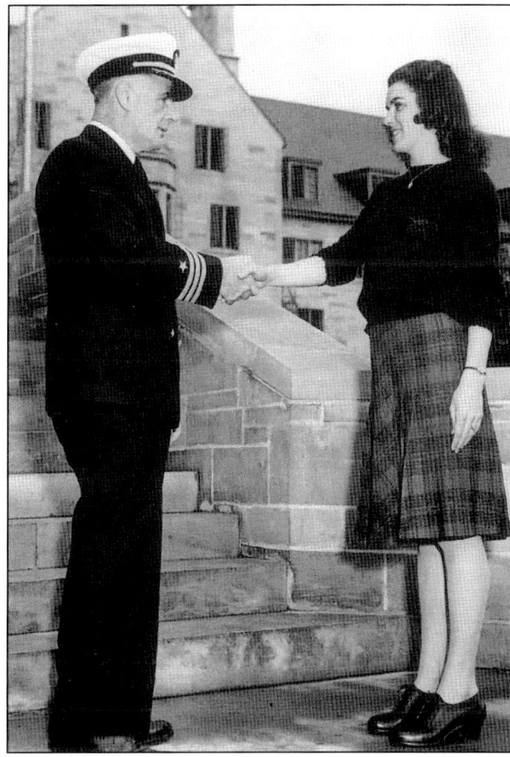

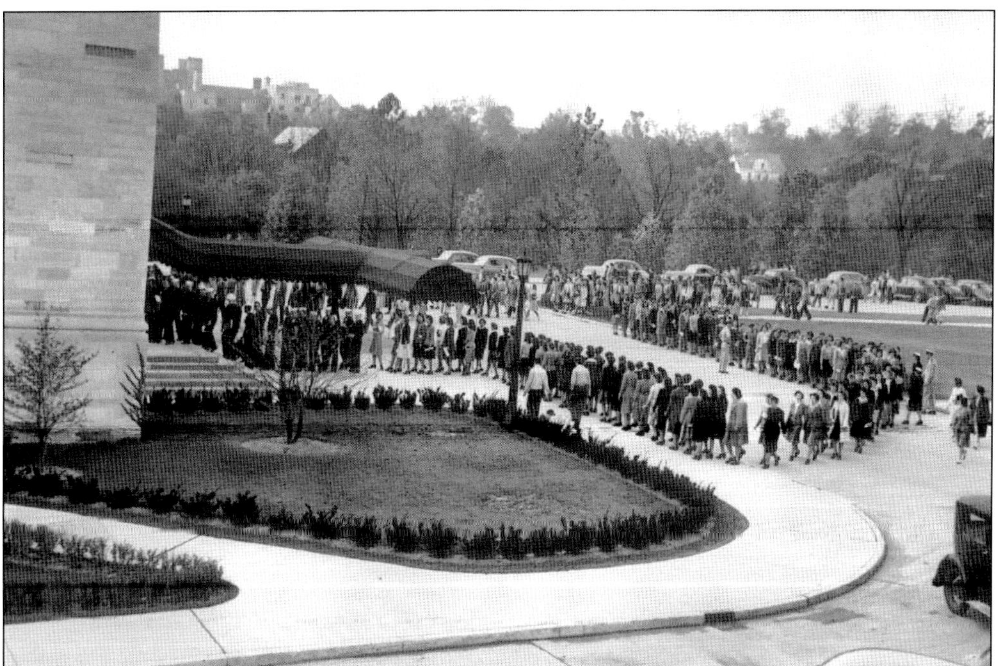

While on campus around 1944, sailors and WAVES (Women Accepted for Volunteer Emergency Service) lined up to be entertained at IU Auditorium by humorist and poet Franklin P. Adams.

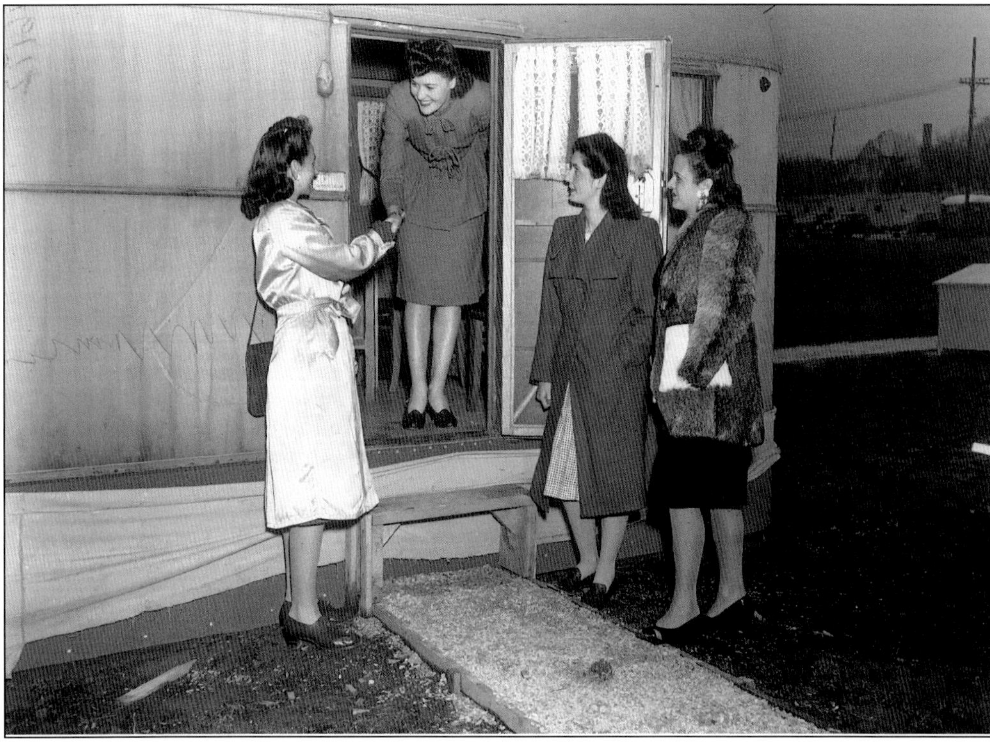

When World War II veterans attended IU, some of them brought brides from other countries. New wives got acquainted at the door of a house trailer in 1946. A sea of trailers formed the Woodlawn Trailer Court (below).

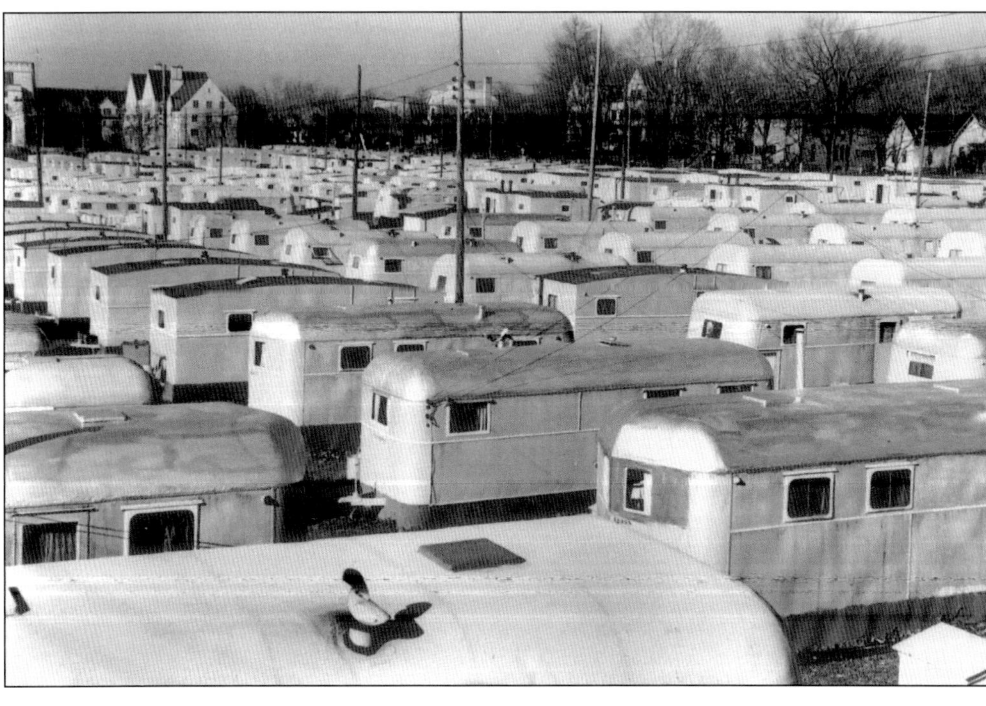

Six

Modern Times at IU

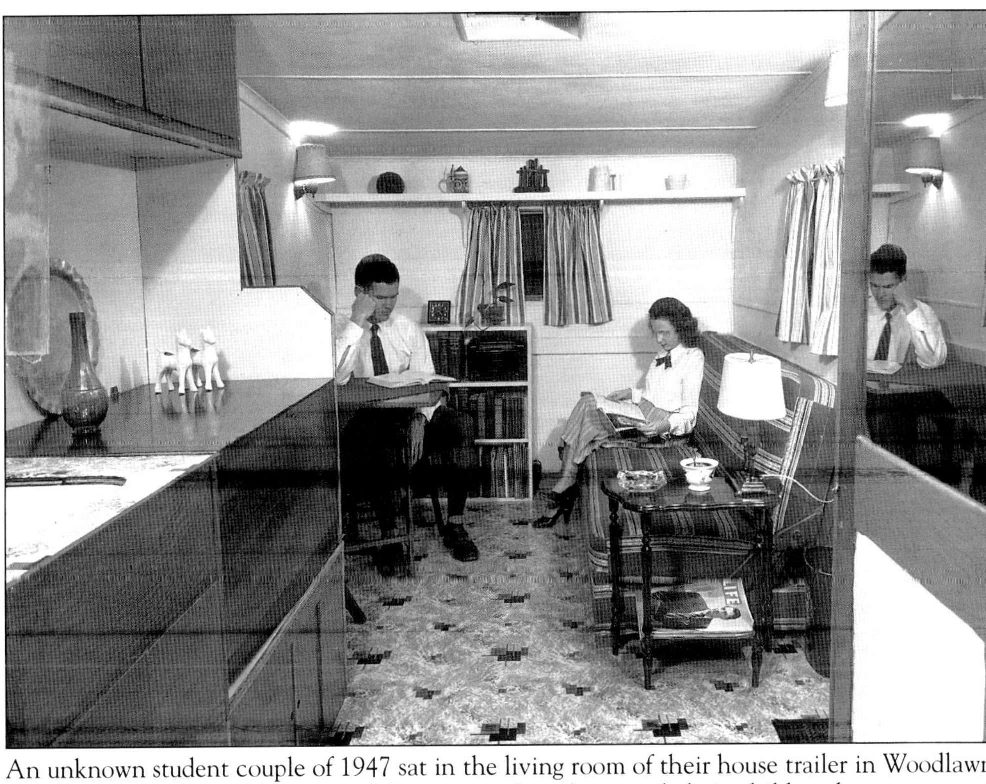

An unknown student couple of 1947 sat in the living room of their house trailer in Woodlawn Trailer Court on the IU campus. Many married students and their children became part of campus life after World War II.

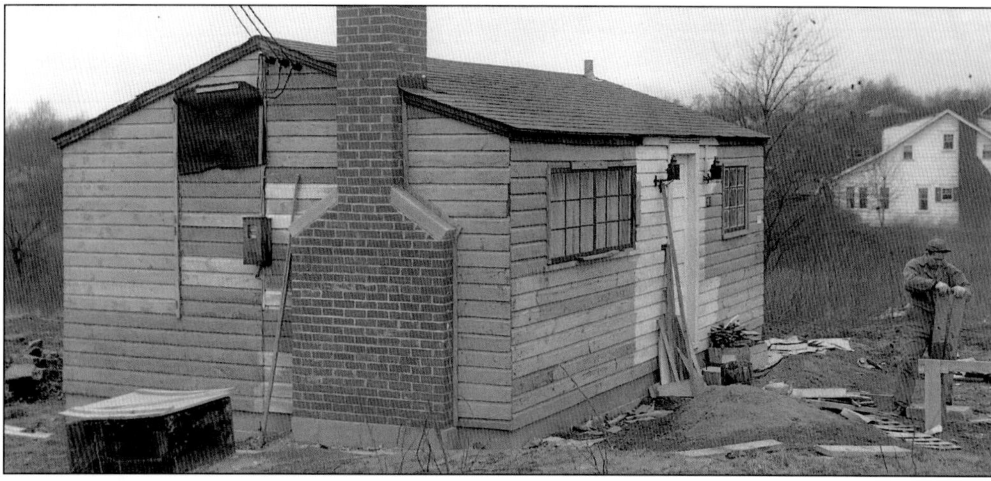

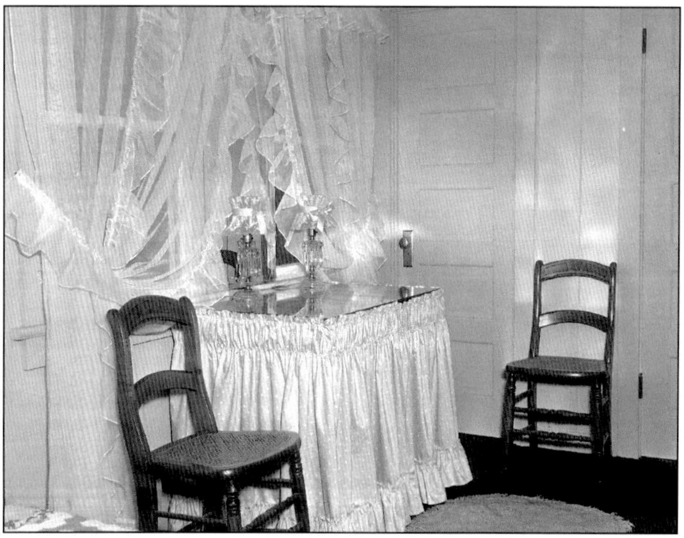

Many solutions were tried to meet the housing shortage that followed World War II. One unidentified veteran (above) posed for an IU publicity shot while completing a home made from two brooder houses, or chicken coops. The interior of the house (left) is shown after it was decorated.

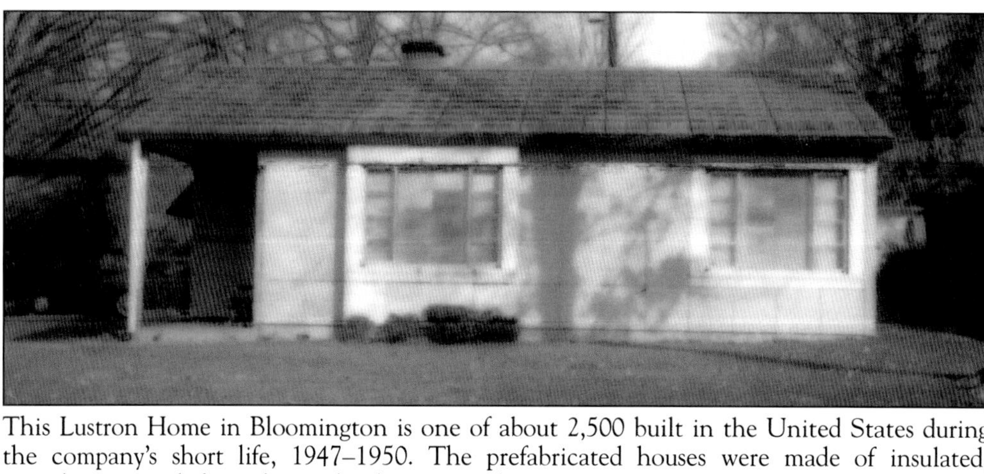

This Lustron Home in Bloomington is one of about 2,500 built in the United States during the company's short life, 1947–1950. The prefabricated houses were made of insulated, porcelain-enameled steel panels that created an interior-exterior wall surface. Built-ins included a "combination dishwasher-clotheswasher-sink."

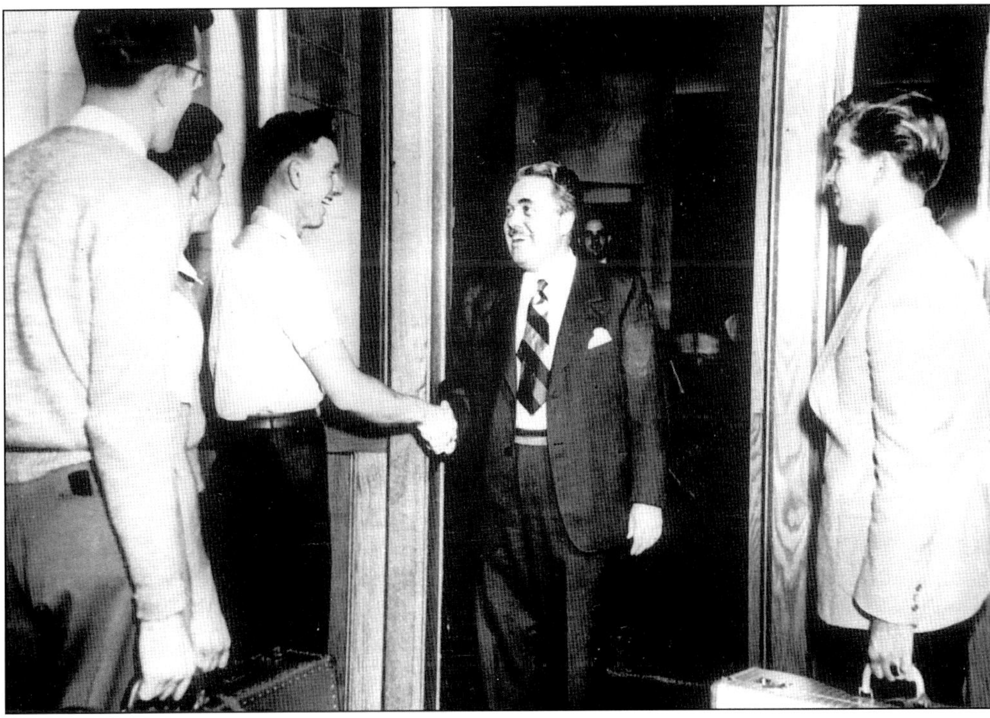

Herman B Wells, president of Indiana University, greeted returning veterans of World War II enrolling at IU. In 1948, Wells took a six-month leave of absence in order to serve as Director of Higher Education in occupied Germany.

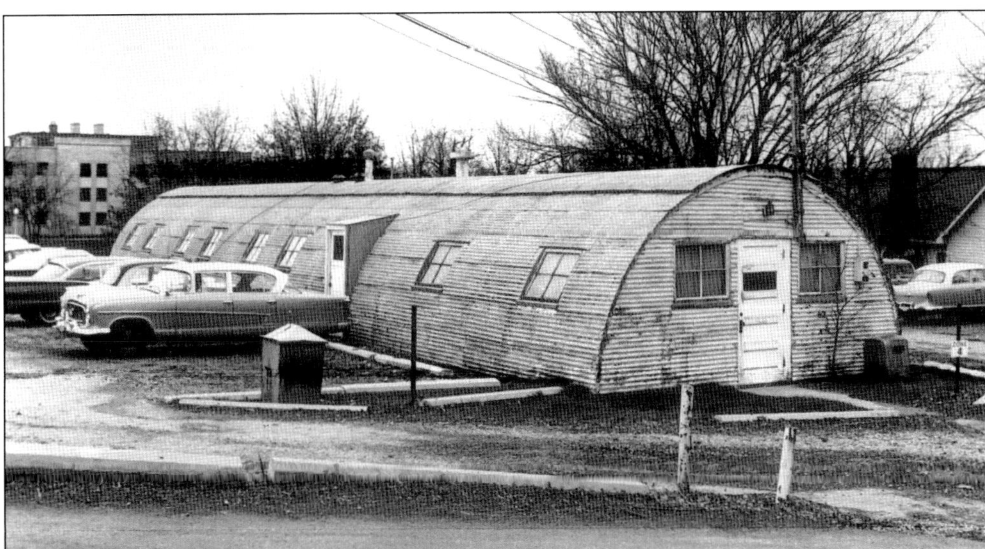

The Quonset hut, named for the town in Rhode Island where it was manufactured, was created by the U.S. Navy in 1941 as all-purpose shelter. The hut was made of steel ribs covered with corrugated metal and had a plywood floor. Surplus Quonset huts remained on IU's landscape and all over the U.S. for many years as classrooms, offices, homes, churches, and business premises.

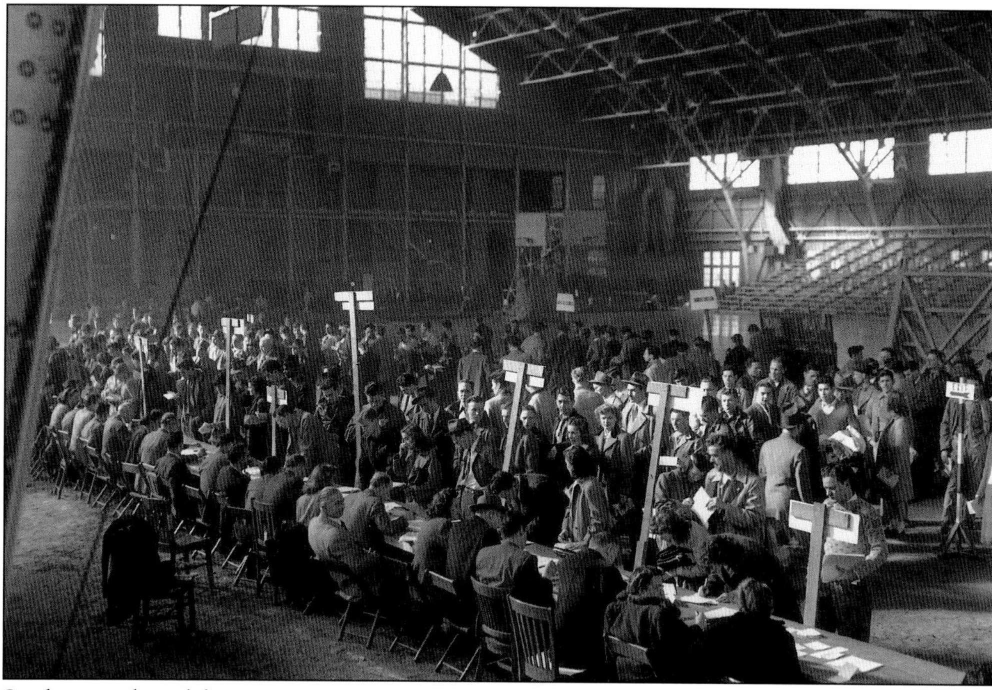

Students gathered for registration in Wildermuth Field House on February 8, 1946. The floor was still unpaved, and those who waited to register long remembered the dust and heat of the field house interior. The student body went from 4,498 in 1945-1946 to 10,345 in 1946-1947, the year after World War II ended.

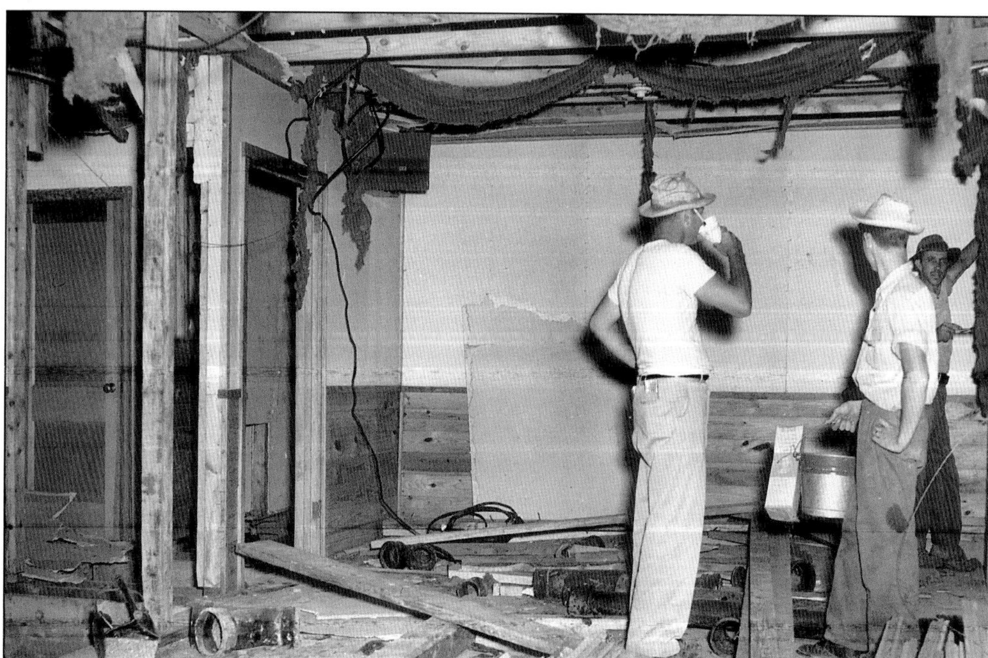

Workers demolished existing buildings in order to construct new dormitories near East Tenth and Union Streets in 1946. The dormitories became part of the John W. Ashton Center in 1980.

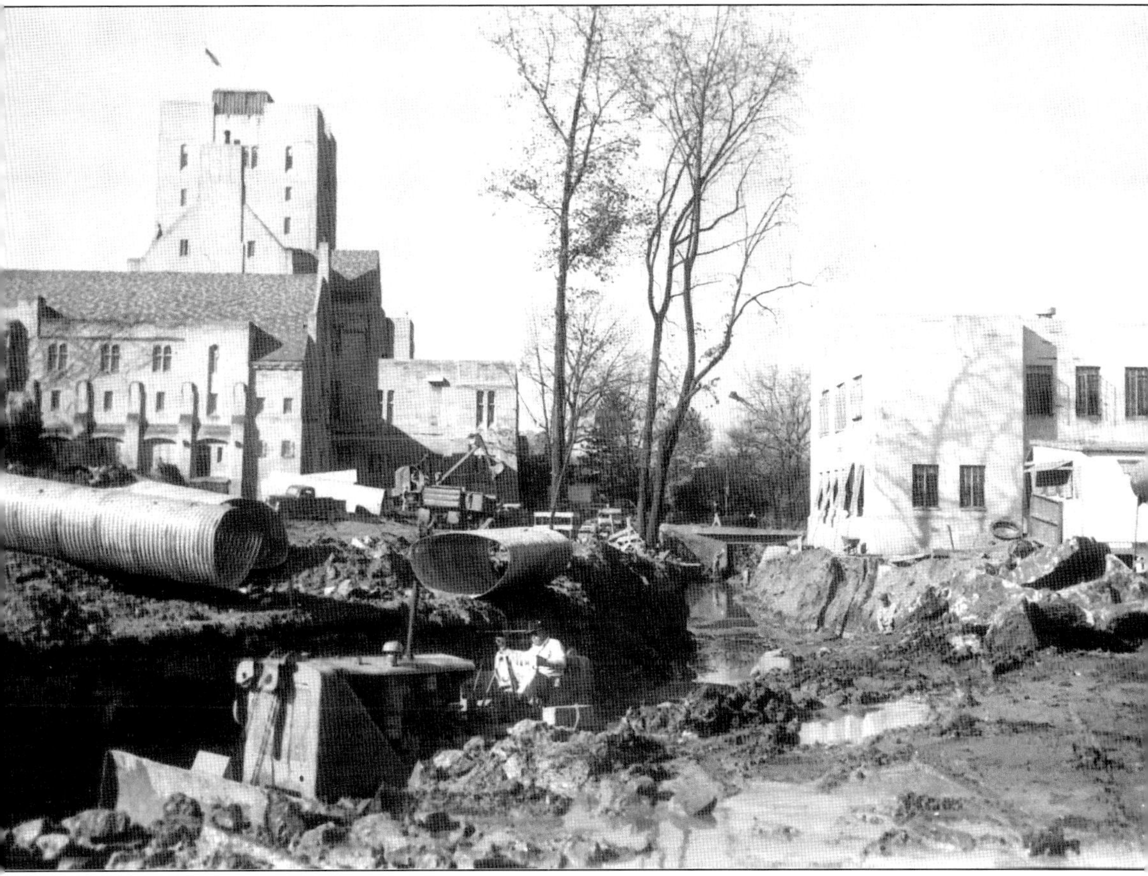

The Jordan River was rerouted in 1956 to allow for construction of the Indiana Memorial Union parking lot south of East Seventh Street. The Indiana Memorial Union is at left of photo and Ernie Pyle Hall (constructed 1938 as the Stores and Services Building) at right.

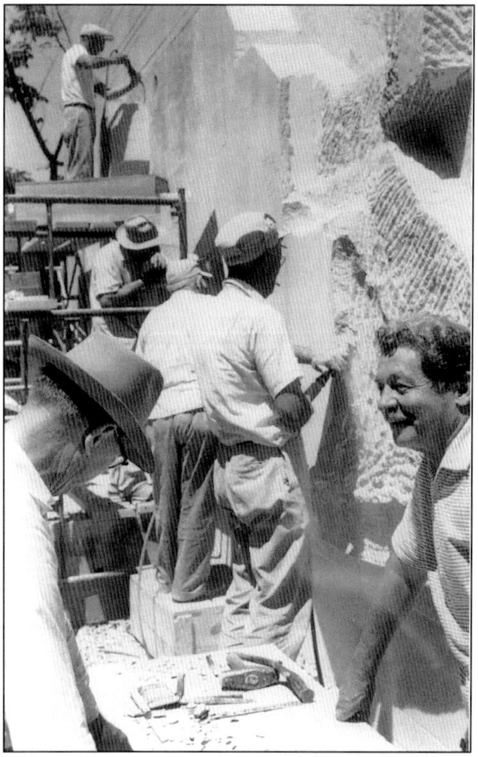

Sculptor Robert Laurent (right) directed limestone carvers using hand and pneumatic tools to create his wall sculpture on the façade of the new Ballantine Hall in 1958-1959. Laurent (1890–1970), born in France, was an IU professor of art from 1942 to 1960. Other works include the Showalter Fountain (completed 1961) in front of IU Auditorium, and a bust of Herman B Wells (1965) for the School of Education.

Ballantine Hall (1959) replaced several rather grand turn-of-century houses on Forest Place that had become university facilities. This section of Forest Place (now Avenue) became a pedestrian path. The 1950s also saw construction of nearby Beck Chapel (not pictured) and Jordan Hall, at right of photo.

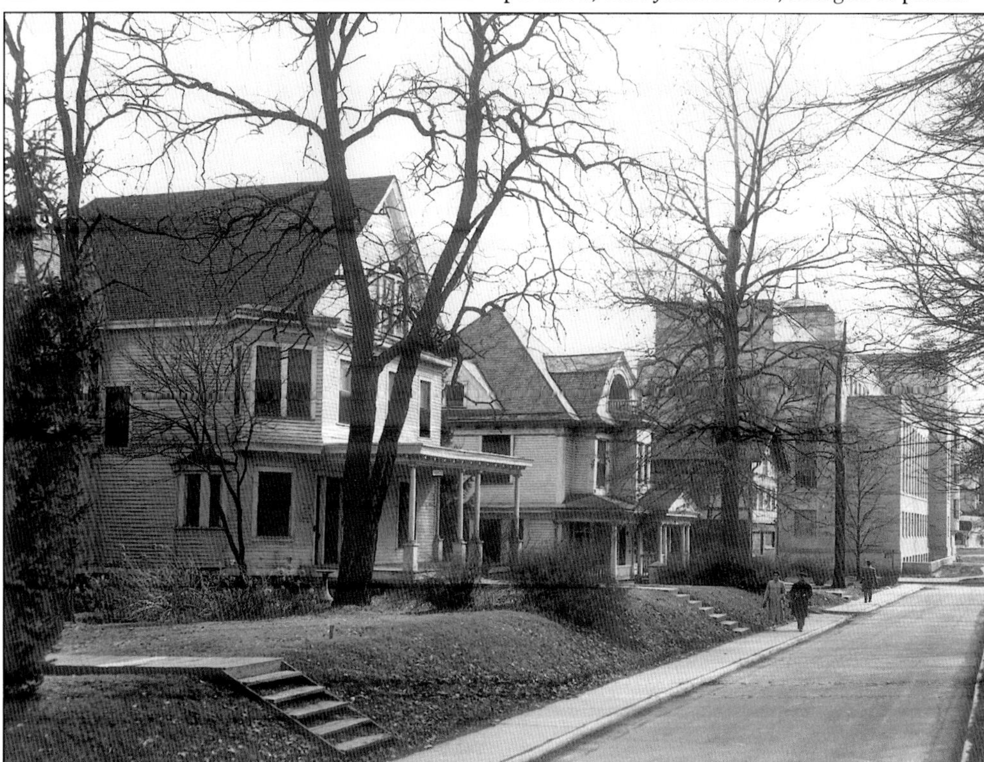

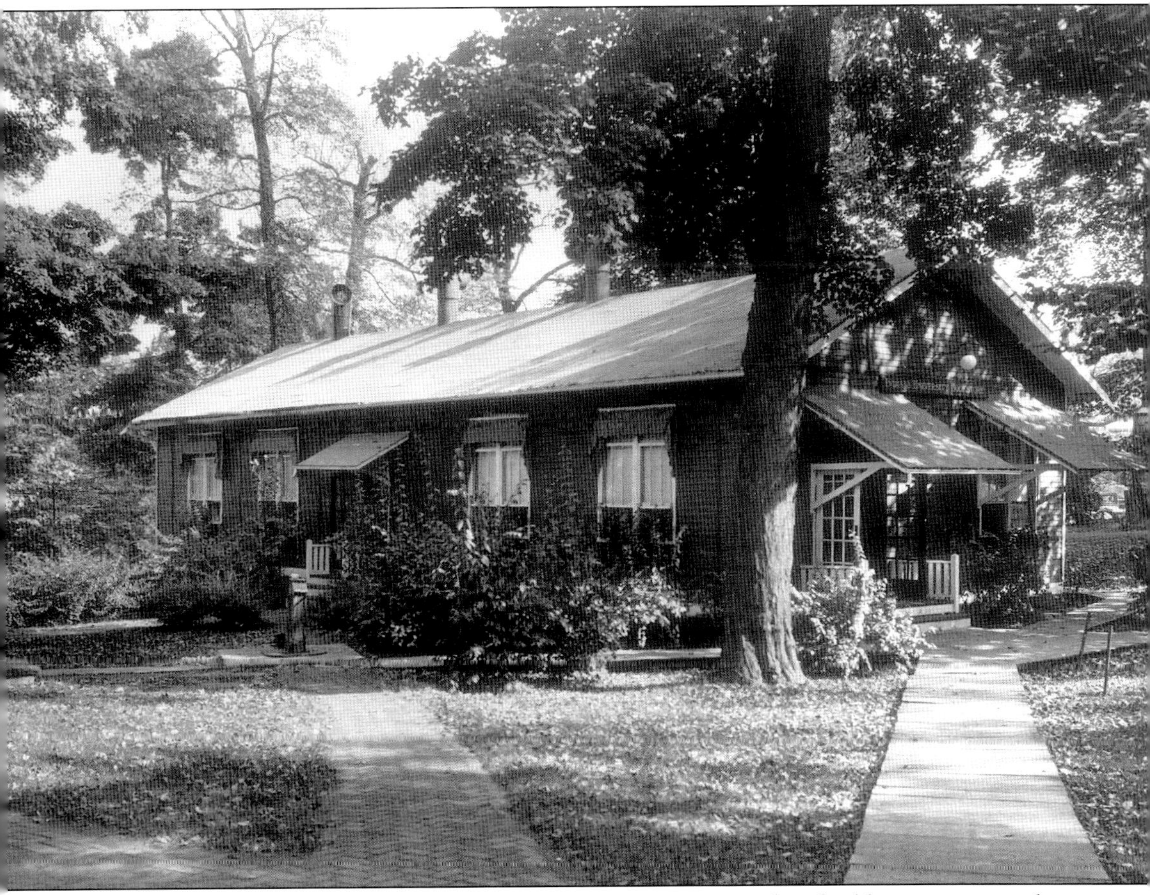

The Indiana University Bookstore (1925) was a one-story wooden building constructed between Owen Hall and Maxwell Hall. The bookstore operation was placed in the Indiana Memorial Union in 1932 and the old building was eventually moved. It was used as a ballet and band practice hall and ROTC rifle range.

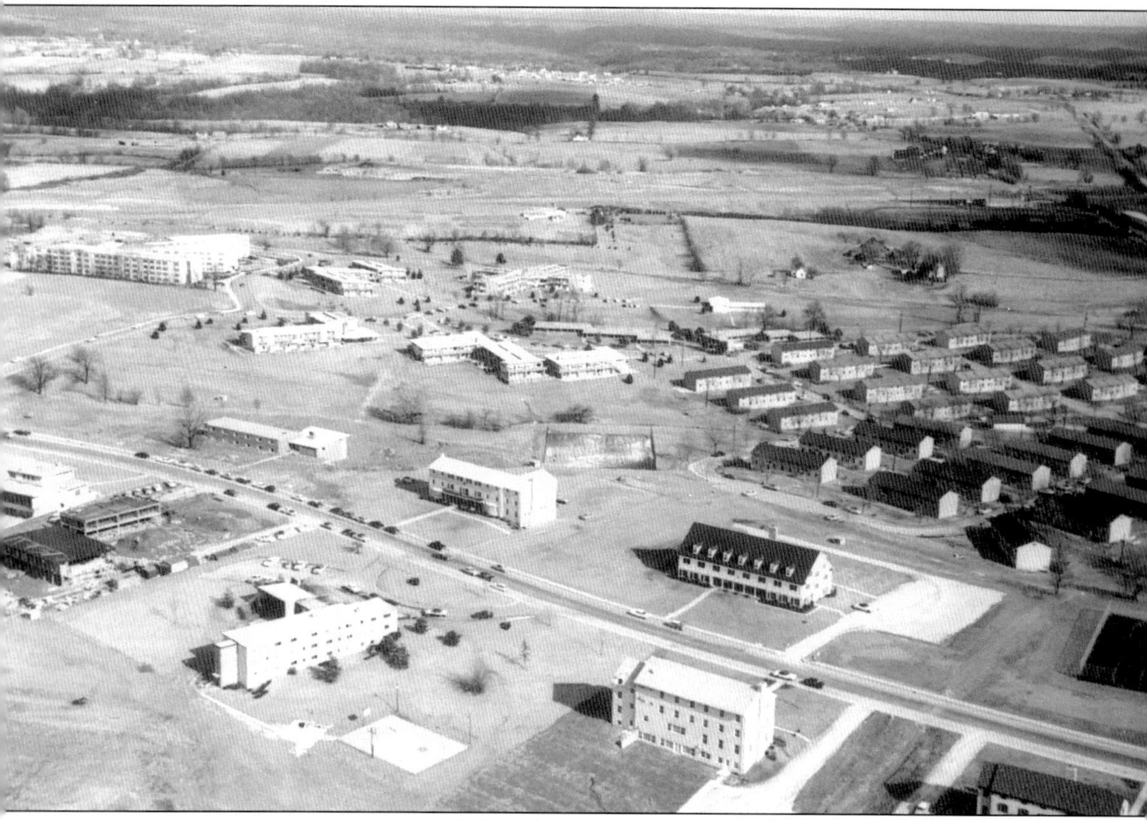

New university development including fraternity and sorority houses on North Jordan Avenue from East Law Lane to East Seventeenth Street during the 1950s and 1960s. On the far side of North Jordan (left to right) are Delta Chi, Zeta Tau Alpha, and Alpha Chi Omega north of the tennis courts. On the near side are the Evans Scholars House (dark building), Sigma Nu, Kappa Delta, and Sigma Phi Epsilon. Married students' housing included the Evermann Apartments (1957), at upper left of photo, and Hoosier Courts Apartments (later renamed) at center. The rows of barracks-like dormitories at right gave way in 1962 to the high-rise Campus View Apartments.

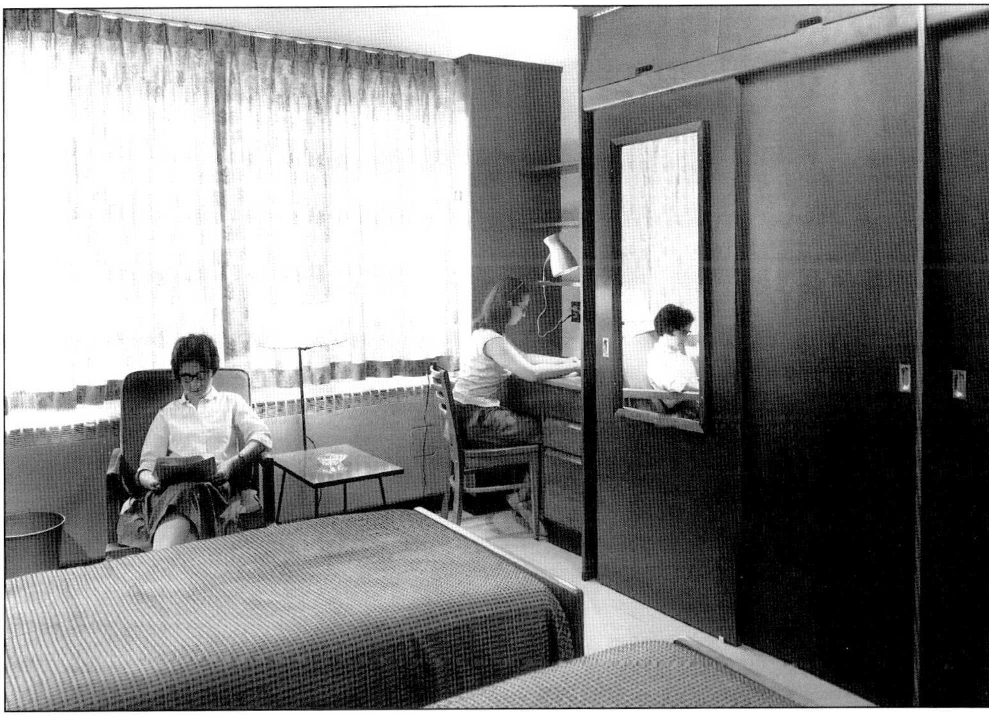

The Wendell L. Wilkie Quadrangle (1965), between East Third and East Seventh Streets, was part of extensive dormitory and apartment construction that developed the southeast corner of the IU campus during the 1960s.

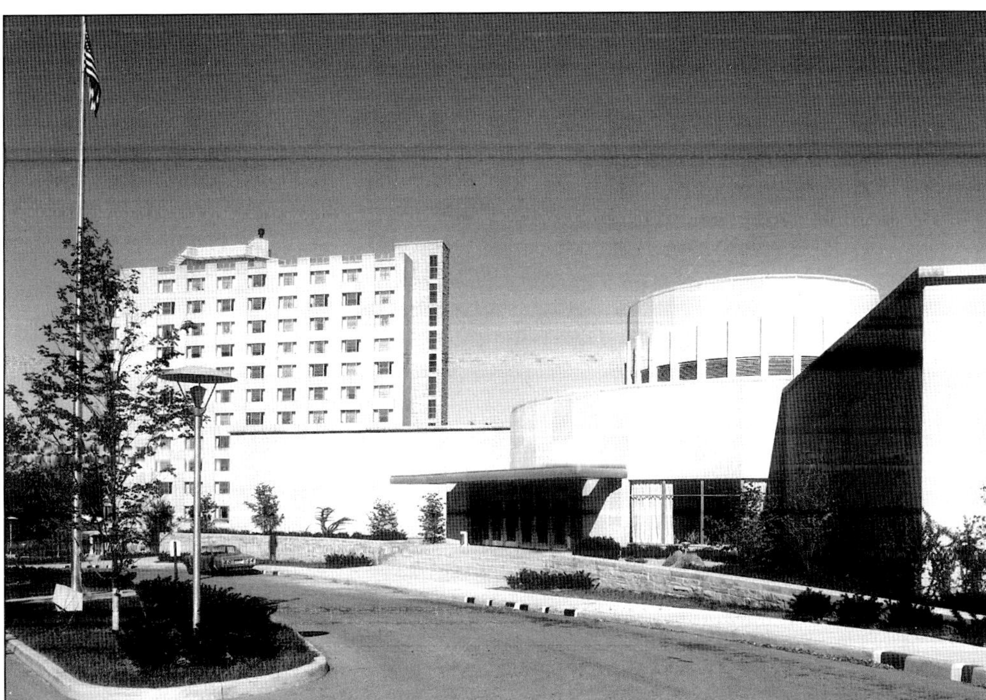

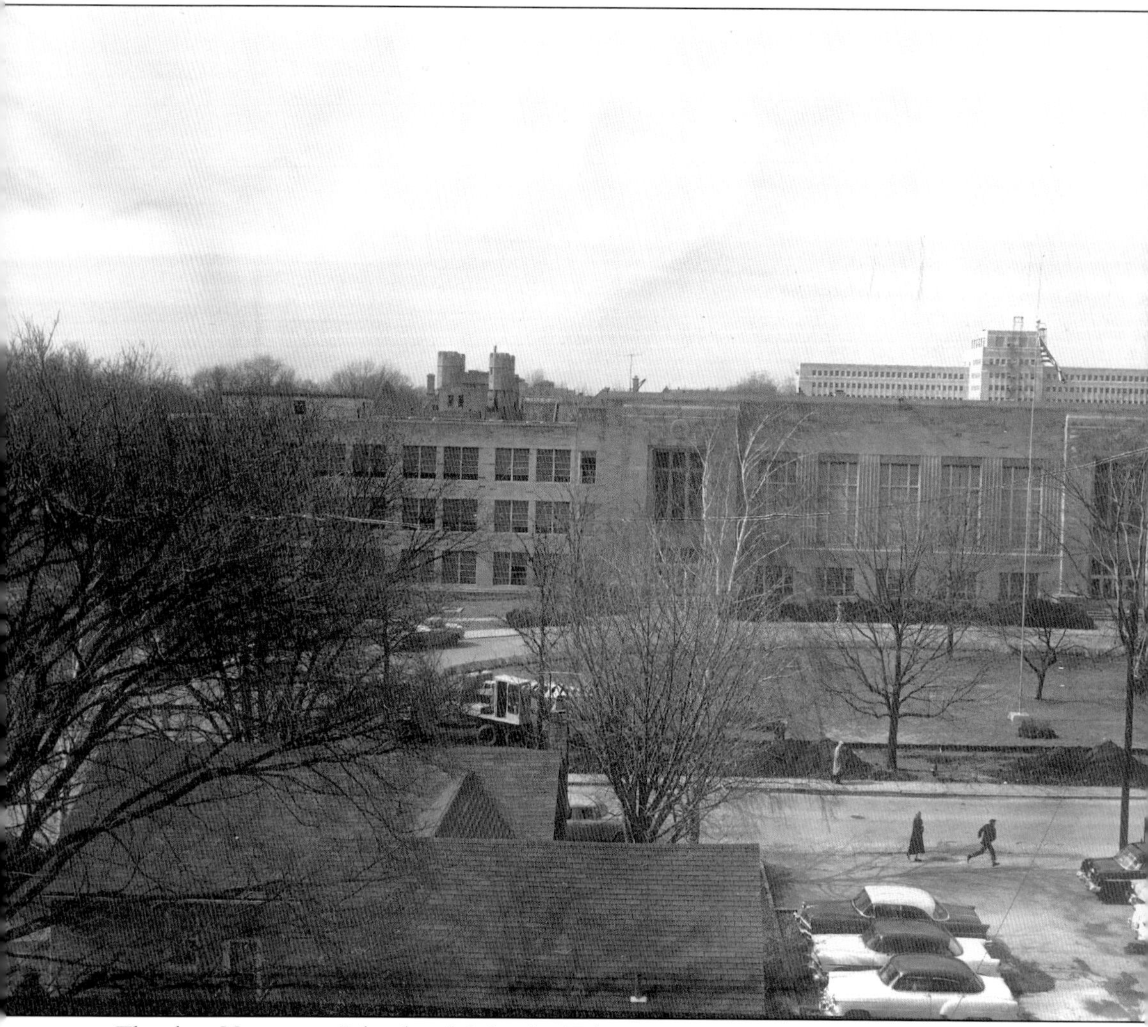

The then University School and School of Education building dominated the corner of South Jordan Avenue at the southern edge of campus in 1959. The building was constructed in 1938 and received the large addition at left in 1951. The building was renamed the Wendell W. Wright School of Education Building in 1979. The School of Education moved to a new building on East Seventh Street in 1993. The old building, extensively renovated, reopened in 1995 as the Bess Meshulam Simon Music Library and Recital Hall.

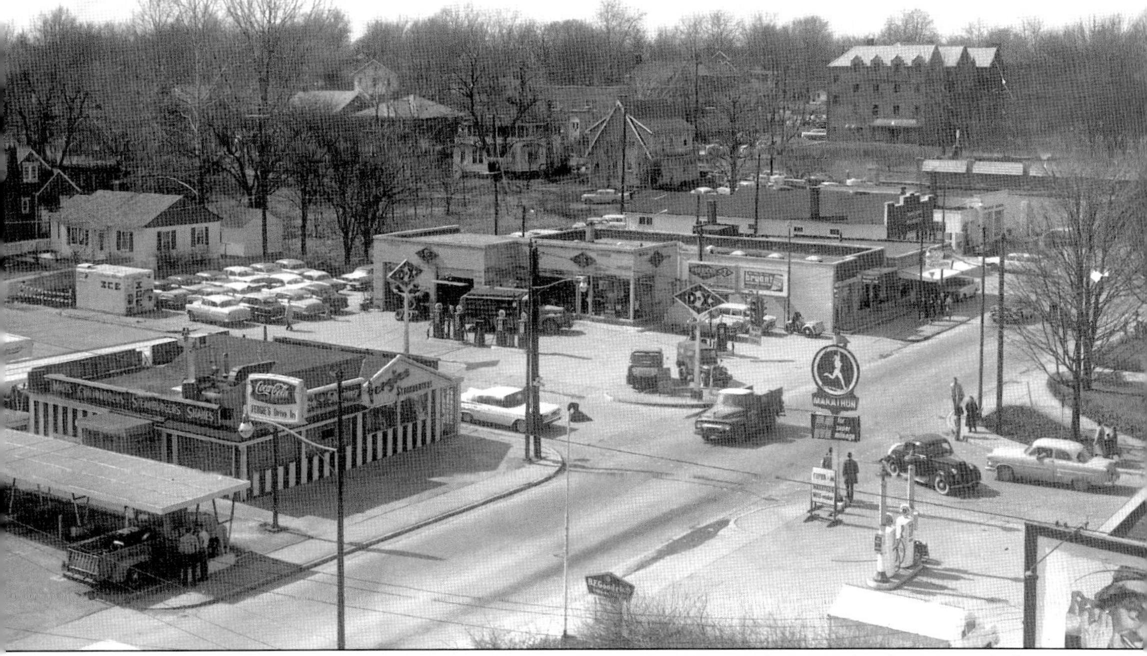

As the viewer looks southwest, East Third Street forms a diagonal from the bottom of the picture to the right edge and crosses South Jordan Avenue. The south side of East Third has changed remarkably little since 1959. The lawn of Recital Hall can be seen on the northeast corner. The Musical Arts Center would be built north of Recital Hall, outside the picture edge, in 1971-1972.

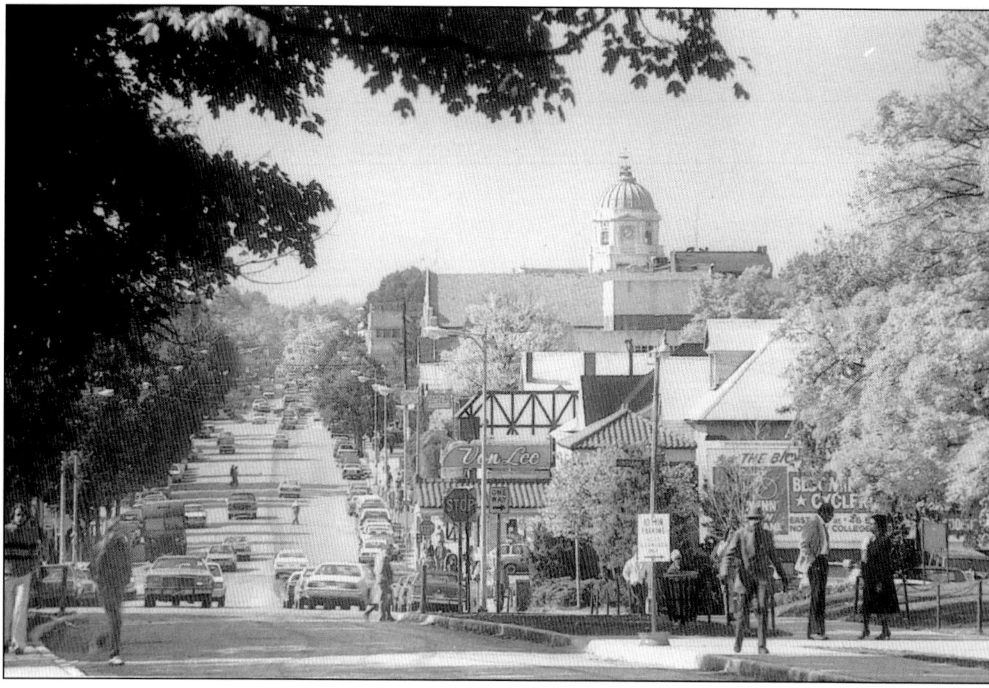

East Kirkwood Avenue, seen from the corner of Indiana Avenue looking west in 1982, has long been devoted to business use. The Westminster Inn (below), built as a residence on the northwest corner of Kirkwood and Indiana, had become a student religious center by 1950 and was later demolished for a parking lot.

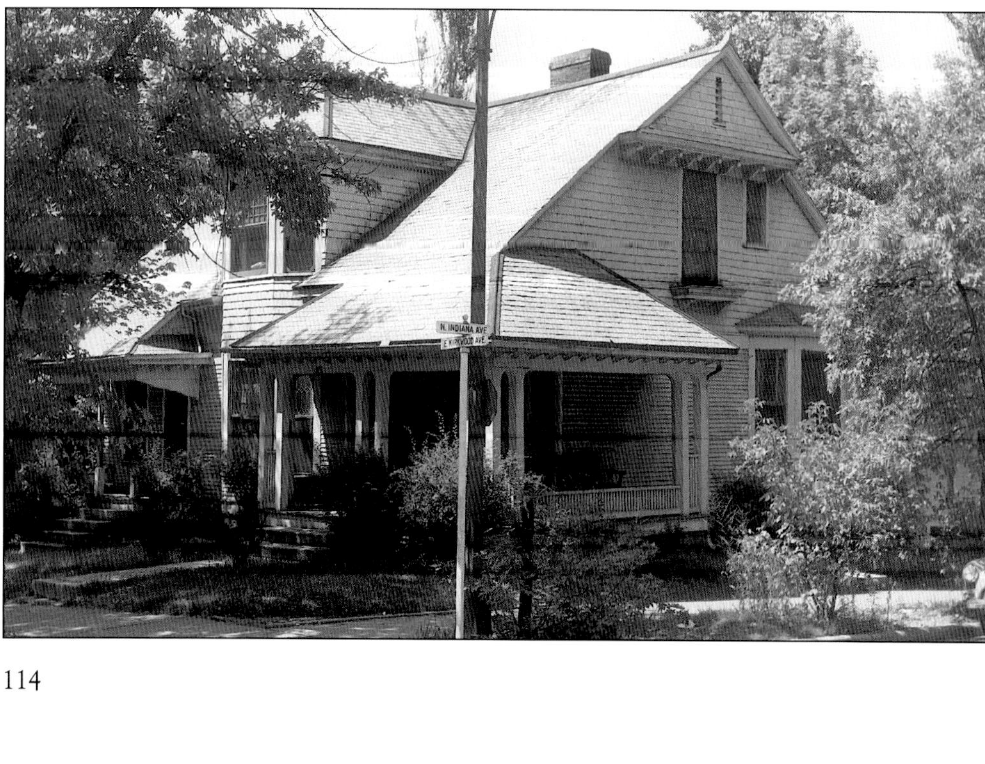

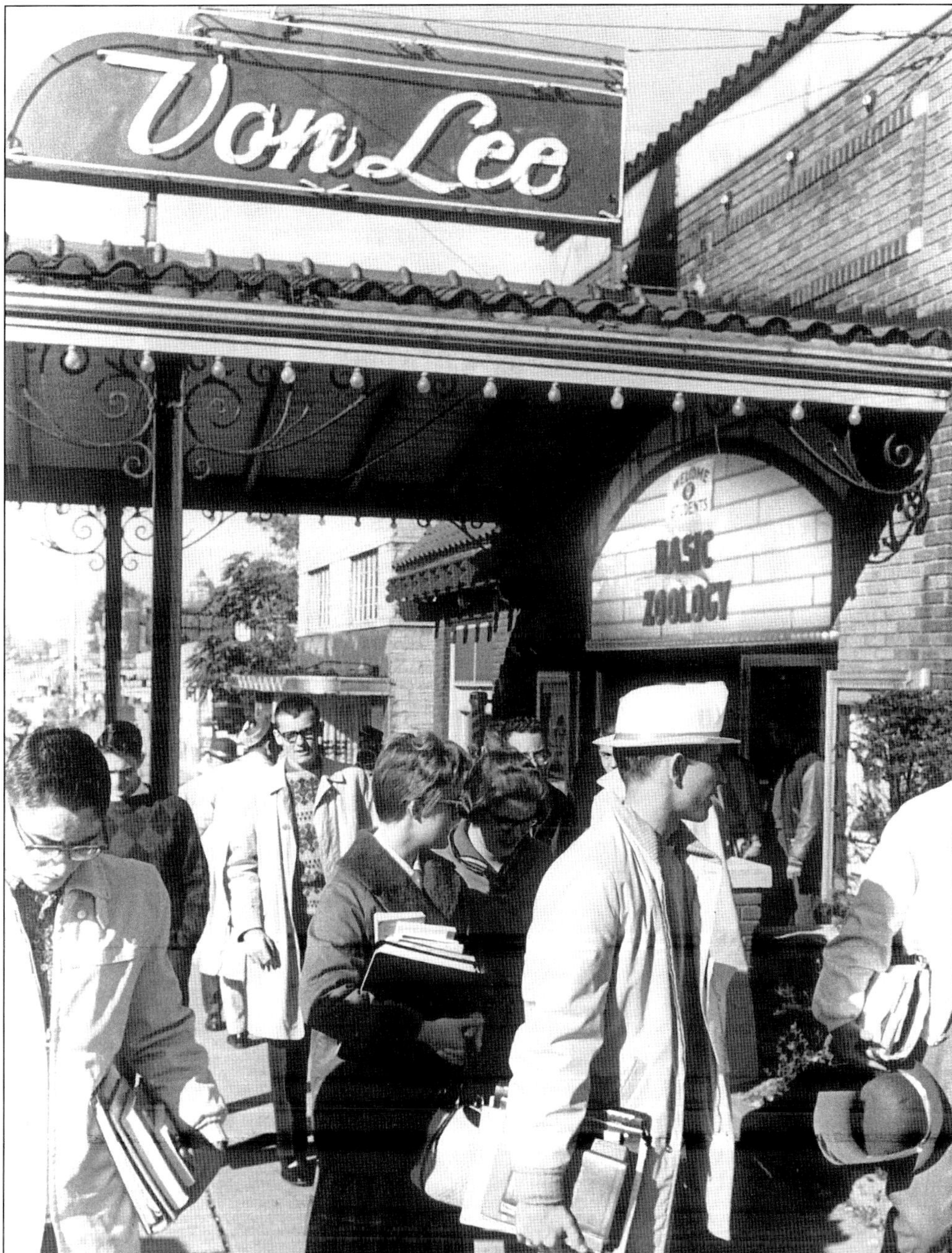

The Von Lee Theatre on East Kirkwood hosted the lectures of a popular zoology professor, William Breneman, during the 1960s while owned by the Vonderschmidt family. The Von Lee opened in 1928 as the Ritz. The Spanish-Colonial-style building was architect John Nichols's last big commission before he died the next year. Kerasotes Theaters, which has owned the building since 1976, replaced its west wing with a concrete structure. The Von Lee received local historical designation in 2000.

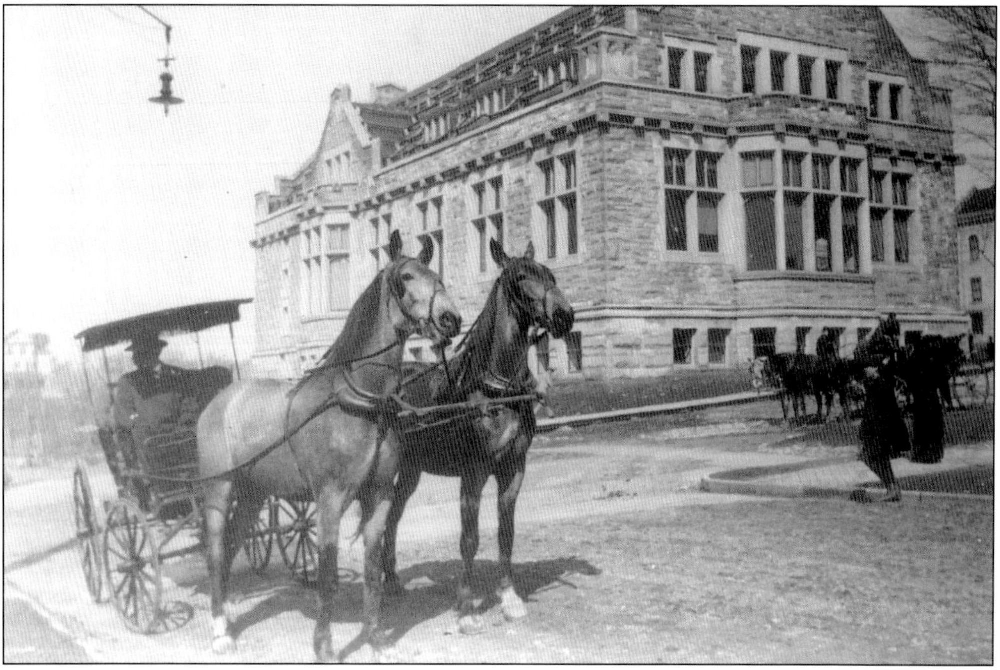

The entrance to Indiana University on Indiana Avenue was not very formal in 1905 when a new university library (now Amos Franklin Hall) was built. East Kirkwood continued east onto the grounds, and Dunn's Woods extended south along Indiana, the direction in which the buggy and horses are headed.

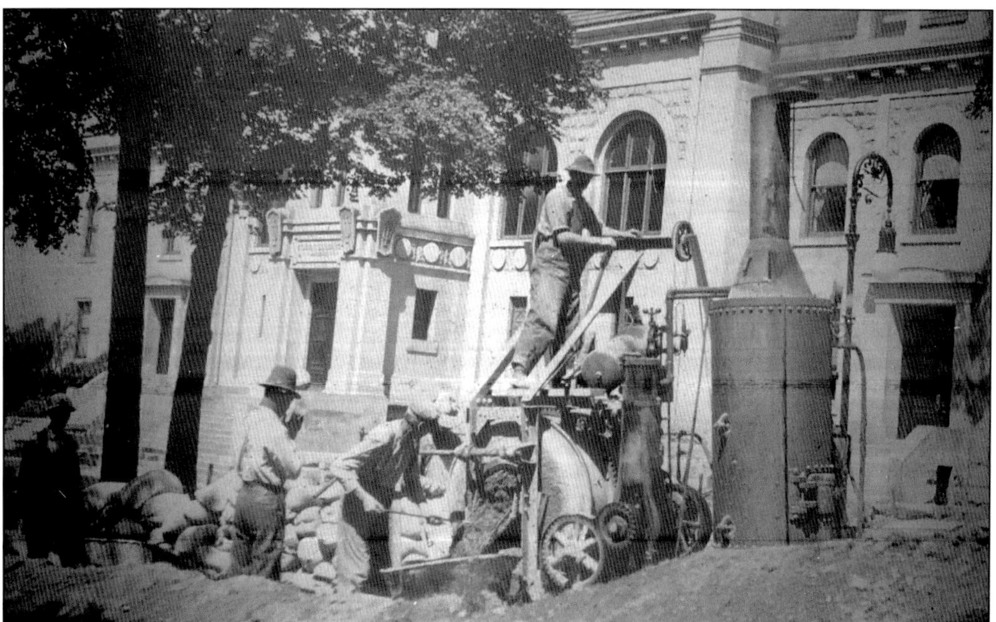

Automobiles were allowed onto campus via East Kirkwood. This crew, using steam-powered equipment around 1915, may have been paving the roadway. The entrance to the Student Building (1905) is at left.

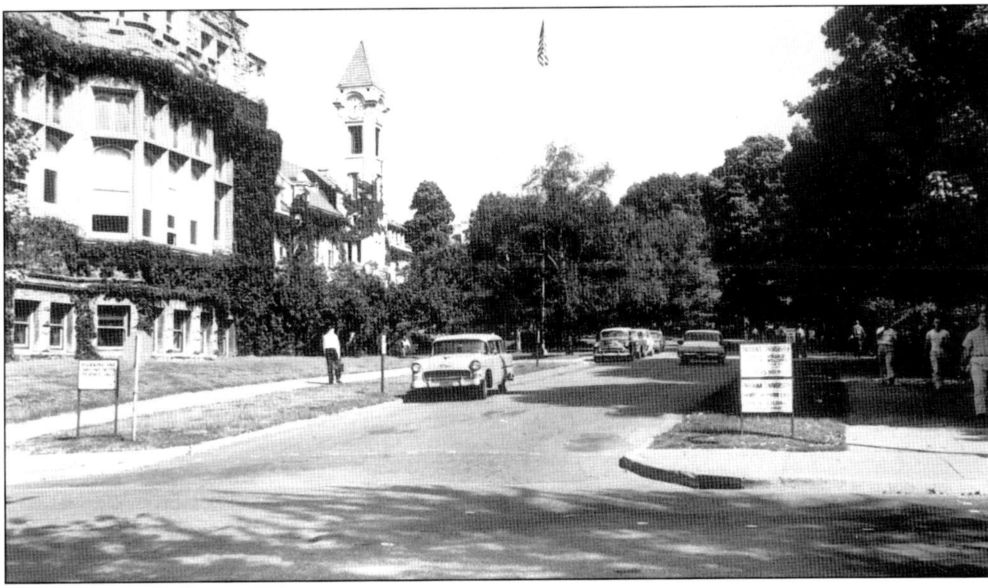

East Kirkwood continued to lead automobiles into the campus until the Sample Gates (below) were completed in 1987, establishing a formal entrance. The buildings of the Old Crescent were listed on the National Register of Historic Places in 1980: Franklin Hall, the Student Building, Maxwell Hall, Owen Hall, Wylie Hall, Kirkwood Hall, Lindley Hall, the Rose Well House, and Kirkwood Observatory.

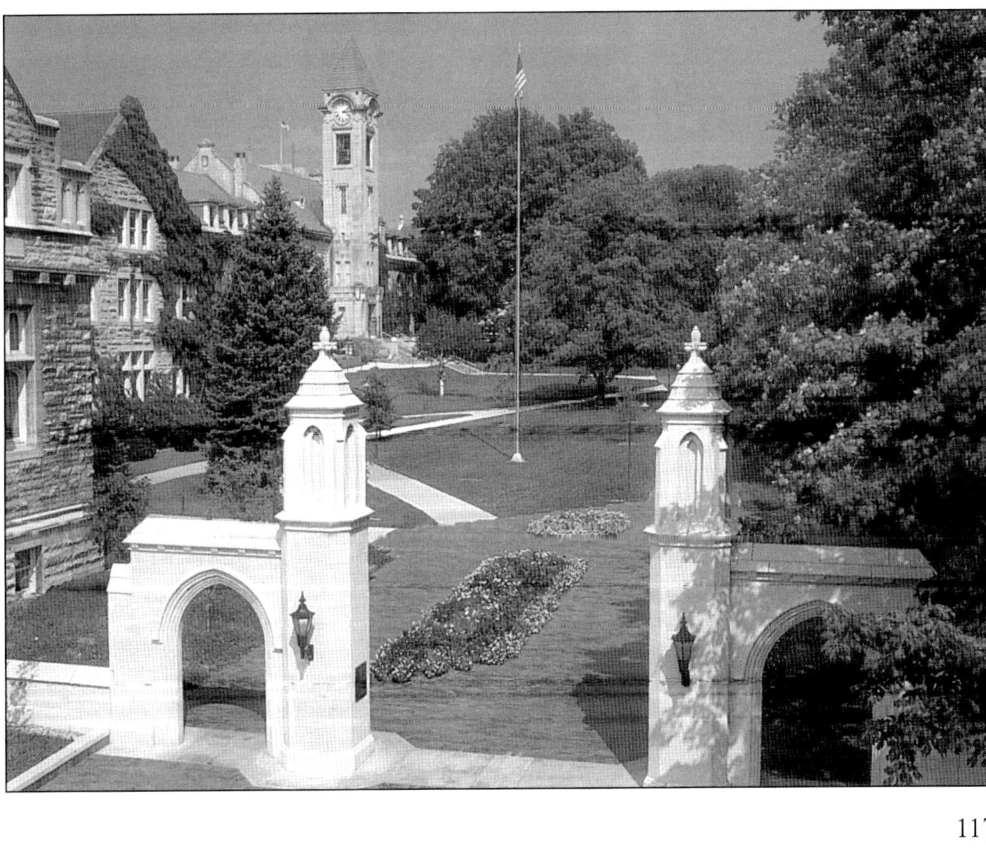

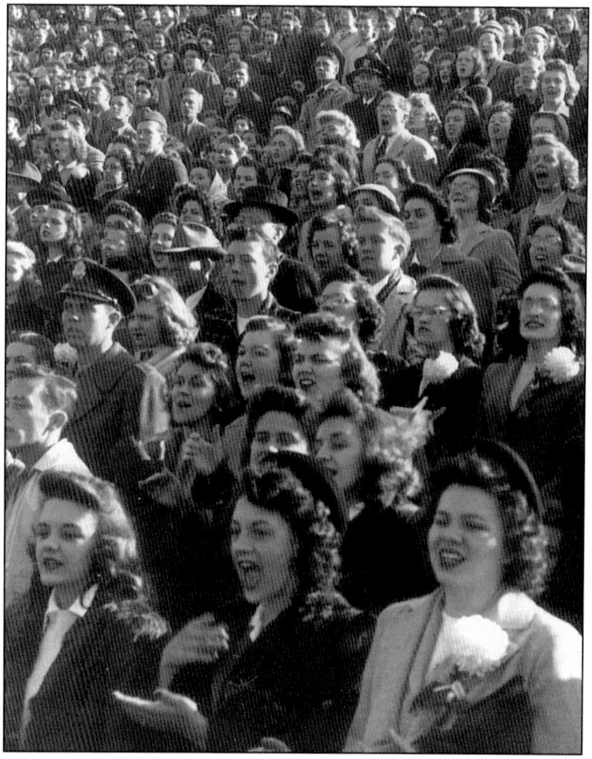

The crowd cheered! IU's first football season after the end of World War II in 1945 garnered a Big Ten championship, 9-0-1, for the Hoosiers. During the Indiana-Tulsa game, Mel Groomes (#57, below) breaks loose behind the block of Howard "Goon" Brown.

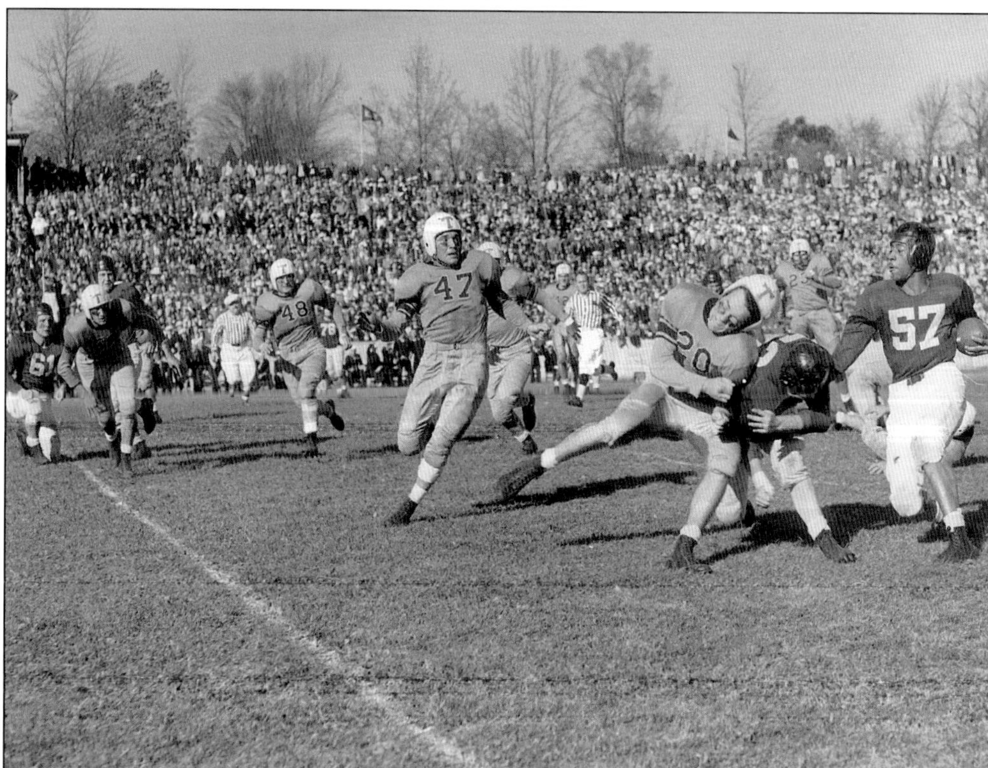

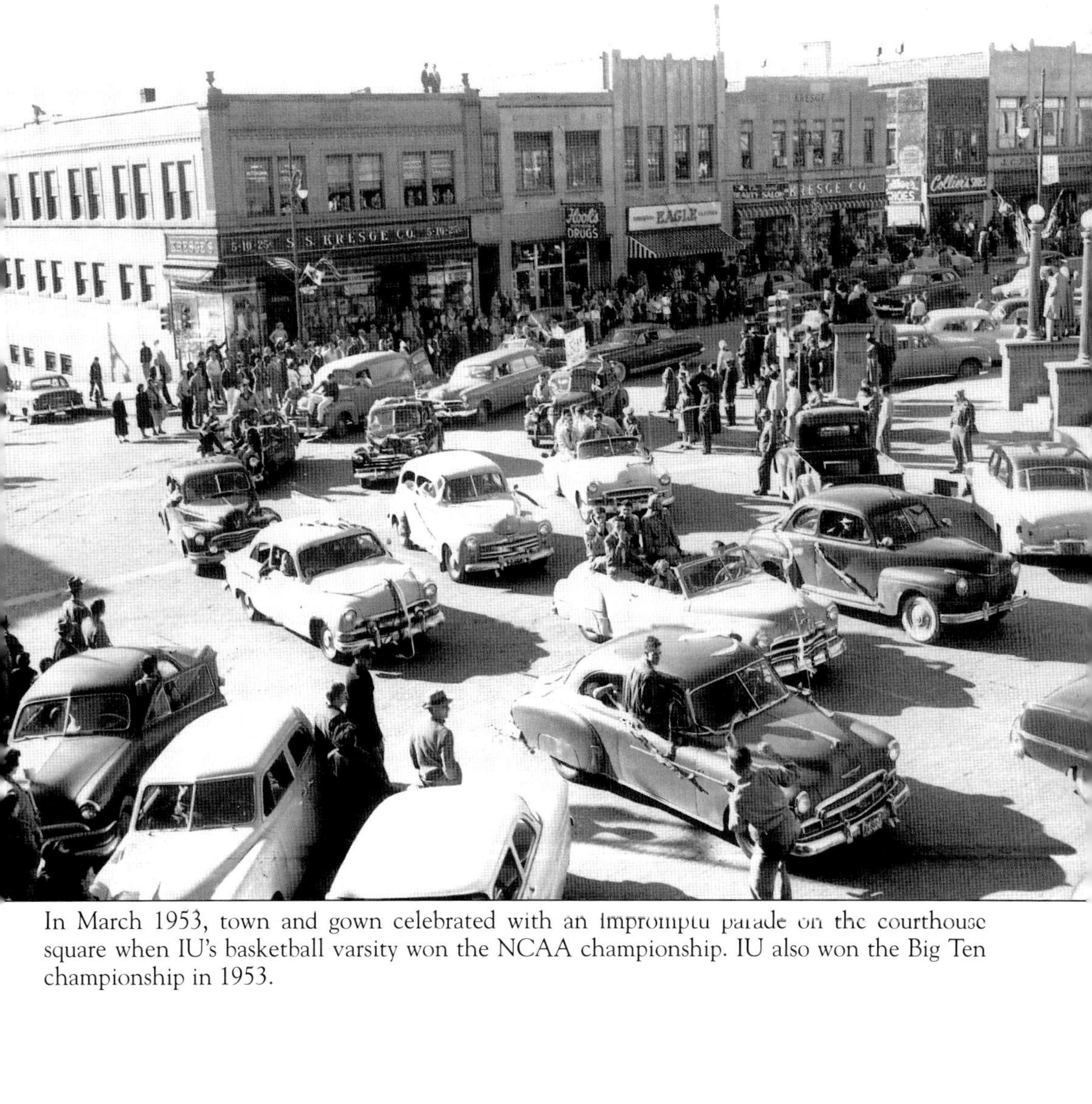

In March 1953, town and gown celebrated with an impromptu parade on the courthouse square when IU's basketball varsity won the NCAA championship. IU also won the Big Ten championship in 1953.

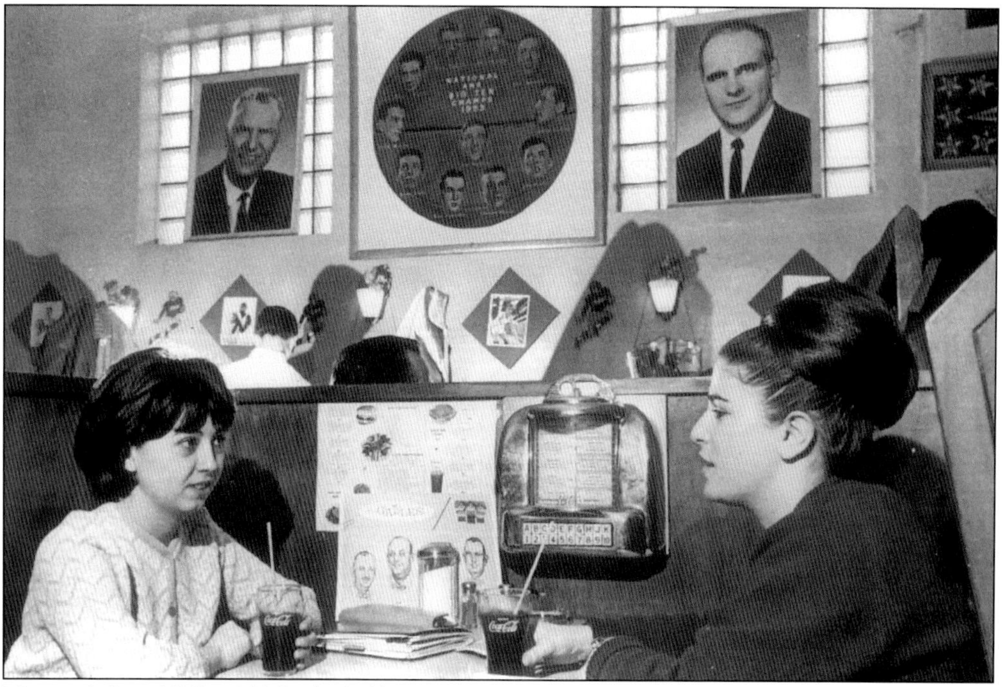

Memorabilia of IU's 1953 basketball season covered much of the wall above the heads of two students enjoying a glass of Coca-Cola at the Gables, formerly the Book Nook. The student hangout was conveniently close to IU's library, located down the block and across Indiana Avenue from the 1920s through 1960s.

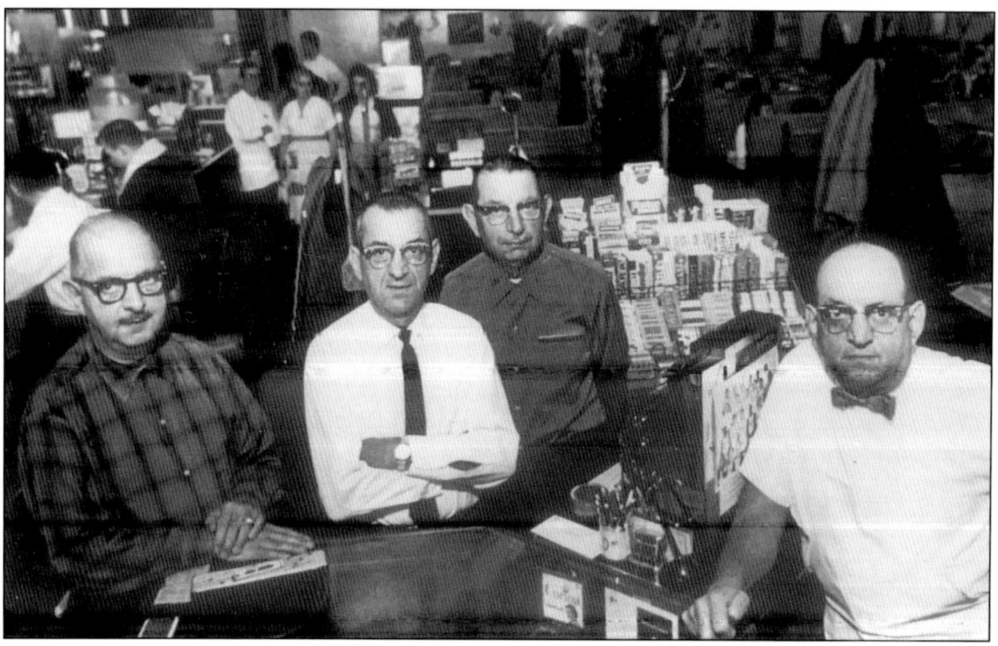

Chris, Charles, Pete, and Nick Poolitsan, sons of the original owner, took over the former Book Nook in 1932 and ran it as the Gables until 1968, when they retired. The brothers were legendary sports fans.

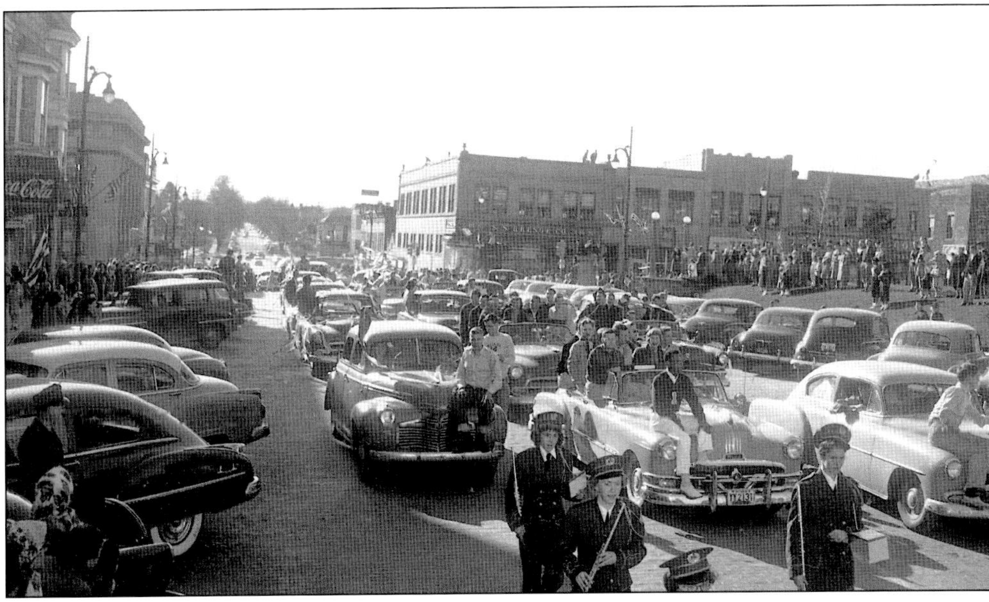

Coach Branch McCracken celebrated downtown after the basketball team's NCAA victory in March 1953 and, below, stood amidst team members Charles Kraak and Bob Leonard on left and Don Schlundt, Paul Poff, and Jim Schooley on right. McCracken graduated from Monrovia High School in 1926 and IU in 1930 (MS 1935). He coached IU basketball (1938–1943, 1946–1965) to 364 wins, 2 national championships, and several Big Ten championships.

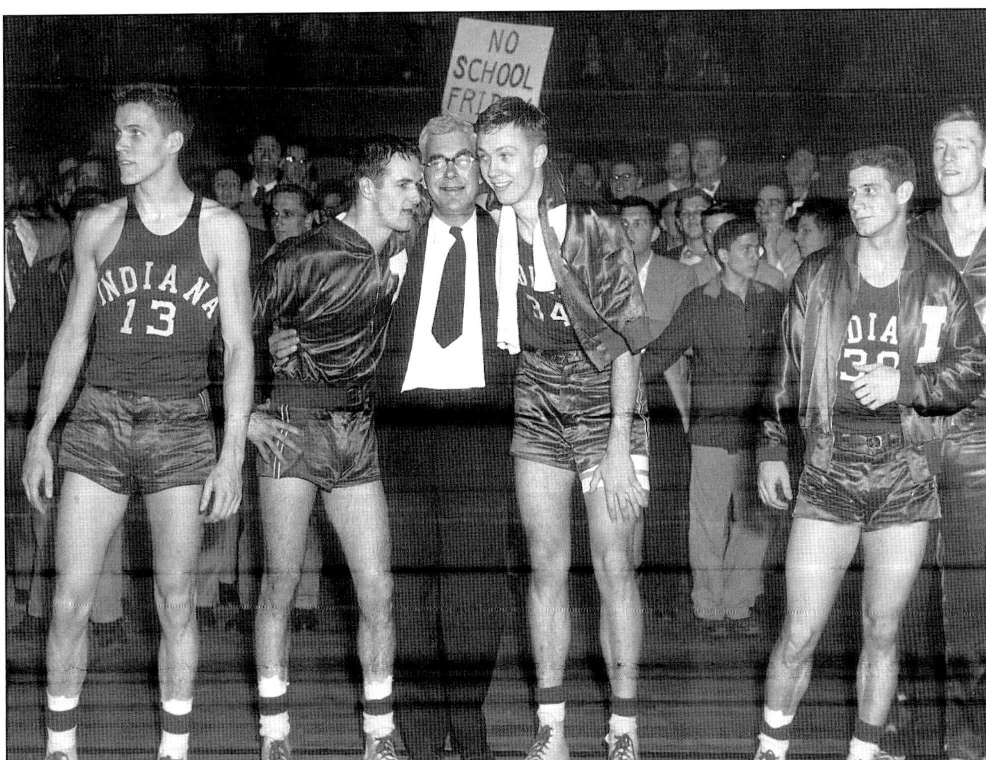

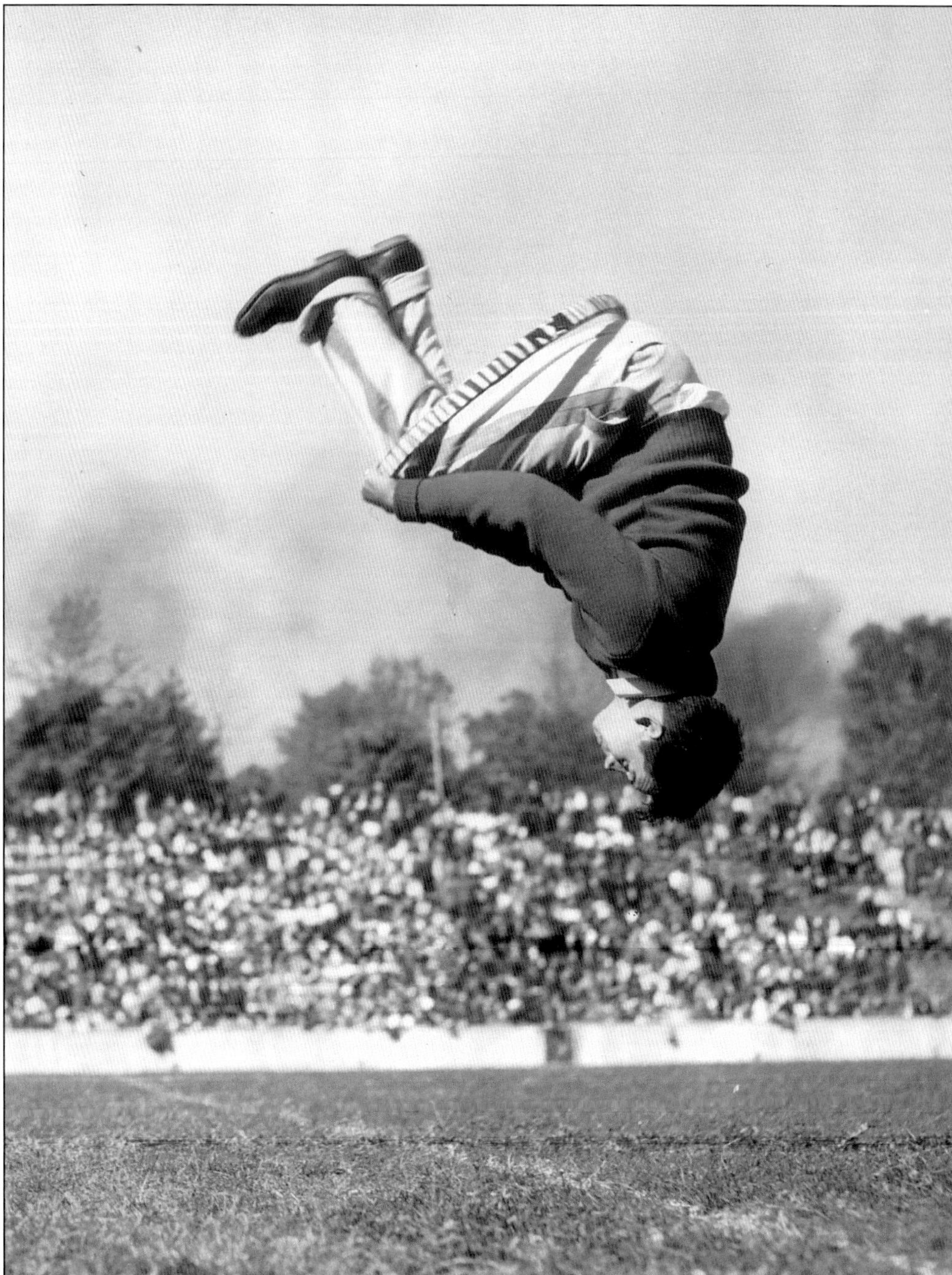

Acrobat Thomas Hampton entertained a crowd at the Old Memorial Stadium (Tenth Street Stadium) in 1944. The stadium was built in 1925 and used for football until the new Memorial Stadium (then Seventeenth Street Stadium) was built in 1960. The stadium was used for Little 500 bicycle races until 1980 and razed in 1982 to create the university's Arboretum.

Seven

Past Meets Future
Neighborhood Success Story

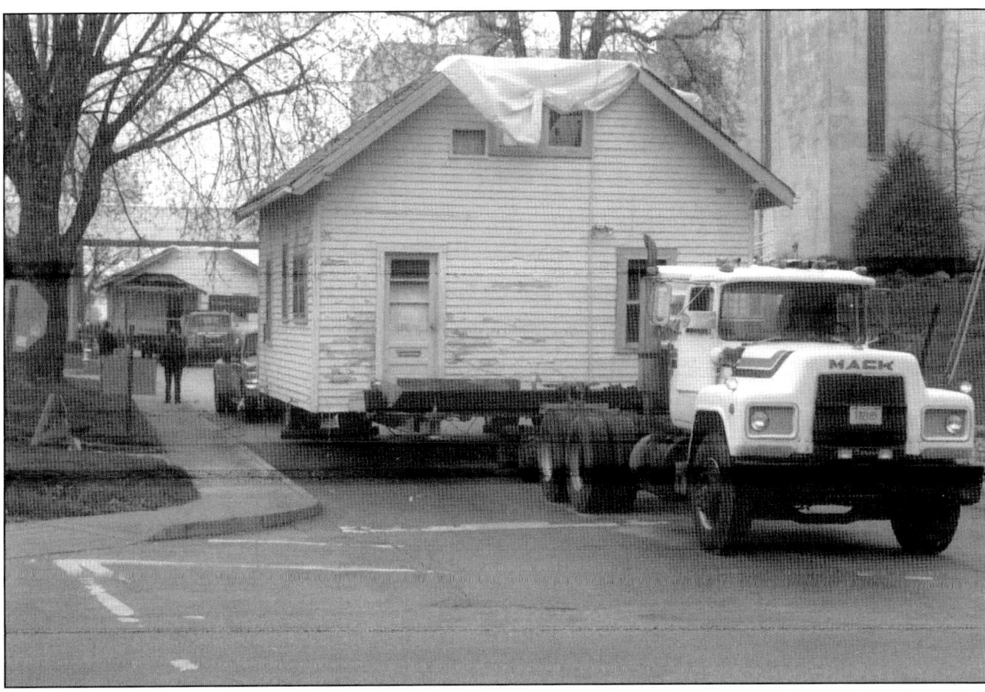

Once slated for demolition, this bungalow was rescued by Bloomington Restorations, Inc. (BRI) for use in its affordable housing program. The bungalow was one of three houses in the 900 block of West First Street to be razed to make way for a parking lot. Instead, BRI moved them from their medically-zoned sites. Overhead wires were temporarily taken down, and the roof peaks of the houses were removed to allow passing under the hospital overpass.

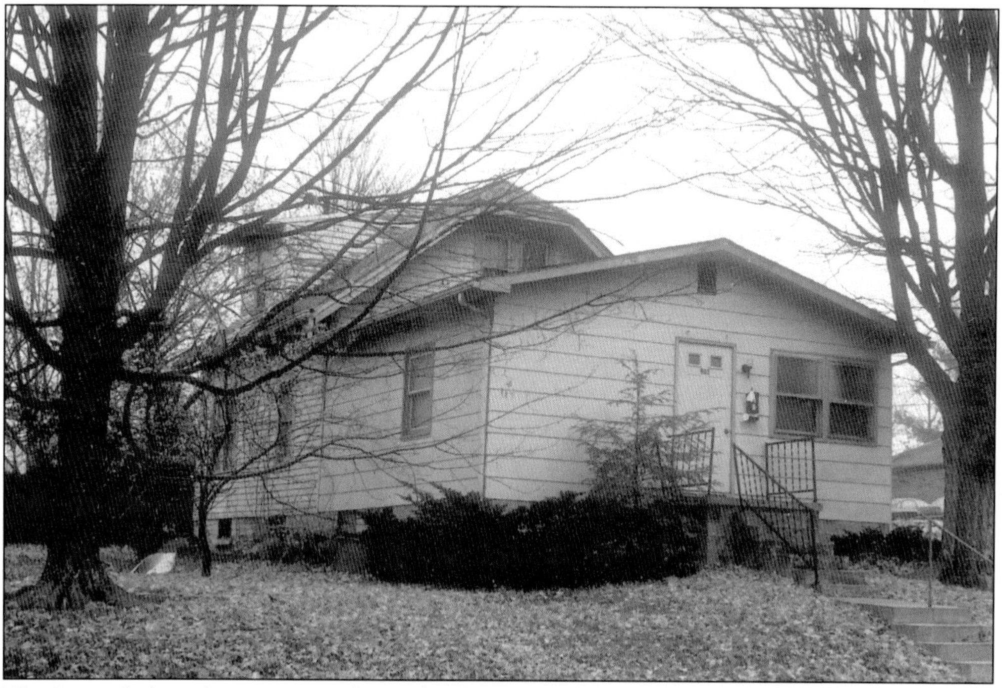

The house before the move was located at 902 West First Street. The house didn't look like much without its porch, and with its front hidden by a commercial addition.

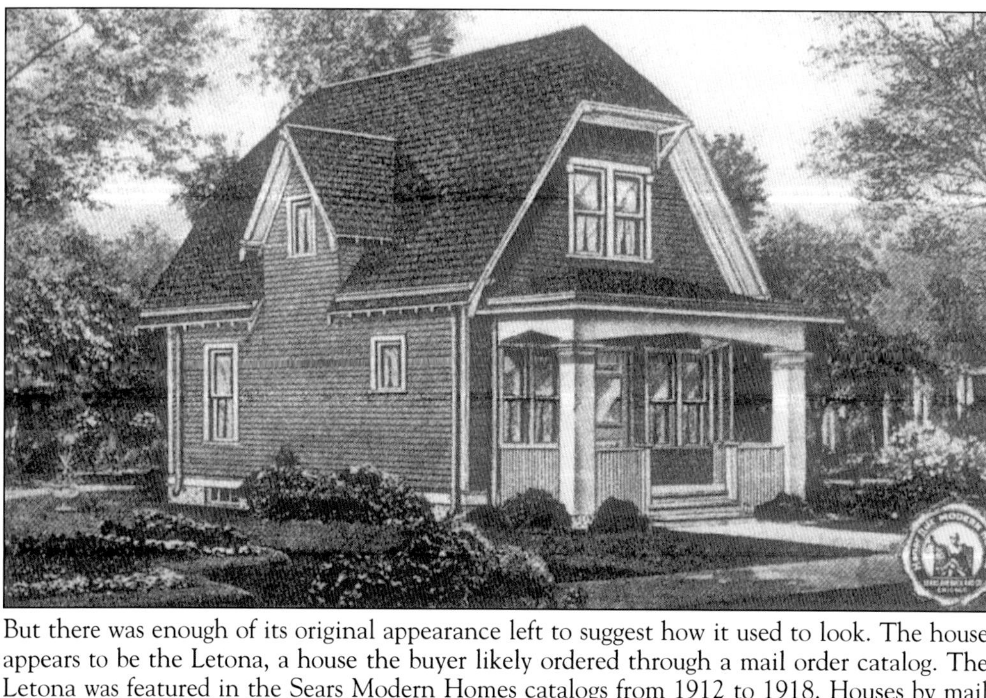

But there was enough of its original appearance left to suggest how it used to look. The house appears to be the Letona, a house the buyer likely ordered through a mail order catalog. The Letona was featured in the Sears Modern Homes catalogs from 1912 to 1918. Houses by mail were shipped in pieces with numbered lumber, trim, roof, windows and doors, and complete hardware, plumbing, and electrical and heating systems.

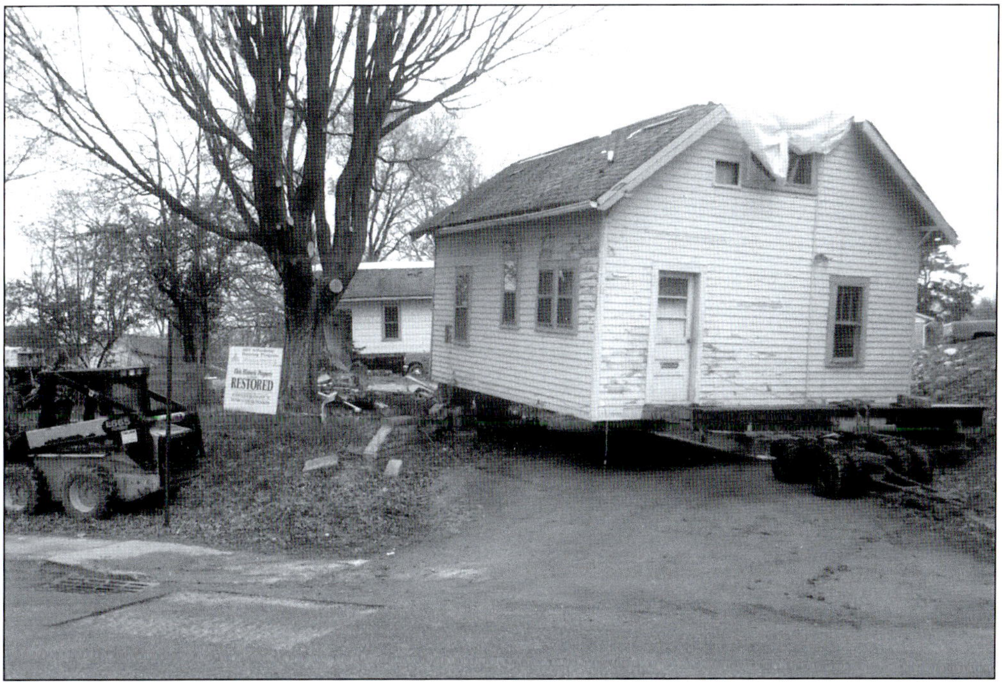

In 2000, Bloomington Restorations, Inc. undertook to move the house, restore it inside and out, and sell it to a lower-income buyer as an affordable home. The house was one of four houses scheduled for demolition that BRI moved that almost too memorable spring. The City of Bloomington's Housing and Neighborhood Development Department provided the affordable housing funding that made the project work.

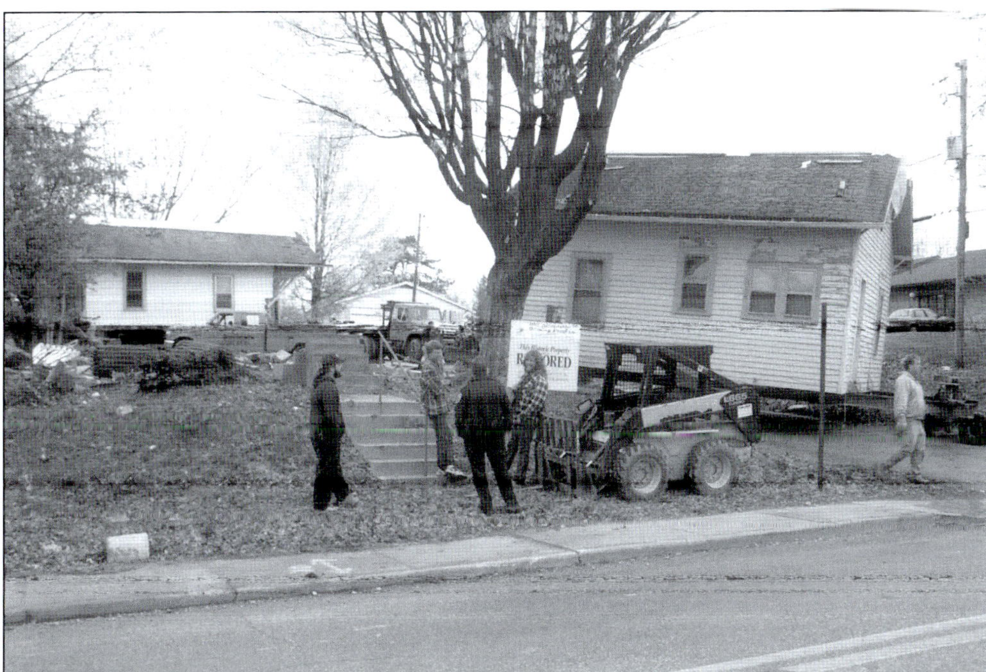

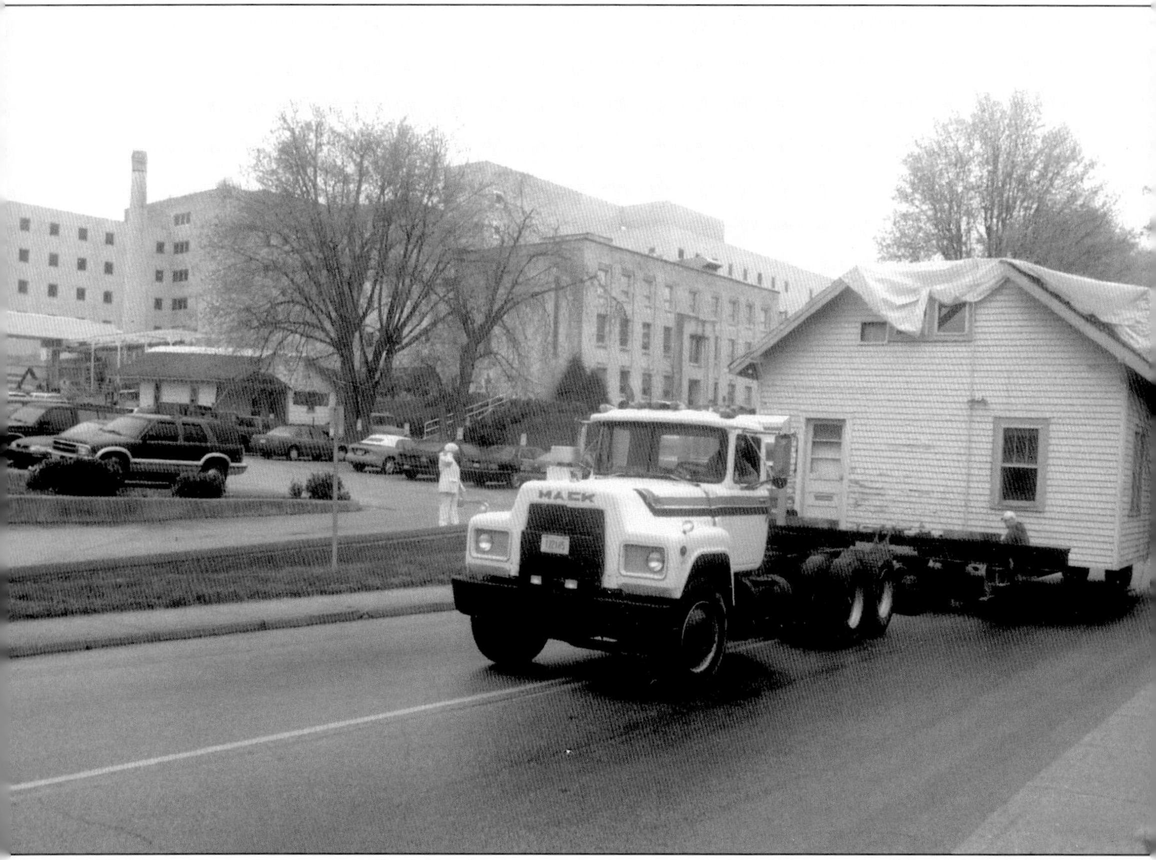

The moving truck trundled the house along Rogers Street south toward West Allen Street. Bloomington Hospital is on the left.

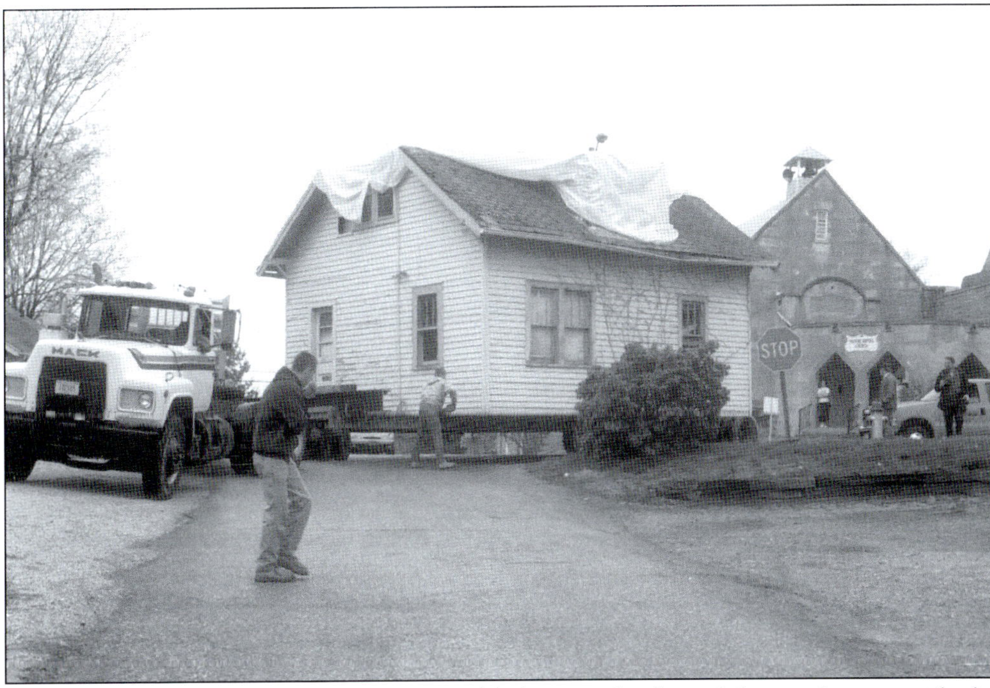

A lead man signaled to the truck driver and helpers as the first of the two houses, with the second following, turned the corner from Rogers onto West Allen Street. McDoel Baptist Church on Rogers is in the background.

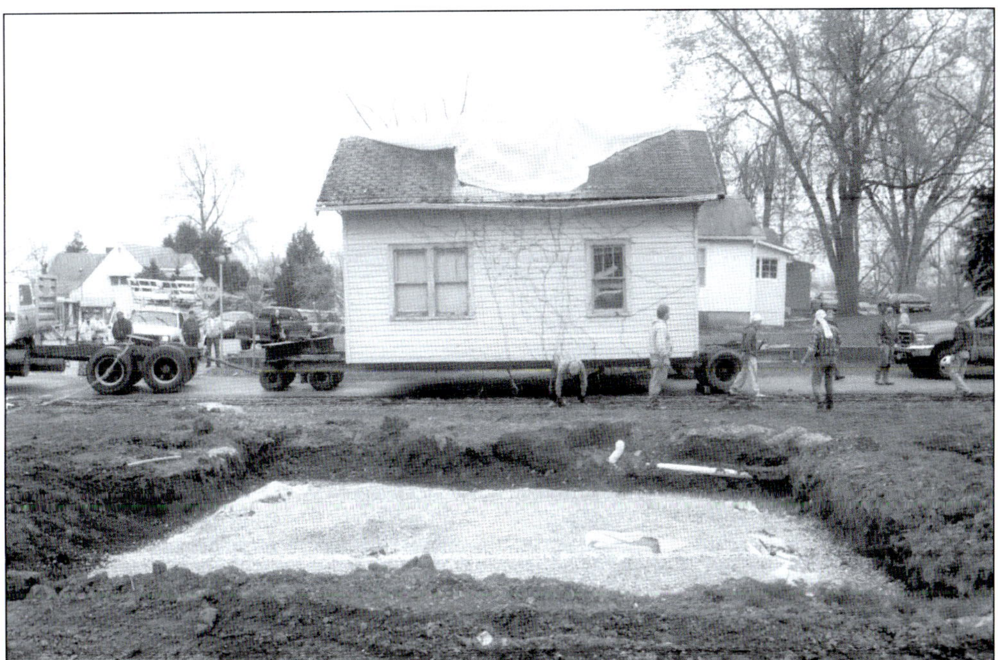
The moving crew parked the house next to its future site at 1020 South Madison Street. For the volunteers and single staff member at Bloomington Restorations, the uncertainties of restoration on a budget lay ahead.

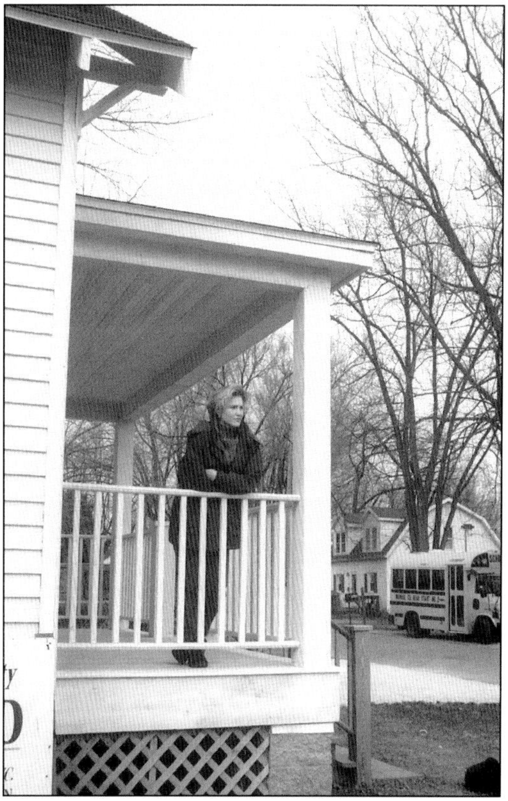

In December 2001, new owner Marian Keith stood on the porch of her home. During the year and a half between being moved and being occupied at its new location, her house was placed on a new foundation and its roof restored. It received new wiring, plumbing, heat, cooling, and restored or new interior elements. Then the house was painted inside and out and a new porch added to resemble the design in the Sears catalog. The house at left of bottom photo, also restored, sold, and occupied, was moved the same day as this one.

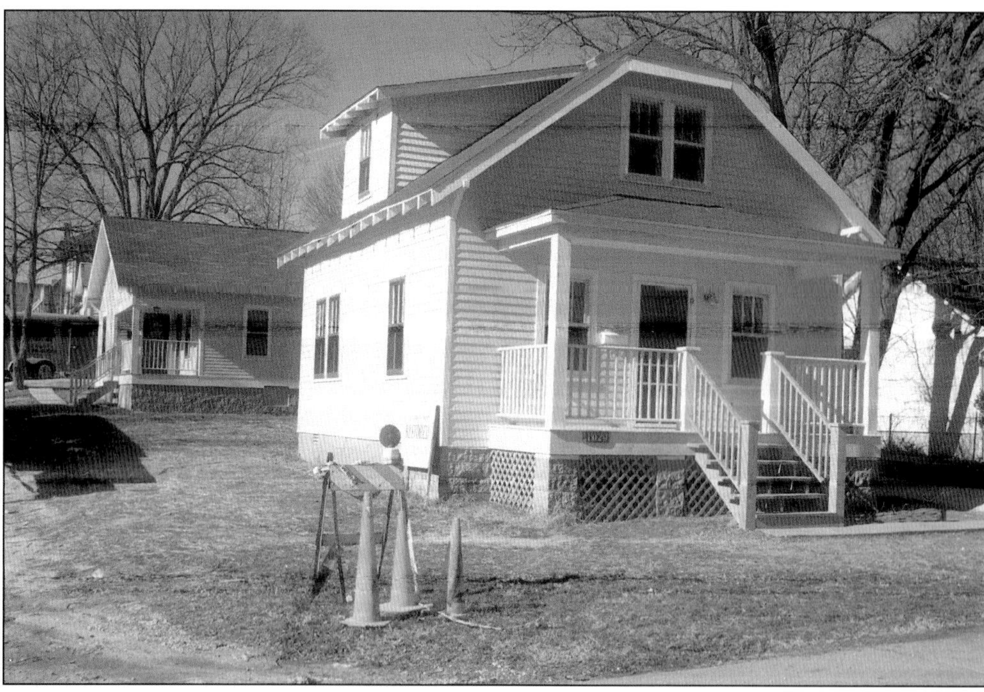